TREE
HERITAGE
OF BRITAIN AND IRELAND

TREE
HERITAGE
OF BRITAIN AND IRELAND

THE LADY OAK, CRESSAGE.

A Guide to the Famous Trees of Britain and Ireland

ANDREW MORTON

SWAN·HILL
PRESS

Copyright © 1998 Andrew Morton

First published in the UK in 1998
by Swan Hill Press, an imprint of Airlife Publishing Ltd

British Library Cataloguing-in-Publication Data
A catalogue record for this book
is available from the British Library

ISBN 1 85310 559 7

Typeset by Phoenix Typesetting, Ilkley, West Yorkshire
Printed in England by The University Press, Cambridge

Swan Hill Press

an imprint of Airlife Publishing Ltd
101 Longden Road, Shrewsbury, SY3 9EB, England

Contents

Acknowledgements

The author would like to thank the many people who have contributed to this publication. Major contributors are – Jim Paterson, for all his work on the Trees of Scotland, researched in meticulous detail, and always shared with those who show interest.

Allen Meredith for his knowledge of yew trees and their whereabouts.

Allan Howard for his work on tree mythology. The chapter on the subject is largely his. Also for his fine drawings, showing the detail and capturing the spirit of the trees.

TROBI for supplying so many of the records for the champion trees. The work they carry out is both voluntary and extremely valuable.

My particular thanks are reserved for my wife Maureen, who has been my companion and constant support over the duration of this project.

All the people who have given information and access to land are too numerous to mention but I would like to thank them all. Wherever we have been, we have been met with courtesy and enthusiasm. Below I have listed some in particular who have helped . . .

David Alderman, Mike Baker, Lord Bathurst, Bicton Agricultural College, Mrs Blanchard, Bill Bowen, Amy Bradshaw, John Bulmer, George Clive, Colonel Corbett, Mike and Penny Cox, Cumbria Broadleaves, Mr Fotheringhame, Nick Gerard, Richard Green, Sir Michael Hanham, Harvest Vision, Mr Hoare, Bryn and Anne Hughes, Michael Lear, Veronica Minshall, Mrs Mitchell, Mr Morris, Percival Morgana, Mrs E Morton, Geoff and Bob Morton, National Trust, Mrs Plumtre, Ben Powell, Oliver Rackham, Royal Botanical Gardens, Kew, Victoria and Tony Schilling, Luigi Scrabarozzi, Mr J Scudamore, Alastair Simpson, Sophie Strickson, Mrs Sykes, John White.

Foreword

There are millions of trees in the British Isles. They grow sometimes where you do not want them to grow! In 1987 and again in 1990, many of them were blown down in southern England during heavy storms. Woodlands were flattened, roads lost whole lines of trees, well-known landmarks disappeared. The great devastation caused people who never thought of trees before to actually begin thinking about them. How could these great, big, living structures be swept over as if matchsticks blown by a giant?

The Midlands too had suffered twenty years earlier with Dutch Elm Disease wiping out hedgerow after hedgerow of stately English elm. Suddenly landscapes were bare.

But of course they were not really. Much remained, and away from the south, the rest of Great Britain and Ireland still had a rich tree cover. These 'acts of God' at least galvanised people into action, and now we see great schemes such as Community and National Forests, as well as initiatives with woodland management, and utilisation of wood products. It is only in relatively recent years, when looking at what we have lost or are losing, that we realise what we have actually got.

Some years ago, an Italian tree recorder visited the British Isles. He had travelled throughout Europe searching out big trees, particularly oaks and yews. He told me that nowhere else in Europe had he seen ancient yews and old burred pollard oaks like those seen here. This started some discussion and thought. Yes, big trees occur elsewhere in Europe, but they are generally timber trees. There are limes in village squares in Germany, there are old plane trees and old olives in southern Europe, but what Great Britain and Ireland have is unique.

When so much of Europe is beginning to look the same, is it not refreshing to still see the regional differences in the British Isles? The ancient yews of Wales, the 'fairy trees' of Ireland, the majestic trees of Scotland, and the old oak pollards of England. Then there are the great tree collections built up over the last few centuries, when the trees of the world began to be brought to these shores. These collections are so special, for where else can you see places like Kew, Westonbirt, the great estate plantings, arboreta, pleasure grounds and the smaller collections, that dot these islands? What we lack in numbers of native species, we more than make up for in historical interest. We have an immensely rich and varied tree legacy. People have recorded, measured and deliberated on our trees over the past few centuries, and the present work of TROBI (the Tree Register of the British Isles) has added greatly to the pioneering work of such people as the late Alan Mitchell, who travelled far and wide measuring trees. Tree recording, though, is only part of the story. What about the glory of trees? The sheer size, colours, myths, legends and folklore associated with these longest living and biggest of plants.

For some people, perhaps more than might admit, these ageing giants provide an uncomfortable contrast to the modern human sense of time. The quiet sense of steady growth and slow development, of yearly renewal and the process of very gradual decay, simply puts them outside the realm of human existence and its in-built concepts of short-term satisfaction which seems to form the basis of present-day culture. The trees themselves appear to live in a different world, and often occur in unexpected places. They are found on unused drovers' tracks, on high open hillsides, in dry stream beds, in ploughed fields, in somebody's garden, or down a narrow, forgotten path. More expectedly, they regularly occur in churchyards, in ancient sacred places where the Druidal yew and Christian stone churches still stand.

They have over the years, and over the centuries, been put to various and unexpected uses. They have served as sacred altars, have performed as temporary churches, been preached under and have heard marriage vows. They have provided convenient hideouts and watchtowers for monarchs, rogues and soldiers alike. They have been, and indeed still are, danced around, bedecked, decorated and feted. They have been built in and played on by children. They have been used as hanging gibbets and as shelters against the elements. Some have been connected with death, others with the power of life, and with healing and restorative properties. They have guided pilgrims, provided landmarks and signposts for travellers, and used to demark astronomical events.

So it was all of these things that brought together this publication, this 'tree tour' of Britain and Ireland. It is not a tree identification book, nor a book on forestry or woodland management. All of those subjects are covered only loosely here, and in greater depth in other publications. In reality, after travelling to every corner of each county, I soon realised that the subject has no end or boundaries. There could be no final completion, since a lifetime, let alone four years' work, would not be long enough to do it justice.

As I said in my previous book, *Trees of Shropshire*, if this publication stimulates public interest, and if people 'look' at trees in a different way, then it will have succeeded. The great enthusiasm shown by virtually everyone who has been visited, written to, or volunteered information, shows that trees do capture the imagination, and that people really do love them.

The trees have been arranged into nine regions, starting in the West Country and finishing in Ireland. Map references are not included, but general descriptions of localities are in the text. Of course, some of the trees are on private land, so special permission is required to visit. Others are on National Trust properties, in arboreta, on roadsides, in public places such as villages, towns and cities, or in gardens open to the public at certain times of the year

Introduction:
Woodland history and mythology

Throughout the last ice age, few trees existed in Britain. Then, in about 8000 BC, the climate changed and became warmer. The ice retreated and the majority of Britain became covered in trees. The low lying lands were almost completely covered, and the forests were home to large animals such as bears, lynx, wolves and reindeer. We only have a scattering and dim knowledge about the activities of man at that time. It would seem, however, that Mesolithic man created clearings mainly by lighting deliberate fires.

In the Bronze Age, stone hoes were used to cultivate the lighter soil when the first stages of settled farming, rather than food hunting, developed. The basic needs were for water and land suitable for cultivation, and when clearing occurred as much of the materials as possible was utilised. Examples of this being timber used for shelters, bark for food, fibres for ropes and even leaves for livestock fodder. Early woodland management started with certain species being favoured and allowed to flourish at the expense of others. When the people had worked one particular area, they moved on to begin the process again.

Some impressive examples of early woodcraft exist in Britain, such as 'The Sweet Track', a hurdle trackway on the Somerset Levels dating from 3000 BC, when knowledge of certain species was used to great effect to create lasting means of communication. Early wooden henge monuments from the south are another example of quite sophisticated use of certain woods such as holly, hazel, elder, oak, ash and lime.

By using pollen counts it is possible to determine roughly the make-up of the virgin forest in around 3000 BC. The dominant species from that time can still be traced today, although it must be remembered that there was much overlapping. The lime was common in south-west England. The elm and hazel in central and eastern Ireland, south-west Wales and western England. Oak and hazel mixed in southern Scotland and northern England and in northern Scotland the pine and birch dominated, as can be seen today in the old parts of the Caledonian Forest.

In the later Bronze Age the climate became wetter and bogs were created, which destroyed some of the forest areas. The activities of woodland interference continued on an ever-increasing scale and the ability of people to control and manage the natural resources at their disposal can be seen with the practice of coppicing, that is, allowing shoots to grow out again from a 'stool'. By coppicing in cycles an ever-present supply of the right wood was available.

Bronze Age man was capable of travelling great distances. This is known from the routes established on the ridgeways and archaeological artefacts from southern Europe on those routes. New species of trees will have been introduced or re-introduced to Britain by these travellers.

The Celtic people who inhabited late Iron Age Britain had a distinctive culture and one that developed independently from their original home on mainland Europe. They had many festivals, two of the main ones being 'Samain', the Celtic New Year in early November (that we now call Hallowe'en), and 'Beltane', the fertility celebration in May (now linked with the May Queen Festival). During the Celtic times the Iron Age carpenter became a skilled craftsman.

The landscape was now a relatively managed one with villages and farmsteads and a framework, although modified during the Roman occupation, that lasted to form the estate and parish boundaries of the late Saxon period. The Romans' arrival in AD 40 brought new forms of timber construction and new emphasis on the coppices for the fuel for baths, furnaces and kilns. The population rose to little more than one million, but it must be remembered that in the remote parts of Britain the effect of the Romans on rural life was minimal.

When the Saxons came, they set up their own administration and the language became the early form of English. Saxon palaces and churches showed a high degree of woodwork knowledge and, over 1,000 years after their construction, doors from Saxon churches are still in use today. A testament to their makers' skill. The land charters of the Saxons list boundary trees with reference to many species such as yew, pear, apple, maple, thorn and oak. Here there is written evidence of individual trees in the landscape being referred to as having specific importance in the culture and management of the landscape. The language told us much of what was happening. An example is the word 'leah' now 'ley' indicating a permanent glade or clearing in the forest, and if we look at today's map many place names will tell us how settlements came into being.

We know that, in those eleven centuries between the Iron Age and the Norman invasion, forest cover in parts of southern and eastern England was almost completely altered, but in the north and west the process was much slower. Suffice to say that by the early Norman period around 1250 it is doubtful whether any significant areas of woodland in England had been left completely untouched. In Scotland and Ireland virgin forest probably remained intact until the seventeenth century, and it was during this century that the classic English lowland landscape of woodlands surrounded by farmland came into being. The medieval landscape became what it was, due to intricate management methods

and strict laws, with well over a third of the country under Royal Forest Law where the King had hunting rights.

The Forest Laws covered everything from wasteland to moorland and woodland. In the remaining land the trees belonged to the lords of the manor, while villagers could only take deadwood and underwood. The classic wood pasture developed. This was a pollarding of trees (cutting off limbs above animal reach) and allowing livestock to roam below the trees. This form of land management allowed certain trees to gain great age and some of the giants seen today are left-overs from this form of management. The forerunner of the parkland with open spaces dotted with big fully developed trees had begun. By the thirteenth century the woodland management of lowland Britain had become either coppicing or wood pasture. Complicated laws existed to protect timber. So as to ensure that a regular supply of wood remained available for the whole population, even the lords of the manor were sometimes unable to fell trees or take timber.

Coppicing remained a practice into this century but it was in serious decline. The First and Second World Wars were responsible for great timber losses. The remaining woods were largely replaced by conifer plantations and the use of large mechanical equipment that could 'grub out' old coppice stools had, by the 1970s, increased the destruction of old woodland.

Since the mid-1980s the decline has halted and much interest has been generated by organisations such as the Greenwood Trust in Coalbrookdale, Shropshire. The Forest Authority now has a much more enlightened view overall on woodland issues and many innovative schemes are in progress. The stimulation of the market for products arising from coppicing being all-important.

The wood pasture, as already mentioned, was a medieval creation that blossomed into the landscaped park, which became such a feature of the English countryside. The production of meat, particularly venison, was the original priority. The continuity of the park in the landscape culminated in the great eighteenth century creations where 'Capability' Brown and Humphry Repton gained their reputations.

To conclude this sketch of woodland history, it can be seen that from deep in prehistory until the present day the use made of the woodlands and their produce has greatly influenced the appearance of the landscape we see around us.

Introduced species

Before the Medieval period, there were very few introductions of new species into the British Isles. It is now known that it is possible to grow a wide variety of trees from all over the world in Britain because there are no extremes of climate. Although the impoverished range left after the ice age has only been added to in relatively recent times.

The main so-called 'native' species list is restricted to the following: alder, ash, beech, birch, box, elm, hawthorn, hazel, holly, hornbeam, lime, oak, pine, yew, and the lesser species of crab-apple, wild pear, bird cherry, gean, field maple, juniper, poplar, rowan, whitebeam, wild service and willow. The native shrub list reads: alder buckthorn, barberry, blackthorn, buckthorn, broom, dogwood, elder, guelder rose, gorse, privet, dogrose, sea buckthorn, spindle and wayfaring tree. The herbalists, many of them monks, began to bring in new species and, over the centuries, these species began to become accepted as natural. Plants that were either a good food source in mainland Europe, or were medically prized, were brought to these islands.

The Roman invasion, it is thought, brought several new trees to Britain. Sweet or Spanish chestnut and the prolific sycamore are now looked upon as part of our landscape. The sweet chestnut is a long-lived tree and monstrous examples can be found. The centuries-old Tortworth Chestnut is at least medieval, and the coppiced Canford Chestnut is one of Britain's greatest girthed trees. The avenue of chestnuts at Croft Castle is another celebrated example. The now common sycamore, which needs controlling in woodlands and gardens because of its invasive nature, is at its best when cultivated as an individual tree, and many fine, fully crowned specimens are to be found in open parklands. The north of England and Scotland boast the best sycamores in Britain. The Scottish trees at Tyninghame, Lennoxlove in Lothian, Posso House and Hirsel in the Borders are matched by the famous Birnam Sycamore near Dunkeld, Perthshire.

Traders opening up the new routes to the Americas between 1600 and 1700 brought more new trees to these shores. The tulip tree, false acacia, swamp cypress, American oaks and Canadian spruces all arrived during that period. The tulip tree at historical Claremont, Surrey, must have been one of the earliest introductions, and as far west as Dyfed and as far north as Coldstream, big old trees can be found. The species has now become popular as a specimen tree and young examples are fairly common around our towns. The swamp cypress, an interesting conifer that sheds its foliage in winter, comes from the southern United States, and one of the earliest specimens can be seen at Deans Court, near Wimbourne, Dorset.

As the Near East and the Orient began to open up to trade, the common and well-loved horse chestnut was brought from Greece and Albania in about 1616. The largest of these species are located in southern England. 'Giants' grow at Much Hadham Rectory, Herts, and Petworth House, Sussex, and the biggest so far recorded is near Hurstbourne Priors Church, Hampshire. Trees with big, layering branches are uncommon, but exist, as at Warwick Castle and Longford Grange, Shropshire.

Of the three well-known cedars, Deodar, Atlas and Lebanon, the latter was the first to be brought in at about 1640. Many claim to be the earliest planted and huge trees can be seen growing as single specimens on lawns close to stately houses throughout England. Notable Cedars are at Blenheim Palace, Oxfordshire, Claremont Landscape Gardens, Surrey, Woburn Abbey, Bedfordshire, and at Petworth House and Goodwood, Sussex. There is also the huge, spreading tree at Rowton Castle, Shropshire.

During the eighteenth century, more and more introductions occurred and forestry trees such as the larch and spruce were planted as experiments to monitor growth and timber quality. Blair Castle, Dunkeld, and Monzie Castle have close associations with these early conifers, and some still stand today as a historic link with their arrival in these islands.

Also about this time, the landscaped park was becoming a fashion. As well as newly laid out landscapes, many older deer parks or wood pasture lands had been altered, added to or tinkered with. Artificial lakes, grottoes, viewing drives, and strategically and aesthetically placed plantations were created. Landowners vied with each other to create the most impressive park. What many assume as the classic English parkland, complete with deer herd, began to appear in every county in the kingdom. Later in the eighteenth and the early nineteenth centuries, the arboretum and the 'pleasure ground' for relaxation and stimulus became essential to the best estate.

These forerunners of the public parks had trees as their main focus. Usually planted with native trees as a backcloth to ornamental specimens, these plantings have given us a heritage of tree culture that many countries do not possess. The great landscape designers such as 'Capability' Brown, Repton and Kent, usually incorporated timber production in their designs, and many a covert and tree clump originate from this time.

The introduction of new species in the eighteenth century were numerous, and well-known trees such as the copper beech,

Turkey oak, weeping willow and Corsican pine are from that period. In the nineteenth century, new species came in ever-increasing numbers. By 1810, Kew had over 11,000 species of introduced plants, with this total continuing to increase. Botanists, scientists, and nurserymen were by this time developing propagation techniques, hybridising, grafting, budding, and were accumulating knowledge of plant families. This accelerated developments and created new species and hybrids.

Plant hunters were sent out, or went themselves, to find new plants from all over the globe. The stories of the great adventurers, like David Douglas, are legion. He was engaged in 1823 by the Horticultural Society of London (later to become the Royal Horticultural Society) to collect seeds from plants in North America. He died eleven years later in Hawaii after introducing, amongst others, the noble tree that bears his name, the Douglas fir. No other collector exceeded Douglas in the importance of his introductions. The most famous of his successors was William Lobb (1809–63), who worked principally for the Veitch family, the enterprising Exeter nurserymen.

Introductions continued apace. Even as recently as 1941, a tree thought of as extinct, the dawn redwood, was discovered growing in a remote valley in West China, and it was brought to Britain in 1948. A specimen growing at Leonardslee in Sussex is already over 30 metres (100 feet) tall.

Wherever we travel in the British Isles, we can now see trees from all over the temperate world.

Fear of the forest

Before the 15th Century England must have seemed one great forest, an almost unbroken sea of tree tops with a thin blue spiral of smoke rising here and there at long intervals. (Hoskins)

From time immemorial and in many

different cultures worldwide, trees have played an important role in religious belief. Strange as it may now appear to the modern mind, trees have unmistakably exercised great symbolic power in earlier, less scientific and rational times.

It has been said that 'the groves were God's first temples' and in Britain we know that the Celts practised religious rituals within sacred groves and particularly venerated the oak tree. The writers of antiquity provide a rich source of information on the magical and spiritual role of trees in Greek and Roman times but the phenomenon is worldwide and goes back into the hidden depths of pre-history.

A paradox of sorts emerges at the outset. Trees *en masse*, in the form of dense forbidding forest, have seldom enjoyed the same divine respect which has been afforded to certain individual trees, or, as with groves, selected groups of trees. In fact, as we know, the felling and clearance of trees is an

activity which has gone on practically uninterrupted for thousands of years and is still continuing unabated in many parts of the world today.

In Europe, the dominance of the forest on early people's lives cannot be overstated. The forest was all-enveloping and all-encompassing and remained so until the start of the lowland clearances by the Saxons in the fifth century.

In the third millennium BC a Neolithic people are known to have settled on the chalk uplands of southern England. They are known to have practised a rudimentary agriculture and to have grazed flocks and herds. They chose to inhabit the most open places which occurred naturally, where there was grass for grazing and few trees.

These naturally occurring islets of space were relatively tiny oases in an immense primeval forest which covered most of Europe. For 2,500 years throughout the Bronze Age and into the Iron Age people lived in very close contact with a trackless fearsome forest full of real and imagined terrors. The forest edge was the edge of civilisation.

For primitive man trees, according to Sir James Frazer, have been one of the primary motivating forces in the evolution of religion, second only to the fear of the human dead. Fear of the forest, therefore, has different motivations than has the reverence of tress and derives from different impulses. The two are nonetheless intimately intertwined.

Tree worship

The tree as a symbol of all Nature and of Life, important though it has been in Great Britain at various times, is nonetheless part of a wider range of religious and spiritual symbols, all of which have been heavily influenced by invading cultures.

The British Isles, located on the Atlantic-facing western fringe of a vast continent, has mainly received its invaders and its cultural influences from the East. In tree-lore, as in all else historically, we have been conditioned, enriched and, to an extent, over-ridden by the culture of the Near East, where civilisations established themselves in much earlier times than they did here.

The worship of trees in the first emerging primitive religions may have been involved with their seeming immortality compared with man's relatively short life span – especially the evergreens which remained changeless whatever the season.

When identifiable deities were slowly crystallising, trees were first identified with God or the Life Force. Given the ever-present human instinct to translate reality into mythic imagery, the tree became iden-tified with God or at least it was imagined to embody a deity. Therefore some trees were singled out for special reverence.

First came the veneration, fear and rever-ence for the tree itself. The image of a great tree with its roots far into the underworld, with a pillar-like truck containing blood-like sap, and with its branches reaching into the heavens became embedded in the human consciousness from very early times. The tree has frequently been seen as an image of the world, or as all of Nature, as the Tree of Life.

We can, therefore, see that many of our ideas on religion are derived from or influ-enced by those of our forebears. When the relationship between trees and religion is studied it can be seen that we are going back to the earliest of early days of human life on earth. Many of the ancient ideas and rituals still linger on and affect the lives and behav-iour of civilised people today.

Trees in art
From the days of mythical Greece until the present, trees have been a source of inspira-tion for artists. John Crowe's *Oak at Poringland* in the Tate Gallery conveys the strength of a mighty tree. Rembrandt's *The Three Trees* gives great atmosphere of grandeur with economy of detail. The major classic landscape painters all use trees as an integral part of their works: Constable, Gainsborough, Hobbema, Cotman as well as

Nash, Bury, Hill and White.

Trees also play a direct part in the art of wood-carving. Carved masks, totem poles of the peoples of North America, or the sophisticated handiwork of Grinling Gibbons, who used pear but mainly the pale soft wood of the lime in his intricate work.

Trees and fertility
The Green Man signifies irrepressible life, an image of renewal and rebirth, and is part of a rich store of vegetation myths but one whose image has persisted above all others. There is a closely related and widespread mythology concerning tree spirits and vege-tation spirits, much of it being imitative magic concerned with attempts to make the corn grow.

The Green Man in popular belief is the sacrificial figure of the old woodland spirit who is killed off by the new spirit of Spring and the new growth. No doubt in a more primitive past a victim was sacrificed before the ceremony became ritualised. The whole complicated ceremony of the Green Man and the May Day observances include the choice of a King or Queen of May, who is almost always symbolically sacrificed and is typically clothed in oak leaves.

It is said that the custom of the Maypole originates from these primitive beliefs in vegetation spirits. In Britain and elsewhere in Europe the Maypole, a standing trunk, was worshipped as a fertility symbol of the vegetation god, and this recognised practice continued into the seventeenth century. The still present custom of the May Queen is a persistent practice which preserves the folk-memory of a sacred marriage to promote fertility of the land.

The Long Parliament of 1644 forbade the Maypole and, though it came back after the Restoration, the leaping and dancing were never quite the same again. Worship of the tree trunk occurs in India, where Hindu women praying for long life for their husbands wind cotton threads around a banyan tree whilst sitting in a circle around it. Speculative comparisons with a weaving of ribbons around the Maypole are difficult to resist.

But what remains? On the surface not a great deal. Interpreting the meaning of remnant practices and fragments of folklore memory is difficult and confusing. Much of the history of such things was branded pagan, and the Puritans and later the Victorians literally rewrote many old stories and suppressed what they regarded as unacceptable to Christianity and good taste.

Nevertheless some things remain still. The face of the mythical Green Man, partly hidden by oak leaves, can be found in medieval churches all over Europe, represented in wood, stone and glass, and there are several instances of annual May Day processions led by a leaf-covered Jack o' Green or Green Jack.

The custom of the Harvest-May is still observed by some peasant peoples of Europe, where a large branch of hawthorn is brought back with the last sheaf of corn. This represents the spirit of vegetation on which depends next year's harvest.

Tree worship was well established by the time of the first known representations, and sacred trees appear on Chaldean and Assyrian engraved cylinders and on temples. The concept of the tree as God's dwelling place appears in both Egyptian and Persian mythology, where the cypress is considered especially sacred.

Tree worship was also widespread in India. To Buddhists the bo-tree (*Ficus religiosa*) is the shrine tree. This extraordinary tree can be found in the grounds of Buddhist temples and where it grows shrines are often constructed. The incredible age of these trees has over the centuries reinforced their sanctity. The greatest of the bo-trees, 'the Mahabodhi tree of Anvradhapura' in Sri Lanka, can be traced back to 245 BC. The tree was grown from a branch brought to Sri Lanka from the original tree at Buddha Gaya on the Northern reaches of the Ganges in India. Under the original tree Buddha attained enlightenment. From that tree cuttings were taken to many places, including the royal park at Anvradhapura. The branch was planted in a special enclosure to mark the King of Ceylon's conversion to Buddhism. The event is recorded in detail in the Mahavamsa, the great historical chronicle of Sri Lanka. The tree still lives, the old shell gone, but the great growth from the original root and branch are still to be seen, making it the oldest recorded living tree on earth. The bristle cone pines, the redwoods, the cedars of Lebanon, the cypresses of the Holy Land, the beobabs of Africa and some of the British yews could be of greater age, but none can match such a continuous and well-documented historical record.

The oldest known, and most famous sanctuary and grove of sacred oaks in Greece was that of Dodona where Zeus was revered in the oracular oak. This sanctuary is thought to have flourished for over 2,000 years. Both the Greeks and Italians associated the oak tree with their highest god, Zeus or Jupiter, the divinity of the sky, the rain and the thunder.

The Lithuanians were not converted to Christianity until the close of the fourteenth century when the worship of trees was still prominent. Remarkable oaks were revered and holy groves were maintained around some villages, where even to break a twig was a sin.

The Celts were Belgic peoples who invaded Britain in the later Iron Age from the neighbouring continent in the first century BC not long before the Roman invasion in AD 40. They occupied south and south-east England and set up powerful small kingdoms some of which stoutly resisted the Roman armies. Boadicea was reported to have released hares from within sacred groves as part of her ritual preparations for battle.

Vernementon 'the especially sacred grove' is recorded in Nottinghamshire in Roman times and Medionementon 'the Middle Sanctuary' is thought to have been located at Cainpapple near the Antonine Wall in Scotland. There are sacred groves recorded in Anglesey where the Druids made their last refuge from the Romans.

According to Laing, most places sacred to the Celts were unmarked by structures so that nothing is left of these natural sacred places except the very occasional remains of a wooden temple, invariably built of oak. With the Celts as with other peoples certain trees and groves of trees (*nementi*) were held sacred and treated with great veneration. The Druids, the Celtic priests, chose groves of oak for the sake of the tree alone and never performed a sacred rite without having a branch of it. Boughs of oak were found in an oak coffin in a tumlus at Gristhorpe in 1834 where mistletoe was also found. The Druids thought that anything that grew on an oak tree had been sent by God himself.

The Druids used 'omen sticks' perhaps made from fruit branches. Such wands and rods, like the willow rods of the Scythians, are forerunners of sceptres, heralds' wands and general staffs. All are symbols of power derived from the original sacredness of the tree. The early Christian missionaries found that they had to contend in Britain as in ancient Germany with the sacred groves, trying to destroy them or build their churches within them in order to subvert their power.

The Roman invasion in AD 40 brought Christianity to Britain and we know that there were Christian churches by the second century. But it was not until the fourth century that the Declaration of Christianity was made by Constantine. We also know that in AD 597 when St Augustine was sent to Britain he was instructed not to destroy the temples of pagan Britain but to establish Christian churches on these sites in order to convert the native British. At the Councils of Auxerne (AD 578), Tours (AD 637) and Nantes (AD 658) the practice of tree worship (*Cultus arborum*) was forbidden.

Pliny the Elder, writing for Roman readers on the customs of the Celts, predictably mentioned only the worship of oak trees. The yew was never mentioned; yet Vaughan Cornish the historian suggested in 1947 that the yew had been a holy tree in Britain before Druidical times and was merely adopted by the Druids. Pliny, like Julius Caesar, may have been indulging in inadvertent praise. Nevertheless, considering the importance of the yew in our ancient culture the omission is surprising.

Tree recording

In the seventeenth century John Evelyn, the diarist and Court official, published his *Sylva, or a Discourse of Forest Trees, and the Propagation of Timber in his Majesty's Dominions* (1664). Through the publication he encouraged landowners to replant neglected woodland for the materials required in shipbuilding and for home timber demands. He argued that improved land husbandry and farming techniques could release agricultural labourers for instruction in Forestry and Woodland practice.

In the Georgian period, it was fashionable to establish timber for investment, although this was something the Victorians were not so bothered about, even though they were keen on establishing game coverts. As mentioned previously, at about this time the acceleration into Britain of plant material from every part of the globe gathered pace. Every garden, estate and newly formed arboretum were planting these imports. In 1838 J.C. Loudon completed his mammoth work *Trees and Shrubs of Great Britain* (*Arboretum et Fruticetum Britannicum*). Propagation, culture and management of most woody plants was written about after extensive travels, and the work contained many illustrations in the four text volumes.

Some sixty-odd years later, in 1906, Elwes and Henry published their private, but great work, *Trees of Great Britain and Ireland*. It has a limited distribution to selected subscribers. The 400 photographic plates of important specimens are valuable records, especially those of trees which still survive. At the 1891 and again at the 1931 Conifer Conferences, records of specimen conifers were published that have given us more valuable information on tree growth.

Later this century, Richard St Barbe Baker, who founded Men of the Trees (now the International Tree Foundation) published several works, including one on famous trees, that highlighted some exceptional specimens. Also L.J.F. Brimble's book, *Trees in Britain* (1948) had special specimens from southern England drawn by the Rev. Lonsdale Ragg.

Alan Mitchell's classic *A Field Guide to the Trees of Britain and Northern Europe* (1974) had a list of some of Britain's tree collections open to the public, as well as measurements of the biggest specimens per species. A few years earlier, he had supplied lists of record trees to J.H. Wilks for his book *Trees of the British Isles*, which contained much folklore and legend and which, incidentally, Mitchell had little time for.

Alan Mitchell, who had worked at Westonbirt Arboretum and at the National Pinetum at Bedgebury for the Forestry Commission, was a most prolific tree recorder. When he left the Commission in the 1980s he continued his work in a private capacity which culminated in the formation of TROBI (the Tree Register of the British Isles). TROBI is a registered charity, with the trustees representing a cross-section of the forestry and arboricultural world. There are currently over 100,000 entries in their data, and it is noted for its value for reference and research purposes. The principal object of the Register is to identify exceptional or champion trees. These are of interest in themselves, but may well have further value for propagation purposes and the checking of growth rates. A network of volunteers supply the information on measurements to keep the records up to date, and these records are available for a small donation to cover administration costs. TROBI has helped considerably with the supply of records for this book. There are many individuals who have held an interest and recorded trees for many years, such as Jim Paterson from Nairn, who is the acknowledged authority on Scotland's champion trees.

Also, since Victorian times, periodicals such as *The Gentleman's Magazine*, the *Gardener's Chronicle* and *Country Life* have included articles on historic and exceptional trees. The various County Naturalists Trusts have also published records and accounts of trees they have seen on their excursions. These have all been valuable in building up the tradition of observation and recording, which is now well established in Britain and Ireland.

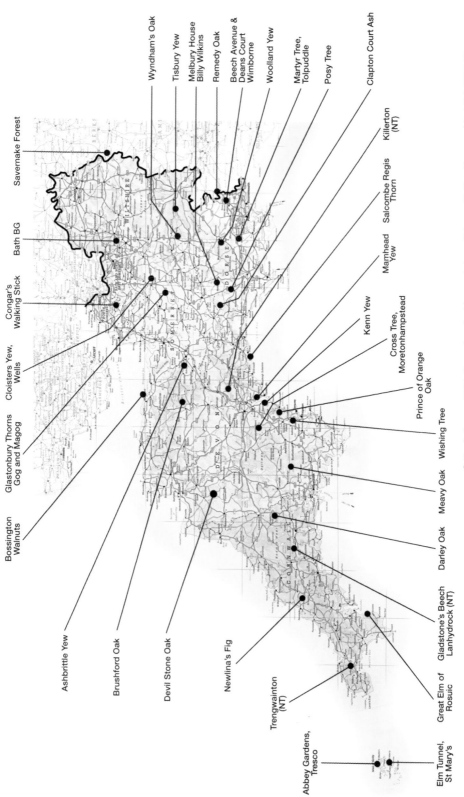

Wyndham's Oak

Tisbury Yew

Melbury House
Billy Wilkins

Remedy Oak

Beech Avenue &
Deans Court
Wimborne

Woolland Yew

Martyr Tree,
Tolpuddle

Posy Tree

Clapton Court Ash

Savernake Forest

Bath BG

Congar's
Walking Stick

Cloisters Yew,
Wells

Glastonbury Thorns
Gog and Magog

Bossington
Walnuts

Killerton
(NT)

Salcombe Regis
Thorn

Mamhead
Yew

Kenn Yew

Cross Tree,
Moretonhampstead

Prince of Orange
Oak

Wishing Tree

Meavy Oak

Darley Oak

Gladstone's Beech
Lanhydrock (NT)

Great Elm of
Rosuic

Ashbrittle Yew

Brushford Oak

Devil Stone Oak

Newlina's Fig

Trengwainton
(NT)

Abbey Gardens,
Tresco

Elm Tunnel,
St Mary's

© Bartholomew 1996. Reproduced with permission of Harper Collins Cartographic. MM-1297–78.

West Country

It is but a short distance between the two coastlines of Cornwall, but they are very different from each other. To the north the wild Atlantic hits the high granite cliffs, topped by ruins of tin mines and punctuated by bays popular with holidaymakers. To the south lies the softer Channel coast, with many deep estuaries that have forced road-building further north, so creating quieter coastal havens. The climate is mild and more sheltered in the south, and it is here that so many renowned gardens have been created. Far older is the ancient and relatively untouched landscape of boundary walls and hedges of elm that is such a distinctive feature of this remote part of England. Off Land's End, the Isles of Scilly have a mixture of the prehistoric and highly exotic.

Across the broad Tamar rises wild Dartmoor, so splendid in sunshine, so menacing in mist. From the strangely shaped tors the land drops north and south to old ports and newer holiday resorts. Beside the Bristol Channel, the small but beautiful Exmoor goes virtually to the edge of the sea cliffs and, in the surrounding villages, old trees still dot the village greens and church-yards. To the east are the Quantocks and, beyond, the flatlands of the Somerset Levels finally rise up to the limestone Mendips, full of gorges and caves.

The red rolling farmlands of south Devon, with their sunken lanes and attractive villages, have a wealth of estates and, like Cornwall, the mild climate has allowed many trees to develop and grow to majestic proportions. Neighbouring Dorset has a green crescent of hills through her centre and the presence of the hill forts lends a timeless quality to this very English landscape. Not only are there rural trees in Dorset but also, surprisingly, a sycamore with a trade union past!

To the north east, Wiltshire has a characteristic appearance of dry chalk uplands, but within the sheltered vales are magnificent houses and estates that contain historically important trees. The river Avon flows into the Bristol Channel beyond Bristol and at the elegant city of Bath are parks, gardens, squares and crescents with rich collections of big trees.

CORNWALL

Within the old parish of Linkinhorne, on the edge of the mysterious Bodmin Moor,

Darley oak, Bodmin Moor – once a look-out tree

Darley Farm was home to Cornwall's greatest oak. The *Darley Oak* still remains, but in its present form is only about half of its original size. It measured over 11 metres (36 feet) in circumference when surveyed in 1958 and had seven stone steps inside its immense hollow bole. It was supposedly once used as a look-out post and also hid a local youth who was escaping from a press gang in the eighteenth century. In the late 1980s the farmer, returning to the house that stands behind the oak, was amazed to see that half the hollow shell had broken away and lay on the lawn by the farmhouse. The stone steps still remain, but now climb a grassy bank that was once the centre of the Darley Oak. The Hoare family recount family tea parties that took place inside the tree only a few decades ago. The Darley Oak is in a prominent position, still very much alive, at the end of the entrance drive from Darley Lodge near to the Darley Forde Garage. It stands on raised ground inside the old garden wall.

The fig tree of West Asia and the Mediterranean has long been cultivated in England. It is usually grown against a south-facing wall but sometimes is grown free standing, especially in the south. After the olive, it has been a fundamental part of the economy of its homelands. In England, Cardinal Pole is popularly credited with having planted the first fig in the grounds of Lambeth Palace in 1548. Those who know *Newlina's fig*, which grows at an angle out of the south wall of the village church in Newlyn East, Cornwall, believe that of all

Newlina's fig – growing mysteriously out of the church at Newlyn East

One of the many great Cornish gardens is Trengwainton where great magnolias grow

figs in England, that is the elder statesman.

The legend tells of St Newlina travelling the south-west peninsula, spreading early Christianity. On the spot where the church now stands she drove a stick of figwood into the earth. The tree took root and around the fig the church was built. A parallel story is that of Joseph of Arimathea and the Glastonbury Thorn. A local simple rhyme reads:

In ancient days Newlina came, the saint
who gave this place its name,
Her staff she planted and she prayed, 'let
here a church to God be made'.
This fig tree is her staff folks say, destroy
it not in any way.
Upon it lays a dreadful curse, who plucks
a leaf will need a hearse.

It is said that four Cornishmen have

suffered bad luck after pruning the fig. One of the most recent was a tree surgeon who broke his leg falling from a tree the day after pruning Newlina's fig! The truth of the legend is open to question, but what is not is the remarkable way the old fig grows straight out of the wall. Looking inside the church, which is in a small village several miles south of the holiday town of Newquay, there is no evidence of disturbance to the walls. It is indeed a mystery.

In a remote part of Goonhilly Down in south Cornwall grows the *Great Elm of Rosuic*. A pollard tree of considerable age, it is considered by the eminent woodland and countryside historian Oliver Rackham to be a possible original tree of one of the elm variants of the Cornish elm (*Ulmus stricta*). The Cornish elm has a distinctive upright growth habit and drops its leaves very late in the year. The more spreading variant, according to Rackham, grows in the Lizard Peninsula and in the Truro locality. The Rosuic elm is found in the hamlet of that name in a valley to the north-west of the

Lanhydrock – part of the double beech avenue leading from the house towards the River Fowey

Gladstone's beech – planted over a hundred years ago at Lanhydrock by the Liberal Prime Minister

National Trust garden Trengwainton has probably the most comprehensive collection of exotic plants of all the gardens. The arrangement is unusual, partly in a series of walled gardens near the entrance where some of the more tender species are grown, partly in woodland and partly beside a stream at the edge of a long drive to the house. Notable trees at Trengwainton are the *Magnolia veitchii* planted in 1936. This is a hybrid between *Magnolia campbellii* and *Magnolia denudata* raised by Veitch's nursery at Exeter. Here too are an excellent dawn redwood and a huge multi-stemmed Campbell's magnolia. This plant was sown in 1926 but the original trees were brought over from Sikkim in 1868. Along the drive some commemorative plantings have been carried out, including on the west side of the meadow a rare but lovely Mexican pine planted in 1962 by the Princess Royal.

Near Bodmin, Lanhydrock is an old estate famed for its towering magnolias and its double beech avenue. The original avenue was planted in 1648 by the second Lord Robartes as a single avenue of sycamores and has gradually been replaced by the beech. One or two of the sycamores have survived however. Lord Robartes is reputed to have directed the planting of the avenues whilst in prison during the Civil War. The walk down the avenue to the River Fowey is a fine one. By the tennis courts are two copper beeches. The larger one was planted in June 1889 by Gladstone, the Liberal Prime Minister. The smaller tree was planted by the Earl of Roseberry in November 1905. Although there is less than seven years between plantings, there is a big difference in their respective sizes, a good example of why one should not be too definite about tree ageing in relation to size. The reason for the plantings? Lanhydrock has always been a Liberal stronghold.

The house, gardens and estate of Lanhydrock cover a total of 450 acres. Very large older trees dot the parkland and a shelter belt surrounds the estate. An interesting and weirdly shaped old Monterey

attractive little fishing village of Coverack.

The warmth of the Gulf Stream, coupled with the natural landscape and imagination of some inspired designers and plantsmen, has helped to create some wonderful Cornish gardens where all manner of trees can be found. The early nineteenth century saw garden owners passionate for exotica and the Victorian plant-hunting expeditions, often financed by the owners, brought many plants to the south-west gardens.

At Heamoor, outside Penzance, the

Pine can be seen whilst approaching the house on the walk from the car park. A huge limb has split from the main bole and rests on the ground still alive. It gives a glimpse of what the crown of the tree looks like close to. The old cones, that can remain close to the branches for many years, are virtually within the reach of outstretched arms. The rugged, deeply fissured bark is another attraction for anyone who wishes to take the trouble of straying off the main path.

There are other gardens in Cornwall that contain trees of such size and rarity that, along with Devon, the south-west peninsula

Tresco Abbey Gardens – exotic trees such as the Metrosideros with its aerial root system grow in this paradise garden

is unique in British tree recording. Some Cornish gardens with record trees are Trewithen, Probus, Trebah, Glendurgan, Trelissick, Heligan, Caerhayes, Pencarrow and Polgwynne.

ISLES OF SCILLY

Some 28 miles further west from Lands End are those wonderful outcrops of rock in the Atlantic, the Isles of Scilly. Within sight of the largest island, St Mary's, is the island of Tresco. Looking from the cliffs of St Mary's you can make out the dark shapes of the conifers, planted in the mid-nineteenth century by Augustus Smith to create shelter from the salt-laden winds. These shelter belts were for his garden, which has become the world renowned Tresco Abbey Gardens of today.

In 1834 Augustus Smith left his home in Hertfordshire to take up residence on Scilly as leaseholder of the Islands in the position of Lord Proprietor. He chose Tresco as the centre of his 'empire', selecting a site for his house previously chosen by Benedictine monks for their priory. The priory had fallen into disuse in the sixteenth century and only the ruined walls remained. They are now incorporated into the gardens of today. The garden was developed across the south-facing hillside in a series of terraces. By the time of his death in 1872 Augustus Smith had produced one of the most remarkable of the Victorian gardens in a setting unmatched anywhere.

A list of all the unusual trees at Tresco would be too great to fill these pages so the exceptional ones are noted as follows. The Tree Fern Glade on the way from New Grimsby harbour contains the largest specimen in Britain of the Mauri pine. Within 'The Hop Circle' are two record specimens of a palm from New Zealand, *Cordyline australis* 'lentiginosa', the cabbage tree in its brown-leaved form. In the Pebble Garden are very rare and prized variegated forms of the same tree. The Chilean wine palm, with its very distinctive barrel-looking trunk, grows close by. It is filled with its own

St Mary's, Isles of Scilly – elms still flourish, like this tunnel of elm between Holyvale and Hugh Town

anywhere, including its home, Australia!

On a very different note, few deciduous trees grow in the gardens but a big mulberry grows near the pools. Was this a survivor from the Benedictine monastery? It is interesting to ponder what sort of response Augustus Smith would receive from the Scillonians if he arrived at Tresco today and proposed a highly exotic garden on a beautiful, if fairly barren Atlantic island. One far different from the nineteenth-century view, I suspect!

Meavy Oak – still clinging to life, the old tree grows near the church

fermented sap, tapped 'in its native land'. for its alcoholic properties.

The Lighthouse Walk contains the pohutawawa (*Metrosideros formentosa*), the New Zealand Christmas tree. This particular massive specimen that straddles the path is regarded as one of the largest of the species in the world and is remarkable for its many aerial roots, some of which have rooted to form props to the main trunk. Throughout the gardens are good examples of the orange bark myrtle from Chile (*Myrtus luma*), a tree that can only survive in the extreme south west. Britain's biggest is at Tresco. Other plants are the largest of their type world-wide. A *Banksia integrifolia* is, according to Australian opinion, the largest to be found

The freak weather in January 1987 caused extensive damage to the gardens and much was lost or had to be cut back hard. Since then replanting and restoration work has carried on without interruption. Tresco can still rightly claim to have one of the world's most unusual and extraordinary gardens.

A feature of the main island of St Mary's is the extensive and healthy elm population. The tree grows wild and suckers freely. It is also used as a hedging plant and windbreak right down to the sea's edge. It is very tolerant of the wind and salt. The nature reserve that runs from Porth Hellick to

Devil Stone oak, Shebbear

Cross tree, Moretonhampstead

Holyvale has pure elm standing for almost the entirety of its route beyond the Higher Moors. There is also a tunnel of elm between Holyvale and Hugh Town. In the Old Town church cemetery, where former Prime Minister Harold Wilson was buried in 1995, elms protect the churchyard and the more exotic plantings within. At Holyvale, in the centre of St Mary's, a black mulberry of some size grows, one of the island's oldest planted trees.

DEVON

On the south-west of the Dartmoor National Park near to Yelverton the small village of Meavy has a very special oak tree. The tree, known as the *Royal Oak* or simply The *Meavy Oak*, was traditionally said to be a Gospel oak used for preaching before St Peter's Church was built close by in AD 1122. The lych gate stands alongside and at one time the original village cross was on the far side of the oak, now replaced with a stone cross.

An 1833 engraving carried the following description of the tree:

It is stagheaded and about 50 feet in height, the trunk which is 27 feet in circumference (no position of measurement is given) is hollow, and has held nine persons at one time. This oak is supposed to have existed at the time of King John.

In the 1970s the old wooden props that had supported the tree from across the churchyard wall were removed due to decay. Steel rods were threaded through the tree about two-thirds of the way up the main structure. These rods were set into concrete stands to prevent them from sinking with the weight of the leaning tree. The crown was reduced and the dead wood removed. The local community rallied around to finance this work. In 1995 the tree was an amazing structure, although very little of the lower trunk remained and was very hollow, the branches were clothed in leaves. One would imagine that at one time the original trunk covered a much larger area. The *Meavy*

27

LEFT:
The present day Cross tree

oak creates a feeling of great antiquity and the measurements in 1833 give a clue to its age. I am sure it has an early connection with the church. Not far from the oak is the mansion where Sir Francis Drake once lived. On the village green beyond the *Meavy oak* is a younger tree grown from an acorn from the original.

In rural west Devon there are many small villages that are seldom seen by the tourists and holidaymakers who either travel the main routes or stick to the coastal areas. Some of these villages are relatively unspoilt, mainly agricultural communities that have kept to their traditions and customs. In the village of Shebbear the *Devil Stone oak* grows on the village green near the church. Beneath the tree is a large boulder that weighs over a ton. Every 5th November a

group of men from the village turn over the stone with staves. This custom is carried out after sunset and after first ringing a peal of bells at the church. Following the turning of the stone the church bells are rung again. The origin of the custom is obscure but one school of thought aligns the activity to the moving of the stone from Christ's tomb, and with this, overtones of the Resurrection come to mind. Stones were revered and worshipped far back into the Bronze Age and the custom may have its origin in pre-Christian times. On the side of the village hall, behind the big old hollow oak, a plaque displays the custom and the powerful shape of the oak tree.

On the eastern edge of Dartmoor in the small crossroads town of Moreton-hampstead, stands the 'Cross tree' or 'Dancing tree'. The copper beech that grows

Kenn yew – ancient yew in St Andrew's churchyard

Prince of Orange oak, Teigngrace

pollarded into a bowl shape, a platform with railings was erected, and a bridge built across to the first floor of the inn. This allowed musicians on to the platform. Paroled French officers played for the townsfolk, who danced below the tree. The name and activities in the tree spread and soon from far and wide, people came to Moretonhampstead for 'merrymaking'.

R.D. Blackmore, author of *Lorna Doone* immortalised the scene in *Christowel*, his book about Devon country life.

Well known local artist Eve Dymond White has captured the romance of the tree perfectly in her fine drawing *The Dancing Tree*.

Salcombe Regis, near Sidmouth in south-east Devon, spreads over a plateau with the central feature of the parish being a narrow combe which slopes down to the sea. This parish was given by a Saxon king to the monks of Exeter Cathedral. In the early days some of the monks occupied the manor house, which is called 'Thorn', taken from a boundary marking tree, the *Salcombe Regis Thorn*. According to Vaughan Cornish, the author of *Historic Thorn Trees in the British Isles* whose family were landowners for many centuries in this area, the thorn at the head of the combe marks the site of a prehistoric place of assembly.

The thorn that stands there today is a replacement of earlier trees that have marked the spot. The nearby plaque reads 'A thorn tree has been maintained here since Saxon times, when it marked the boundary between the cultivated field of the combe and the open common of the hill. It has given the name Thorn to the adjacent house where the Manor Court was held, and to the surrounding farm.'

In recent years much exhaustive research and recording work has gone into the yew trees of the British Isles by such people as Allen Meredith, Bill Bowen from Bath and Percival Morgan from Devon. Percival Morgan has spent many hours visiting churches, recording their woodwork, and whilst visiting he has become fascinated by

today beside Cross Street is a 1912 replacement for the massive old elm that once stood by the remains of the old market cross. It finally blew down in a severe gale in 1903.

The old market cross had stood on raised ground well into the seventeenth century. A wych elm seeded itself into the ground beside the cross. It grew on into a large tree, which eventually ousted the cross, breaking the shaft in the process. The head of the cross was then positioned in front of the tree. It still stands in the same manner today.

The alternative name of 'Dancing tree' originates from the work of one John Hancock, who turned the nearby dwelling into a public house in 1799. He had the elm the churchyard yew trees. To quote:

I go around old churches looking at the wood carving of the old craftsmen and it was on these visits that I came to look at the yews in the churchyards. To date I have recorded over 950 yews in over 200 churchyards, the largest being 40 feet in girth at 3 feet above ground in a little churchyard about 8 miles south of Exeter.

The churchyard referred to is Kenn, a few miles west of the Exe estuary. The yew is located approximately 40 metres (44 yards)

south-west of the church of St Andrew. It has part of the crown missing, probably due to wind damage, but it is generally in a healthy state. Of course the very nature of an ancient yew makes measurement a chance affair and can only ever be a guide to age in comparison to a similar girthed tree but it is nevertheless fascinating.

Not so far away, now on private ground, is the old church at Mamhead. The yew here was struck by lightning in the 1940s but has recovered despite this, having been cut back severely to about 12 metres (39 feet). It has a girth of 10.36 metres (34 feet) and appears to have a sound trunk, very unusual for such

Killerton – superb Lucombe oak near the lake

a big girthed tree.

The *Prince of Orange's oak* takes its fame from a story relating to the Prince, later to become William III or commonly 'King Billy', resting by the tree after his landing at Brixham on 5 November 1688. With him were his Protestant troops from Orange. Tradition says the oak was eighty years old at the time. It grows now on a relative byway in the village of Teigngrace near Newton Abbot. At breast height the tree is over 10 metres (33 feet) in girth and has a very distinctively shaped trunk with many hollows, which, in 1995, included a colony of wild bees.

A few miles north of Totnes, at the castle at Berry Pomeroy, an old beech goes by the name of the *Wishing Tree*. For a wish to be granted it is necessary to walk backwards three times around the tree. If you are not too dizzy, you have a chance of your wish coming true!

In 1995 the Old University College of the South West expanded to become the University of Exeter. It needed more land for buildings so a number of large old houses and gardens were purchased. Some of these had well established, and in some cases unique, trees growing in them. One had an arboretum that had been planted in about 1866 by the famous nurserymen Robert Veitch and Sons. They were active in introducing new species from all over the world but particularly from the United States of America.

In another garden grew some of the earliest Lucombe oaks, hybrids between the Turkey oak and Cork oak, which dated from about 1762. All this wealth of tree

LEFT:
Tulip tree of immense size growing in one of Britain's earliest arboreta at Killerton, Devon

growth was imaginatively grown by William Lucombe of St Thomas, Exeter and was eventually incorporated into the new campus. Some of the trees have now gone but the mixture of these early plantings and later additions have created a new arboretum in its own right. There are over 600 species of trees and shrubs now growing at Exeter University.

The Lucombe oak is a semi-evergreen that grows in several forms. One of the largest girthed trees can be seen in Phear Park, Exmouth, and all around the Exeter area are early examples of this oak. Some particularly fine ones grow at the National Trust garden at Killerton, near Broadclyst between Cullompton and Exeter. This garden is largely the result of the collaboration of two family dynasties. The Aclands, who have owned Killerton since early in the seventeenth century, and the Veitch family,

already mentioned as local nurserymen. The Veitch family were also landscapers and plant introducers of high note and had a major influence on this very early tree collection started around 1800.

The informal arboretum spreads up the south face of a ridge. The Terrace has a fine free-standing tulip tree, while the South Lawn contains a Lucombe oak and a weeping silver lime. The main grass path has cork oaks and a beautiful, and very large for the 'type', deciduous camellia (*Stewartia pseudocamellia*). Other record trees abound and a huge *Magnolia campbellii* can be seen when in flower from over three miles away. The zig-zag path is home to a Coast redwood, raised from seed in about 1843 and planted in 1860. The path to the chapel grounds passes a rare hybrid oak (*Quercus hispanica* 'Crispa'), the biggest in Britain, planted along with a grove of tulip trees in 1808 and near the chapel is a hop hornbeam

Glastonbury thorn – legendary tree near the Abbey ruins

Wearyall Hill – a lone Glastonbury thorn growing on the original site

(*Ostrya carpinifolia*), the tallest in Britain. Within the parkland is a fine Lucombe oak near the pond and impressive evergreen holm oaks can be found near the buildings and chapel.

The good trees are too numerous to mention but this very early tree collection is covered well by the National Trust publication and gives an indication of what the younger collections may, from this mild climate, look like in time.

Elsewhere in Devon many collections contain outstanding trees: Endsleigh, Powderham Castle, Knighthayes Court, Bicton Park and beyond Plymouth on Torpoint the parks of Anthony House and Mount Edgecumbe. Of the National Trust properties, Cotehele north of Plymouth has a record Davidia, Coleton Fishacre near Kingswear has a rare Catalpa and holly species, Arlington Court at Barnstaple has good examples of garden trees. Also, the RHS new national garden at Rosemoor south of Great Torrington is a rapidly developing enterprise with good young trees. In addition Dartington Hall, Totnes also has Lucombe oaks and a good Davidia tree.

Clapton Court Ash, Somerset – extraordinarily shaped old ash tree

SOMERSET

In the famous and mystical Somerset town of Glastonbury, amongst the treasures that pilgrims visit, are the *Glastonbury thorns*. The legend tells us that in the land called Avalon, Joseph of Arimathea, an old tin trader from Phoenicia in whose tomb the body of Jesus was laid, fled his native land and sought peace in Avalon. He and twelve followers climbed a hill to survey the scene and then he drove his thorn staff in the ground to signify the journey's end. The staff took root quickly and on the sixth day of January by the old calendar, which was the original Christmas Day, the thorn flowered. The miracle of the thorn was celebrated by the building of the first Church of Christ on foreign lands and was dedicated to the Virgin Mary.

Scions were taken from the Arimathean Thorn and planted firstly in other parts of Glastonbury and then other locations in England and beyond. The oldest thorn today is on Wearyall Hill overlooking Glastonbury, the traditional place for Joseph's first planting. Others can be seen in the Abbey grounds and in front of the parish church. The thorns now growing are not particularly old. The one in the Abbey Grounds is no more than eighty years old. People expect to see huge old trees and are sometimes disappointed. The thorns' continuity is from cuttings taken and planted to continue the line. As one of the brethren described it to me 'the Thorn is like the Christian message – same church throughout the ages represented by different people, just as the Glastonbury thorn is the same tree, but represented by different specimens; both have death and then new life'.

The *Glastonbury thorn* (*Crateagus oxyacantha biflora praecox*) is double flowering, depending on the weather, from mid-November to January and again in May. Strangely some of the trees retain leaves throughout the year. The large tree on the lawn in front of St John's Church has recently died but younger trees remain.

To the east of Glastonbury and the distinctive Tor, a footpath leads over the flat surrounding farmland. In a hedgerow by the path grow two old oaks known as 'Gog and Magog'. Information regarding their location and names is available from the publications to be found in the Tourist shop

Brushford Oak, Exmoor

by the Abbey grounds.

In Southern England, despite the beauty of the ash tree, there are few trees of great note or fame, apart from the *Winchelsea ash* in Sussex, preached under by John Wesley and drawn by Lonsdale Ragg in 1933. However, the tree that stands within the garden at Clapton Court is very special. The *Clapton Court ash*, looking for all the world like an ancient old pollard oak with burrs, hollows, contorted limbs and lichen covered bark, is in fact a native ash which lays claim to being the biggest girthed and possibly the oldest ash in England. Huge trees in Glen Lyon, Scotland and Talley Abbey, Wales rival its girth size but look nothing like the squat-shaped Clapton Court tree. At 1.5 metres (5 feet) the ash has a girth exceeding 8.90 metres (29 feet) and has been estimated at 220 years old, although it may well be a lot older, even up to 500 years old.

Originally the tree would have grown in the fields and only relatively recently incorporated into gardens. This may well have protected the ash from the chainsaw. There is no doubt this is a 'character' tree and worthy of its fame. For several years its hollow stem housed a colony of wild honey bees whose combs lay exposed over successive winters. Following on from the bees, wasps had a considerable colony when the tree was viewed in the summer of 1995 and rabbits also burrowed deep below the root buttresses.

Not far from the ash can be found an early planting of the dawn redwood (*Metasequoia glyptostroboides*), a tree only rediscovered in Central China in 1941. Seed from the discovered stand was sent to the Arnold Arboretum in Boston and further seed distributed by them through Kew brought a seedling to Clapton in 1949. It stands at over 20 metres (65 feet) tall and is one of the United Kingdom's tallest dawn redwoods.

Also close by is a beautiful acer palmatum that contains the ashes of Mr Martineau, an earlier developer of these splendid gardens. The hollow where his ashes were placed has now sealed over, so locking the remains forever inside the tree. Clapton Court, at the time of writing, has been purchased by new owners. It is not known what their intentions will be regarding opening to the public.

The *Ashbrittle yew*, found in the small village churchyard west of the Somerset town of Wellington, grows on a tumulus. The yew is multi-stemmed with a healthy central stem and six others all well decayed. The mound on which the churchyard now stands is roughly oval and aligned east to west. Legend tells of the churchyard being originally a druidical site and nearby battles with Roman soldiers ended with the heads of defeated Romans being buried on the mound.

On the south-east corner of Exmoor,

Bossington, Somerset – walnut trees, a feature of village scene

Palm Churchyard, Wells Cathedral

near Dulverton and the Caernarvon Arms, the churchyard at Brushford does not have a yew but an old oak in a prominent position. In the reign of Elizabeth I an oak growing in the churchyard of St Nicholas is mentioned in local descriptive passages. The *Brushford oak* is very hollow and has timber props under its largest limbs. It does, though, sport a healthy crown of leaves and has become a symbol of the village's endurance.

Within the church is a chapel designed by the famous architect and garden designer Edwin Lutyens. It was dedicated in 1926 to the Hon. Aubrey Herbert, son of Henry the fourth Earl of Caernarvon, whose fame came from his discovery of Tutankhamun's tomb in Egypt.

The attractive and unspoilt little town of Dulverton, home of the Exmoor National Park Headquarters, had the *Belfry tree* until 1975. This great sycamore, which dwarfed the tower, was split by lightning in the early

Black walnut by croquet lawn, Bishop's Palace, Wells

nineteenth century. In one of the earliest recorded examples of 'modern' tree surgery a local blacksmith held the trunk together with iron bands. Those bands are still resting against the tower walls. The trunk eventually broke in a gale in 1975 when the tree was more than 300 years old.

On the far side of Exmoor the picture postcard village of Bossington, near Porlock was once famed for its *Bossington walnut tree*. It must have featured on countless holiday photographs standing as it did at the centre of the village near the thatched cottages. From the old walnut, younger trees have been grown from the nuts propagated by nurserymen and local gardeners. These trees of various ages are dotted around the village, particularly on the green. They maintain the link between the walnut and this enchanting north Somerset village.

In the square formed by the cloisters of Wells Cathedral is a yew tree surrounded by graves. The place is called 'the Palm Churchyard', the name coming from the custom of using the branches as palms on Palm

Sunday. At the Bishop's Palace in Wells a fine and very old Ginkgo grows close to the wall. The tree was drawn in September 1938 by the tree artist Lonsdale Ragg. By the croquet lawn is an impressive black walnut that is similar in stature to the Much Hadham specimen.

At the east of the churchyard at St Andrews, Congresbury, stands a spreading beech tree. Closer inspection will reveal iron bands around the trunk. Within the beech can be found the remains of a yew tree. The old pieces of yew spill out on the ground below the spreading beech branches. An extraordinary sight! Was the beech planted very close to the yew and in its shade grew to dominate the fading yew, eventually circling the old tree and tightening its grip on the ancient yew? Did the beech grow actually within the yew's hollow centre eventually to spread right around it?

For many centuries the yew was known as *Congar's Walking Stick*. Research has revealed that the name derives from St Congar who, according to legend, came to Britain and his travels brought him eventu-

LEFT:
Congresbury – remains of 'Congar's walking stick' inside beech tree

ally to a spot where he built and dedicated an oratory to the Holy Trinity. He planted his staff and it spread its leaves to provide shade. By tradition that tree was the yew that became *Congar's Walking Stick*. According to Collinson in his *County History of Somerset* 'a fine yew existed in the churchyard in 1790'. Allen Meredith located the old remains from an 1829 engraving which showed the yew in relationship to the church.

King James II and his Queen Mary visited Bath in 1687. Local tradition states that the Queen, anxious for an heir to the throne, visited St Winifred's Well in the town to seek the holy waters for 'help' with fertility. She bore a son the following year and the delighted Queen gave a present to the town of a number of mulberry seedlings to be planted in the locality of the well. St Winifred's Well is on Sion Hill and in the 1970s several of these mulberries were

Wyndham's oak – sinister past (drawing by A Howard)

tracked down by Lonsdale Ragg. The largest was found at Lyde House although this tree was damaged in 1942 air raids.

In the elegant squares and crescents of Bath some splendid early tree plantings took place to complement the architecture. There are particularly fine London planes and in the Botanic Gardens, off Victoria Park, are large hornbeams, a tree of heaven, cucumber tree, snakebark maples, a rare and much sought after variegated table dogwood (*cornus coutroversa* 'variegata'), and the infrequently found Sweet Buck Eye from the southern United States. Towards the city centre are other rare chestnuts and in Henrietta Park is a very large purple sycamore.

DORSET

In a field next to the churchyard at Silton, in the northern tip of Dorset, stands *Wyndham's oak*, named after Sir Hugh Wyndham, whose statue dominates the parish church. Sir Hugh was a well-known circuit judge who lived at the Silton Manor House in the seventeenth century and was known locally for his habit of sitting underneath the tree contemplating. It is also

understood that two of the Duke of Monmouth's followers were hanged from the tree during the Bloody Assizes in the 1600s. There were many such hangings in Somerset and Dorset associated with the infamous Judge Jeffreys. It is most likely that the old gnarled Wyndham's oak, now 9.75 metres (32 feet) in the girth, was a boundary or marker tree from the original Gillingham Forest. It has stood the test of time and now stands alone overlooking the beautiful rolling countryside.

Deep within the Dorset countryside is the village of Woolland. Its yew tree is one

Wimborne Minster to Blandford Forum – famous beech avenue near Badbury Rings, Dorset

Posy tree, Mapperton

of the best specimens in Britain, growing quietly in the corner of the churchyard. It has a beautifully fluted bole and measures over 10 metres (33 feet) in the girth. There is plenty of evidence of badgers regularly visiting the base of the tree and close by is the grave of Count Alexander Csaky 1921–93. In 1994 wild bees were inhabiting the roof of the church.

In neighbouring Wiltshire another huge yew grows in the village churchyard of Tisbury. This tree is spoilt by the concrete inserted into the hollow trunk, a misguided attempt to prolong the tree's life. Sometimes it is better to leave trees to their own devices.

At anytime of year, but especially spring and autumn, when travelling between Wimborne and Blandford Forum, Dorset you cannot fail to be impressed by the beech avenue that runs alongside Badbury Rings hill fort. There, trees were planted by the French prisoners-of-war in the early 1800s. The idea was to plant one beech for every day of the year on each side of the road. Since then the trees have died off, but others have been planted and the overall effect,

Remedy oak – (drawing by A Howard)

particularly when in leaf, is of driving through a leafy tunnel. The area either side is open and at times windy, but there are lovely and popular walks near the beeches and over the hill fort.

At Deans Court, Wimborne, grows Britain's biggest swamp cypress, measured in 1986 at 1.88 metres (6 feet) diameter 5.91 metre girth (19.4 feet). It has since been remeasured with a greater girth recorded in 1994. Two big branches broke away from the tree in the gale of January 1990, but otherwise the tree is intact. It is believed that the tree was brought over from America in the seventeenth century, either by Thomas Hanham, who led an expedition to the New World in 1606, or more probably by John Tradescant, who was gardener to the Cecil family who still own nearby Cranborne Manor. Interestingly, in Tradescant's lists, preserved at The Museum of Garden History at Lambeth, the first items entered are the swamp cypress (*Taxodium distichum*) and a tulip tree (*Liriodendron tulipifera*). A tulip tree stands immediately adjacent to the swamp cypress at Deans Court. The court is still owned by the Hanham family and is open to the public at advertised times.

At Mapperton, near Beaminster, Dorset grows a tree known as the *Posy tree*. The sign on the tree reads: 'It was past this tree that local victims of the Great Plague were carried to a common grave by the surviving villagers'. The tree is a very hollow sycamore, at one time filled with concrete but now only remnants remain. Severe pollarding in the past has reduced the size of the crown and many cavities, hollows and wounds are visible. Also dead branches suggest that in future years tree surgery will be required to keep the tree intact.

The *Posy tree* stands on a small island of grass down a quiet lane on a ridge above Beaminster. Nearby is the renowned Mapperton Gardens. This is indeed a beautiful part of rolling rural Dorset. It is a far cry from 1665 when the Plague was at its peak.

RIGHT:
Remedy oak, Woodlands, Dorset

Then the people of the parish gathered at this spot holding posies of flowers and herbs. These, it was hoped, would ward off the terrible disease. It was common practice in many parts of Britain to try this 'remedy' as a last resort. The nursery rhyme 'Ring a ring of roses, a pocket full of poses, tischoo, tischoo, we all fall down' is a sinister reminder of the Great Plague. Few children can now associate such a quaint song with its origin. The tree measured 3 metres (10 feet) in 1994 at 1 metre (3.3 feet) from the ground, so raising doubts as to the possibilities of the present sycamore being the original. I would think the tree now standing is no more than 200 years old. It is probably a replacement for the old original *Posy tree*.

At Woodlands in Dorset is a tree with similar traditions. It is called the *Remedy oak*. The sign under the tree reads 'According to tradition King Edward VI sat beneath this tree and touched for King's Evil'. In 1551, a year before his death, the 15-year-old King Edward VI visited Dorset and dispensed his 'priest king' therapy at the roadsides of the county. He stopped at the junction of two roads in the wooded area near Verwood. That area is now called simply 'Woodlands'. The magical powers of being touched by the venerated king were seen as a cure for illness and evil. This association goes back into pre-christian times.

The curative powers of the oak were also very strongly believed and that an oak tree was chosen as the place to distribute therapy is no surprise. King's Evil or scrofula was a form of glandular fever, or severe tonsillitis. It was a major disorder up to 100 years ago. The 'scrofa' is the name for 'sour', which describes the look of someone's face when suffering from scrofula.

Customs have changed over the centuries and the belief in the divine powers of the monarchy have gradually been eroded. The link between the oak and healing powers is based much more on chemical fact. The tannin and astringent properties of the bark were used in the treatment of sore throats.

Water found in pockets in oaks was taken and tried as a cure for sore throats and skin problems.

The remains of the *Remedy oak* are an amazing sight. They are little more than a piece of bark with branches hanging over a road, secured by a cable. From the roadside it looks healthy and indeed has a good covering of leaves. From the woodland side it is completely decayed and only half the trunk remains. It is an intriguing tree and its story goes a long way back. At one time it would have been huge and heavily trunked, now it is a shell that still survives.

The *Martyr tree*, in Tolpuddle, Dorset is a sycamore where, it is reputed, five men, James Brine, Thomas Stansfield, John Stansfield, George Loveless and James Loveless – met to plan their Union. In 1833 wages for a farm labourer were cut from 9 to 7 shillings per week – this led to extreme hardship. Local agricultural labourers, led by George Loveless, set up the Friendly Society of Agricultural Labourers, their agreement being made at Thomas Stansfield's Cottage.

An informer betrayed the men after the meeting, which was held on 22 February 1834, and posters were put up locally, and probably on the tree, warning that anyone caught joining illegal Societies or Unions to which they bound themselves in illegal oaths, could be transported.

The Vicar of Tolpuddle supported the men and further unrest was discussed in the evenings at the tree on the village green. The men eventually turned to the GMC Trade Union. Two delegates visited Tolpuddle and, after their visit, the Friendly Society of Agricultural Labourers was formed by George Loveless. The local magistrates and employers arrested George along with six close associates, including the other original four men. They were tried at Dorchester for offences under the Mutiny Act and were sentenced to transportation to Van Dieman's Land (Australia) for seven years. Some stayed

RIGHT:
Oriental plane, Corsham Court – an incredible tree covering a vast area

Martyr tree, Tolpuddle

Martyr tree, Tolpuddle (drawing by A Howard)

in Australia, some returned.

The story of the Tolpuddle Martyrs is seen as a landmark in workers' rights as there was such an outcry from the population about their treatment, and their case was used as a 'bench mark' in the trade union movement. The sycamore tree, known from then onwards as the *Martyr tree* because of its association with the men on the green, has survived well, although the main trunk became very hollow and the big limbs became dangerous as it spread over the green. In 1969 the TUC were informed that the tree might have to be felled. The National Trust commissioned a tree survey and, along with the Parish Council, requested help from the TUC. Together an action plan was drawn up. Tree surgeons banded the tree to prevent splitting; the hollow bole was cleaned out and filled with vermiculite; the dangerous branches were cut back; cables, rods and bolts were inserted; ivy was removed and young growth given room to develop. In the early 1970s the tree began to recover and its girth was measured at 5.40 metres (17.7ft).

To commemorate 150 years since the Tolpuddle Martyrs' struggle, another sycamore was planted in 1984 by the Secretary of the TUC, Len Murray (Lord Murray). The second tree was grown from a seed of the original. It stands close to its parent and close to the thatched shelter built in 1934 to mark the centenary.

The *Martyr tree* measured 5.75 metres (18.9ft) in the girth at 1 metre (3.3ft) from the ground in May 1994 and now the filler has largely been removed from the hollow bole. The tree's crown is quite healthy and sometime in the future the branches will need thinning out to allow it to develop its crown more fully. Then it will once again spread over the green, as it did when the men originally met to discuss their grievances.

Six miles south of Yeovil, on the Dorchester road (A37), Melbury House has a fine arboretum and beautiful deer park. Britain's largest Caucasian oak (*Quercus macranthera*) grows here, and one of the most celebrated old pollard oaks, named *Billy Wilkins* stands near woodland out in the park. This ancient oak is amongst the best old 'burred' specimens to be seen anywhere, and resembles the Lydham Manor tree both in size and appearance. *Billy Wilkins* got his name from a local character who was known on the estate.

WILTSHIRE

The small town of Corsham in Wiltshire has grown considerably in recent years. But the old centre retains its character with seventeenth and eighteenth century golden-stone houses, old weavers' cottages and almhouses. Near the church of St Bartholomew is the impressive entrance to Corsham Court with its history stretching back to Anglo-Saxon times. The house with its gables and mullioned windows was largely built by Thomas Smythe who bought the property

in 1582. Paul Methuen became the owner in 1777 and began a collection of paintings by sixteenth and seventeenth century Italian and Flemish Masters.

The gardens were designed by Lancelot 'Capability' Brown, who planned to include a 13-acre lake, and was completed by Humphry Repton nearly forty years later. Brown built the Gothic Bath House, laid out the avenues and provided for the specimen trees. In particular he has been credited with planting the Oriental plane known as the *Corsham Court plane*. This tree is one of the greatest planes in England. Its most remarkable aspect being the 'layered' branches that have touched the ground, rooted and spread, and thus created a huge spreading crown. It is truly a magnificent tree. The vigour in the tree is now transferred into the newer branches and not the old original trunk. The circumference around the crown is over 240 metres (780 feet). The Oriental plane was introduced into Britain in about 1550 and it may well be that the Corsham plane was planted earlier than its present suggested date.

Other trees at Corsham include a black walnut, close to the plane and a young arboretum area out in the parkland and a pleached hornbeam hedge closer to the house. In the 1990 storm many trees were lost from the grounds but mercifully the plane remained relatively unscathed.

Just to the east of the attractive town of Marlborough one of England's oldest forests can be enjoyed. Savernake Forest covers over 11,330 hectares (28,000 acres) and its Saxon name is derived from 'Severn Oak'. At one time, during King John's reign, the forest covered 255 square kilometres (98 square miles). These days Savernake is mainly large beechwood interspersed with old pollard oaks. Some of the beeches are very tall and the greatest specimens in the 'High Trees' locality can be found close to the A346 Burbage Road. The *King oak* and *Queen oak* have now gone but a drive or walk down the Grand Avenue will still reveal huge old beech trees.

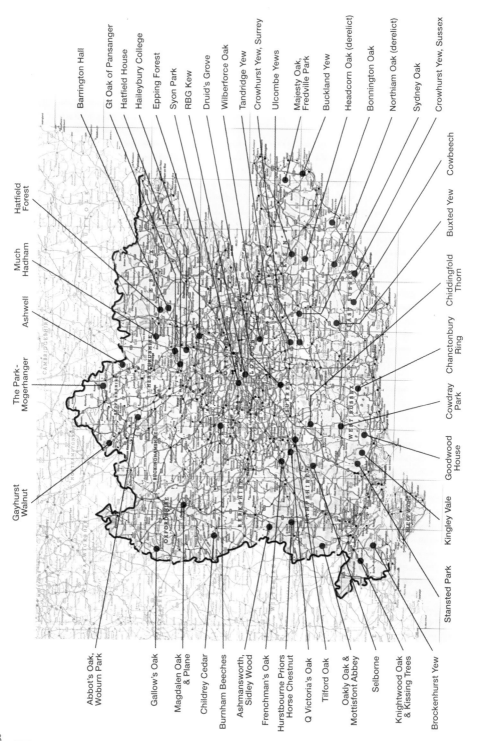

Barrington Hall

Gt Oak of Pansanger

Hatfield House

Haileybury College

Epping Forest

Syon Park

RBG Kew

Druid's Grove

Wilberforce Oak

Tandridge Yew

Crowhurst Yew, Surrey

Ulcombe Yews

Majesty Oak, Fredville Park

Buckland Yew

Headcorn Oak (derelict)

Bonnington Oak

Northiam Oak (derelict)

Sydney Oak

Crowhurst Yew, Sussex

Hatfield Forest

Much Hadham

Ashwell

The Park-Mogerhanger

Gayhurst Walnut

Cowbeech

Buxted Yew

Chiddingfold Thorn

Chanctonbury Ring

Cowdray Park

Goodwood House

Kingley Vale

Stansted Park

Abbot's Oak, Woburn Park

Gallow's Oak

Magdalen Oak & Plane

Childrey Cedar

Burnham Beeches

Ashmansworth, Sidley Wood

Frenchman's Oak

Hurstbourne Priors Horse Chestnut

Q Victoria's Oak

Tilford Oak

Oakly Oak & Mottisfont Abbey

Selborne

Knightwood Oak & Kissing Trees

Brockenhurst Yew

© Bartholomew 1996. Reproduced with permission of Harper Collins Cartographic. MM-1297-78.

South-east England

Chalk downland straddles the south-east coast of England. The summits of the ridges have been used by mankind since pre-historic times. Evidence of this early occupation of the land is given further credence by the existence of so many ancient yews in the south-east. Only Wales has more.

Near the coast, the New Forest spreads over 36,500 hectares (90,000 acres) from the Hampshire Avon to the Beaulieu river. East of the delightful Test Valley, the North Downs begin to curve in a broad sweep across to the east shores of Kent, embracing as they go the diminishing orchards and hopfields of the Weald. Below them is the low and mysterious Romney Marsh.

North, the river Thames cuts through between the Berkshire Downs and the Chilterns where the beechwoods roll northwards towards the Bedfordshire plain. Here are the greatest beeches in England, and at Burnham, the great pollards are contorted into the most weird shapes. Farmland and leafy lanes spread to the east above the London suburbs, finally reaching the rivers and creeks of the Essex coast. This sometimes maligned county still has many treasures that await the tree explorer.

South-east England is the foundation stone of modern Great Britain. On the Kent shores William brought his Norman army into a land ruled under an uneasy Saxon throne. From Winchester he ruled his new land, and at Windsor he built a castle and enclosed a great deer park that still contains medieval trees, recently saved from felling by a public outcry. William's hunting forests in Hampshire also grow trees of great age and provide recreation for thousands of visitors annually.

The region has the greatest concentration of parks, estates, gardens and arboreta in Europe, where record and historic trees abound. Here, London has a tree heritage second to none, with a garden that was, and still is, at the forefront of the botanical world.

HAMPSHIRE

The hamlet of Mottisfont, near the River Test and close to Romsey in west Hampshire, is home to Mottisfont Abbey, set on green lawns amidst vast old trees and bordered on one side by the watermeadows of the Test. The house, as it became after conversion in the sixteenth century, is open to the public and was, together with some 800 hectares (2,000 acres), given to the National Trust in 1957. Some huge London planes growing along the boundary of the Abbey grounds spread out into the road, such is their immense girth. There is also a huge plane near the Abbey.

North of the Abbey across the fields and by the idyllic Test Valley footpath stands the *Oakly oak*. Few trees could stand in such a setting as this old oak, next to a track by a fast flowing chalk river spanned by a small bridge that carries Oakly Lane towards Oakly Farm. The girth of the tree well exceeds 9 metres (29 feet) and twenty people could once stand inside the hollow trunk. Tradition says that the oak is seven centuries old and has one or two legends attached to it. The most famous one is the nursery rhyme 'Hey Diddle Diddle'. A countryman observed one night the silhouette of a cow, tilting at the moon as it appeared from behind the tree. It promptly fell inside the hollow oak, causing a premature birth of its calf. It sounds fantastic, and probably unlikely, but the story creates a powerful image!

To the east, Selborne is one of Hampshire's most famous villages and was made so by Gilbert White. Born in 1720, he

The huge burred bole of the Oakly oak

Gilbert White's simple grave is in the churchyard. Nearby on the main road the empty shop, the village butchers until the 1914–18 war, was recorded by White in 1756:'I planted 4 limes in the Butcher's Yard to hide the sight of blood and filth from ye windows'. Two well pruned limes from the original four remain to this day. Opposite, pleached limes decorate the small front gardens of the cottages.

Behind the village is a steep hill called 'The Hanger', which is mainly covered with beech. It is topped by a boulder called the 'Wishing Stone' and was a favourite haunt of Gilbert White. Over 100 hectares (250 acres) of land around Selborne belong to the National Trust. The walks around here are all splendid.

South-east of Selborne, on the northern outskirts of Liss, near Burgates, an old oak stands on the village green outside the Spread Eagle pub. The oak is completely hollow but much work has been done to continue its life, and its good health is treasured by the local community.

was a scholar and sometime vicar of Selborne. His classic work, *The Natural History of Selborne*, was published in 1788. The village itself is gathered around the green, named the Plestor, and was once a market place. Gilbert White refers to the big oak as a meeting place for the villagers on the green. The original tree has gone but a younger oak, complete with a seat around the trunk, sits attractively in its place.

The *Selborne yew* was measured 7 metres (23 feet) in the girth by Gilbert White in 1789 and exceeded 8 metres (26 feet) when blown down in the second great gale in 1990. It is the most famous of the many yews mentioned by Gilbert White and remains as an epitaph to the naturalist. A desperate attempt to save the tree was carried out in 1990. The blown tree was righted and the hope was that some unbroken root may rekindle the life in the tree. Unfortunately this did not happen and a plaque on the side of the church tells the story. Luckily the tree did not severely damage the church when it fell.

Selborne village, the present day Plestor oak on the green

The Frenchman's oak – the old boundary tree near Winchfield

In north-east Hampshire a well-known landmark still stands between Winchfield and Odiham close to Junction 5 of the M3. Known as *The Frenchman's oak* it was used as a 'limit' or 'parole' tree for the French prisoners billeted in nearby cottages during the Peninsular Wars. The prisoners worked in local quarrying and could not stray beyond the tree on their recreational walks, otherwise they would be severely reprimanded. Similar 'limit' trees are *The Honour oak* near Tavistock and *The Prisoner's bush*, Selkirk, in The Borders.

The Frenchman's oak has been variously propped and lopped over the years but it is still very much alive. A younger oak stands close by and the well preserved '40 mile London' marker, painted distinctively white, stands between the oak and the road on the common land that surrounds the tree.

Only a few miles away, just off the A287 close to Farnham and down a lane opposite the Queen's Arms inn, *Queen Victoria's oak* is a fairly insignificant tree that stands on the westerly side of the lane. On her regular visits to Aldershot the Queen would be driven to this high spot by the oak to admire the magnificent view of the Hampshire countryside spreading out below the tree and hillside.

At Ashmansworth, off the A343 north of Andover, the finest hornbeam coppice in Hampshire stands within Sidley Wood. This is a hilltop site with many of the coppice stools contorted into fantastic shapes, some more than 2 metres (6.5 feet) across. The biggest is estimated to be a minimum of 500 years old. It is suggested that this wood was of natural origin.

The pleasant village of Hurstbourne Priors, at the crossroads of the B3048 and B3450 east of Andover, is home to one of Britain's biggest horse chestnuts. Growing in a field behind St Andrew's church is a huge, very old chestnut. It is surrounded by a wooden fence to protect it from horses that graze the field.

A famous corner of Hampshire is known as the New Forest. Over more than nine centuries ago, William the Conqueror set aside his 'new' hunting lands to guard against any threat to his chase of the Royal deer.

The forest is still very much a working and living community, where ponies and cattle have right of way as they freely graze the land. The main difference in present days is that it is a recreational haven for thousands of people each year. For the tree enthusiast it is essential to go deeper into forest areas to experience the true unchanged magic of the ancient woodland. Here, wild deer browse the oaks and beeches and huge old pieces of timber are host to a myriad of wildlife.

In recent years the management of the forest has been reinforced. Now planning powers equivalent to those of a National Park give added protection, and a partnership of agencies, authorities and organisations work together to run the whole area.

Much has been written about the history of the forest for those who wish to find out

Knightwood oak – the New Forest's most celebrated oak

of some considerable height. It is variously estimated as being between 300 and 400 years old and it is ringed by a wooden fence that has protected the ground below the tree from compaction, and has also created excellent conditions for younger growth to flourish. It is well worth visiting.

This whole area gives a taste of the true New Forest experience. Walk for a few hundred metres from the car park and you have your own company. Around you are huge broken and weird pieces of timber, superb beeches and oaks covered in lichens.

Near the *Knightwood oak*, the incredible sight of the *Fused* or *Kissing trees* can be found, where an oak and beech embrace each other. Botanically known rather unpoetically as 'inosculation' – the growing together of two different species – this rare happening is as equally worth seeing as the *Knightwood oak*. Also in the area are oaks planted by royalty in recent times.

more, and the guide entitled *Explore the New Forest* and the Hampshire County Council booklet *Ancient Woodland* are excellent guides for walkers and the naturally inquisitive.

The forest is divided by 'walks', old segments of land like parishes in a town. These regions make an ideal way of exploring. Major walks are Bolderwood Walk, Rhinefield Ornamental Drive and Oberwater Walk.

Two of the most famous trees in the New Forest were the *Queen beech* and the *Knightwood oak*. The *Queen beech* has now gone but the *Knightwood oak* proudly remains. It can be found by travelling down the A35 from Lyndhurst and taking the ornamental drive heading for Bolderwood Walk to the west. A path leads from the signed car park towards the tree.

The *Knightwood oak*, named after the enclosure in which it stands, is an old pollard

Kissing Trees – oak and beech embrace in the New Forest

The weird-shaped trees in this area are reminiscent of Burnham Beeches, and the ancient rights of estover, or collecting firewood from the forest, was practised until 1698. Then, an act of William III made the feeding of deer by pollarding an offence, thus helping to create this forest scene. At the village of Brockenhurst in the middle of the New Forest there is an ancient churchyard yew estimated at over a thousand years old and with a branch spread of over 20 metres (65 feet). The grave of Brusher Mills, the forest snake-catcher and local character who lived in a hut in the forest, is nearby.

WEST SUSSEX

One mile east of Midhurst, in West Sussex, Cowdray Park is home to many impressive trees.

An avenue of Wellingtonias a 300-year-old Lebanon cedar, as well as a huge variety of other species, makes for a wonderful treescape. It is, however, the *Durmast oak* (over 9 metres (29 feet) in girth at the buttressed base, and 7 metres (23 feet) at 2 metres (7 feet) high) and the Sweet chestnut, with a girth exceeding 9 metres (29 feet), that make Cowdray even more well-

known in tree circles. The oak is thought to be one of Britain's oldest surviving oaks.

A few miles east of Cowdray, Petworth House and Park were originally laid out during the Elizabethan period. 'Capability' Brown redesigned the grounds in 1751, but the gardens and park suffered badly in the great storm of 1987. However, 10,000 new trees have been planted by the National Trust as part of the restoration scheme.

Above Chichester, the beautiful downland scenery has many attractions for the visitor. As well as the Weald and Downland Open Air Museum, there are the various appeals of Goodwood – the 'Glorious Goodwood' racecourse, the motor-racing track, golf course and other sports facilities of Goodwood Park itself.

Close to Goodwood House, are several Cork oaks of varying ages. Their appearance perfectly matches the notable Sussex flint building. Goodwood is the seat of the Dukes of Richmond and Gordon, and was built between 1780 and 1800, but the biggest and oldest trees pre-date the house. Opposite the front of the house, across open parkland, the

Goodwood – the cork oaks complement the flint house

beautiful cricket ground sits happily amongst some huge, magnificent Lebanon cedars. They are amongst the earliest and biggest in Britain, the greatest having a girth exceeding 10 metres (33 feet).

By early in the 1700s the Cedar of Lebanon had become quite an established introduction and was found in the grounds of a number of country seats. The Duke of Richmond planted many specimens later in the eighteenth century, not for timber but for ornament.

In 1761, Peter Collinson, according to his diary, paid £79. 6s on behalf of the Duke for one thousand 5-year-old cedars, which were planted at Goodwood in the same year. The young trees had been raised by a butcher named John Clarke from Barnes, London.

Loudon wrote of the Cedar of Lebanon: 'the cedar is one of the most magnificent of trees, uniting the grand with the picturesque, in a manner not equalled by any other tree in Britain' and 'it confers dignity on the park and mansion to which it belongs'. Loudon gave statistics and a list of impressive specimens in his work entitled *Arboretum* (1838, pp. 2426–7).

The three other cedars seen in Britain arrived in the nineteenth century: the Deodar cedar in 1831, the Atlas cedar in about 1843 and the relatively rare Cyprus cedar in 1879.

A well-known landscape feature on the south Sussex Downs, between Steyning and Washington, is the Chanctonbury Ring, greatly affected by the great gales of 1987 and 1990. The beech circle that grows on the hill fort above the village of Wiston was originally planted by Charles Goring of Wiston House, the great Elizabethan mansion at the foot of the Downs. He lived out his own version of the classic tale 'The man who planted trees'. As a boy, he held the dream of planting the whole of the top and northern slopes of the Downs above his home at Wiston.

In 1760, while still relatively young, in order to realise his ambition he persevered up and down the 800-foot hill, carrying not only the trees but also the water in cans and bottles which would help the beeches to establish. He died at the age of 85, having spent the best part of his life watching the gradual transformation of the hillside above his home. His grave, in Washington church-yard, is within sight of his life's work. The trees are not loved by all, however, as they grow over the well preserved embankments of an Iron-Age hill fort, as well as the remains of two Roman buildings. 'The ring', not the description of the trees but of the hill fort, can be seen from far and wide and the views from the hill are extensive. The long-distance footpath, the South Downs Way, crosses the hill.

Four miles north of Chichester, high on the Chalk Downs, lies Kingley Vale, one of the strangest and least known nature reserves in England, and the site of one of Europe's finest yew forests.

It is different from Reenadinna, the wild yew wood near Killarney, yet it does have obvious similarities. It is drier and the oldest trees are estimated to be approximately 500 years old, but some may be quite a lot older.

Car parking is about one mile away from the reserve at West Stoke, near Mid Lavant. As you walk, the landscape changes from chalk scrub to the yews on the higher ground. Some trees were killed or shattered by rifle practice during the Second World War. Approximately twenty large old yews are thought to be the parent trees of all the numerous offspring now to be seen.

The dense shade created by the yews eradicates almost all other plants. The remains of dead junipers, shaded out as the yews have grown, can be seen.

On some of the trees, there is a distinctive bristle of hard, thin leaves, where they have been browsed by animals, noticeable on some wild specimens but not on churchyard yews. One of the great yews in Kentchurch Park in Herefordshire has such bristles, caused principally by the deer herd. In the autumn, the female trees are covered in fruit.

The red ovils are harmless, and in days gone by were eaten by humans, when not

Old Cedars of Lebanon by the cricket field at Goodwood

taken by the birds. It is the foliage in quantity, dead or alive, that is deadly as the leaves contain taxin.

In the nineteenth century, Lowe, the great 'recorder' of yews, conducted experiments with the foliage on himself, and his account of the results makes fascinating if not sombre reading:

The tracings of the pulse show beyond doubt that it is a cardiac tonic of no mean value. The heart's action is decreased in frequency by small doses, such as one twentieth to one eighth grain, at the same time that the cardiac pressure is distinctly increased.

and finally:

On the whole it contrasts favourably with digitalis and convallovia, and is worthy of more extended observation.

Recent findings on the uses of taxin in relation to the treatment of cancer, have borne out Lowe's comments on the need for more experimentation.

As well as the yews, Kingley Vale has interesting archaeological remains as the site has been used by man over many millennia. At the head of the Vale, the Tansley Memorial stone commemorates Sir Arthur Tansley who pioneered the study of woodland ecology in the twentieth century. The book *The Great Yew Forest* by Richard Williamson (son of Henry Williamson, author of *Tarka the Otter*) is a complete account of the nature reserve in all its forms. The Victorians loved the forest and considered it both sinister and fantastic. Today it holds a special attraction as a unique, woodland ecology.

To the west, past Funtington and north of Havant, the village of Rowland's Castle is a convenient place to stop to take the public footpath into Stansted Park. Walking on rising ground, you are suddenly confronted by a wonderful open piece of land bordered by long avenues of trees. At the far end of the vista is Stansted House itself. At the

Rowland's Castle end of the avenue, a cross marks the spot where, on 7 May 1944, an airman crashed his plane and was killed. The man who found the remains of the aircraft had returned fifty years later on VE day to leave a commemorative card (1994). The double line of beeches to the north of the open ground were planted on the day that the unhappy and long-suffering monarch,

Stansted Park – the great beech avenue

George III, died. The trees were dedicated to his memory. Another beech avenue leads along the main drive by the house, and there are many other walks through the fairly extensive Stansted Forest.

EAST SUSSEX

The name Crowhurst has close links with ancient yews, since Crowhurst, Sussex has such a tree, and so has the neighbouring county of Surrey. The Sussex tree has had a series of measurements taken for over more than 300 years. John Aubrey visited the yew in 1680 and found it to be 8.20 metres (27 feet). When measured in 1879, the girth was less than the 1680 recording, at 8.10 metres (26.6 feet), and John Lowe's 1894 measurement was 8.15 metres (26.7 feet). A Mr Papillon had the iron band around the trunk loosened and was probably also responsible for the iron railings placed around the tree in 1907. Measured in 1982, it had grown to a 8.55 metres (28 feet) in the girth.

A theory well researched by Allen Meredith explores the possibility that the tree played a part in the story of the Battle of Hastings (1066). According to Mr Meredith, the section of the south coast around Hastings has changed over the last 900 years and Hastings was once protected on three sides by water. At that time an inlet extended towards Crowhurst.

The chroniclers of the time describe the battle thus: 'Harold gathered a great army and came against them at the great apple tree'. The theory is that the apple tree was in fact the yew tree and that the reference was to the red fruit of the female yew rather than that of the short-lived apple. The battle having been fought in October, would have coincided with the fruiting of the female yew. It is generally accepted that King Harold owned the land on which the yew grew at the time of the battle.

At Buxted Park, now a hotel, and leisure complex, standing majestically, if slightly uneasily, amongst the trappings of the late twentieth century grows the *Buxted yew*. Chroniclers have recorded that branches from this tree were used to create arrows used in the Battle of Hastings.

Inland from Eastbourne on the Sussex coast, and north-west of Herstmonceux, the village of Cowbeech is named after the beechwoods that once were dominant in the area. Several large beech trees have, over the years, been credited with giving the village its name. The old land which forms Cow Farm has a large beech growing at the top of the bank leading down into the hamlet from the southern end. This tree is known locally now as the *Cowbeech*. In the 1970s, it was under threat from a new line of electricity pylons that crossed the village from east to west. After vociferous local protests, the Central Electricity Generating Board agreed to re-route the lines to avoid interference with the tree. This is an excellent example of a local community having a constructive influence on their village surroundings.

The *Queen Elizabeth* or *Northiam oak*

finally died a few years ago. Northiam lies in east Sussex on the road from Hawkhurst to Hastings. It was, however, to Rye that Queen Elizabeth I was travelling in 1573 when, on 11 August, she stopped to picnic below the oak on the village green. She inadvertently left a pair of her shoes behind. The Trewerne family kept the shoes at Brickwall Manor for many years, but no one is now sure of their whereabouts. The *Gentleman's Magazine* of 1816 describes the tree and mentions storm damage to the crown. The remains of the tree, complete with ironwork, are still to be seen at the north-west corner of the green.

Sussex has many record trees, and in recent years much work has been done to search for big trees of all species.

KENT

From Igglesden's book *Saunter Through Kent* (1913) come the words 'it is famed far and near – the *Fredville oak*', and one hundred years earlier Hasted wrote, 'though it must

'Majesty' – 'elephant's feet' on the giant oak at Fredville Park

have existed for many centuries, yet it looks healthy and thriving, and has a most majestic and venerable appearance'. The real name of the tree is *Majesty*, and one hundred years ago it had two consorts *Beauty* and *Stately*.

Majesty used to stand on a lawn in front of the house at Fredville Park. It has been quite hollow for at least one hundred years and managed to escape destruction in the great storms of 1987 and 1990. The lawn and gardens would have come much later in the oak's history though. The house at Fredville was accidentally burnt down during the Second World War by the army who occupied the house in 1939.

The present-day owners of the park are the Plumtre family, who first took claim to the land in 1750. They now live close to the park at Little Fredville.

Majesty is Britain's greatest maiden oak (that is unpollarded). Measured over many years, in 1994 it had a girth of 12.04 metres diameter (39.5 feet) and a height of 20 metres (65 feet). Children from the village measured *Majesty* for themselves in 1983. According to the *Kentish Gazette*, 'they stood on tiptoes and this time it was spot on

the claimed girth of 11.4 m (37.4 feet)'. Previous measurements are:

Year	Measurer	Girth	
1822	J.G. Strutt	8.55m at 2.40m	(28ft. at 8ft.)
1907	Elwes & Henry	10.05m at 1.0m	(33ft. at 3ft.)
1940	R.O.B. Gardner	11.12m at 1.5m	(36ft. 6ins. at 5ft.)
1966	A.F. Mitchell	11.38m at 1.5m	(37ft. 4ins. at 5ft.)
1973	A.F. Mitchell	11.60m at 1.5m	(38ft. 1in. at 5ft.)
1993	Mrs Plumtre	12.04m at 1.5m	(39ft. 6ins. at 5ft.)

The whole of Fredville Park is covered in a wealth of impressive timber, including several mighty chestnut trees, one of which is called the *Step tree*. Its name is taken from the steps and platform that once adorned the tree. The park is close to the small village of Nonnington, and is private apart from public footpaths. Permission to see the oak, which is surrounded by self-seeded, over-grown woodland, must be sought from the owners.

The Step tree – sweet chestnut of mighty proportions at Fredville Park

On the edge of Romney Marsh overlooking the flatlands that stretch down to the sea, the tiny hamlet of Bonnington has an old oak that once, according to local tradition, acted as the gathering place for the local court. The tree is known as the *Lawgiver* and Samuel Bagshaw, writing his *Directory of Kent* 1848, calls the *Bonnington oak* 'the ancient Court Leete tree'. Under the tree, meetings were also held to choose new constables for the Bonnington and Hamme area. The faded village sign not far from the tree depicts the oak in the Middle Ages. The oak is now an old burred trunk, with much deadwood, but it is still alive, and stands testimony to its prominence in the history of Bonnington village.

One of Kent's most famous oaks was unfortunately set on fire in 1989. The very hollow *Headcorn oak* grew in the boundary land of the fifteenth century church and was propped up with timbers. It had a girth exceeding 10 metres (33 feet) and was reputedly one of the last survivors of the great Forest of Andredsweald. It was, like the *Bonnington oak*, a 'court' tree, and the legend still exists that King John held bull-baiting contests around the tree.

Not far away and inside the churchyard, grows a vigorous young oak, growing from an acorn from the original tree. Hopefully this new *Headcorn oak* will be looked upon and admired by future generations, just as the old tree was.

Only a few miles from Headcorn lies the village of Ulcombe and on the side of the hill above the small village the *Ulcombe yews* grow in the churchyard. There are several ancient yews and the biggest is one of Britain's greatest girthed yews. The slightly smaller tree, growing to the right of the path, is, however, the more impressive. It has beautiful smooth yet red, fluted bark and is an outstanding tree.

Moving large trees is a practice that has gained in appeal over the past few decades. The idea of having an 'instant' landscape fits in well with the pace of the present times. It is, however, not new and in the latter part of

the eighteenth century it was considered practicable to move quite large trees with the aid of specially built two-wheeled trailers, aided by a large gang of readily available labourers who dug carefully around the whole root systems of trees.

Sir Henry Stewart and the celebrated Lancelot 'Capability' Brown used the method. Sir Henry wrote of the best practices in *The Planters Guide* in 1828. However, the most famous 'mover' of big trees was William Barron of Borrowash,

Buckland in Dover – the ancient yew that was moved in 1880

Derbyshire, one time head gardener to the Earl of Harrington of Elvaston Castle. He had much success with his transplanting exploits. He was called upon in the 1870s to work out a way of moving the churchyard yew in Buckland in Dover, Kent.

The tree was growing very close to the west end of St Andrew's church, and it had been shattered by a lightning strike which had also damaged the church steeple. Also, in 1878, a decision had been taken to extend the west end of the church. The tree was a genuine ancient yew with a girth exceeding 6 metres (20 feet). In 1879, William Barron was contacted and asked for his opinion on the possibility of moving the *Buckland yew* to the east end of the churchyard.

The move was to take place in February

Buckland yew

1880 and the churchyard was to be closed during the operation. However, spectators were to be allowed to view at a cost of twenty-five shillings and sixpence per person! Barron boldly proclaimed that the other large trees that he had moved were 'chickens compared to the Buckland yew'.

On 24 February the trenching started and was dug around the tree to a depth of 1.5 metres (5 feet). A cutting was made along the 19 metres (62 feet) distance to the new site. Using timbers and chains, the entire root system was freed from the surrounding ground. Rollers were placed under the huge root ball and the estimated 55 tons were ready for moving. A bathing machine haul system was set at the planting spot and the tree was gradually pulled. Unfortunately, as the operation began, the chains snapped under the strain. Stronger chains were desperately sought and eventually on 3 March, the tree began to be moved. It took the whole of that day and the next to complete the move before the root system was dealt with.

Even after the trauma of the move, more was to happen. A hidden brick vault, close to the main trunk, caved in taking with it a large portion of the earth that was attached to the root system. Undaunted, Barron constructed a support and, despite all the cynics who said that he would not succeed, the tree still lives today, one hundred years later, in its new position.

The cost of the operation was put at £1,862, a lot of money in 1880, but the admission charge, plus income from other publicity and reporting, helped considerably to close the gap in funds. One hundred years of blizzards and storms, particularly the gales of 1987 and 1990, have failed to destroy the Buckland yew. It stands, a testimony to Barron's extraordinary exploits. The churchyard is now surrounded by houses and factories, yet it is still an oasis of tranquillity and home to an extraordinary tree.

North-west of Royal Tunbridge Wells are several well-known estates including Chiddingstone Castle, which has impressive old oaks, Hever Castle and Penshurst Place. Penshurst, the ancestral home of the Sydney family since 1552, was the birthplace of

Sir Philip Sydney, the Elizabethan poet, diplomat and courtier. He was also author of the romance *Arcadia*, and his home was the inspiration for the Arcadian house described in the story. The house has a superb state dining room much loved by Elizabeth I, and in the grounds, beyond the formal Italian gardens, are the remains of the *Sydney oak*. According to Lord de L'Isle the tree is over 900 years old. The famous artists Landseer, Nasmyth, and others have portrayed the tree. In 1879 *Country Life* gave its girth as 10 metres (33 feet) at ground level, and 9 metres (29 feet) at 2 metres (6 feet). The oak has suffered over the last ten years in the storms,

Sydney oak – 900-year-old remains of the tree portrayed by famous artists at Penhurst Place, Kent

and although still alive in 1995 it has lost much of its former glory. From its position overlooking the lake towards the magnificent house, it now shelters the odd sheep in its hollow shell. An impressive old gingko can also be seen growing very close to the main door of the house at Penshurst.

In the London borough of Bromley, on a public path between the Keston to Downe road, is the heavily supported *Wilberforce oak*. At this spot, William Wilberforce tried to think of a way to realise his ambition of abolishing slavery. A stone seat was erected in 1862 by Earl Stanhope, bearing the following inscription from Wilberforce's diary of 1786:

> *I well remember, after a conversation with Mr Pitt, in the open air at the foot of an old tree in Holwood, just above the steep descent into the Vale of Keston, I resolved to give notice on a fit occasion in the House of Commons, of my intention to bring forward the abolition of the slave trade.*

SURREY

William Cobbett (1763–1835) was a controversial politician, agriculturalist and writer. On one of his frequent rural rides he passed through Tilford, near Farnham, Surrey. He was taken by the huge proportions of the *Novel's oak* or, as it is now called, the *Tilford oak*. In Cobbett's day the tree had a girth of 5.20 metres (17 feet) and when measured in 1970 was 8 metres (26 feet 4 inches). In front of the tree by the roadside is a stone seat with a plaque that reads, 'by far the finest tree that I ever saw in my life'. It also claims that the tree was 800 years old, which is undoubtedly an exaggeration. The *Tilford oak* is now not as fine as in Cobbett's day as it has had its top pruned back.

Nearby are other planted oaks. One planted in 1901 already has a girth exceeding 2.70 metres (9 feet). Then there is the *Jubilee oak* planted in 1897 and *King George V's oak* at the top of the green, planted in 1911.

At the castle in Farnham are cedars grown from seed brought from Lebanon by Bishop North in the late 1700s.

On the edge of the green in the attractive village of Chiddingfold, 8 kilometres (5 miles) south of Milford, the well-known *Chiddingfold thorn* is thought by some to be as old as the nearby Crown Inn. This is claimed to be the oldest inn in Surrey, first mentioned in 1383. The village itself was recorded in the twelfth century when the last remnants of the surrounding forest were being finally colonised for farming. There is, however, still much woodland in this area of the county.

A more realistic assessment of the thorn's age is that it cannot be much more than 400 years old. The base of the old tree is tunnelled with age and it now grows in two distinctive halves held together by iron-work. The thorn was first shown on a centuries old map. There is no documentary evidence to link the *Chiddingfold thorn* to any historical fact but because of the care taken to look after it, including a wall built around it, it must have been held in much reverence for many a long year. It may well be that the thorn had a particular religious

Crowhurst yew, Surrey – in which a cannonball was found by villagers in 1820

significance for the locality.

Surrey has two of the greatest yews in England at Crowhurst and Tandridge. The very hollow and very large *Crowhurst yew*, not to be confused with the yew at Crowhurst, Sussex mentioned earlier, has had much attention over many centuries. It is also very photogenic, probably because of its hollowness and the door placed in the cavity on the main trunk.

In 1820 villagers excavated earth within the base of the yew and found a cannonball that had gradually been enclosed by the tree. This was believed to be a relic of the Civil War in 1643. The ball was left inside the tree. During the Second World War the cannon-ball was found to be missing one morning. Some time after the war a cannonball was discovered when a former Canadian camp site was being cleared. The ball was handed over to the church authorities. Presumably a soldier had removed the cannonball as a prank or meant to take it as a souvenir.

The church of St George at Crowhurst has been restored several times since the seven-teenth century but there are still traces of the original Norman work. The churchyard occupies a hill top position, which must look very different now from those times when the ancient peoples met below the yew.

The Crowhurst, Surrey tree was recorded in Brailey's *History of Surrey* published in 1850; it was then measured at 9.35 metres (30.7 feet) at 1.5 metres (5 feet) from the ground. It was fitted with a table and bench. John Lowe measured the tree with Reverend Mr Curters in April 1889 when it was 10 metres (32.9 feet) at 1.5 metres (5 feet), so it appeared to have grown 20 cm (8 inches) in 40 years. According to the rector, an old parish record in the church at the end of the nineteenth century states that at the time of Charles I (1630) the tree was 9.15 metres (30 feet) around the middle. Also of interest is that during the big storms in 1845 'large destruction' was caused to the top of the tree. In 1984 the tree was remeasured and had grown 46 cm (18 inches) in 354 years.

The *Tandridge yew* is one of the most

Tandridge yew – 'the red tree on the hill' one of the greatest yews

splendid yews to be seen anywhere. It has beautifully fluted bark, particularly on the side of the bole facing the church. The tree is unlikely to be as old as the Crowhurst tree but who knows! When dealing with yews there are more questions than answers. Measured by John Lowe in April 1890, it was 6 metres (20 feet) in the girth at 1.2 metres (4 feet). Low enthused: 'there is a magnificent head of foliage extending over 24 metres (80 feet) in diameter. The entire girth at 0.6 metres (2 feet) from the ground is 9.2 metres (30.3 feet)'.

The *Tandridge yew* is particularly tall for a yew and when measured in 1990 stood at over 10.6 metres (35 feet). Its estimated age as in excess of 2,500 years. The most extraordinary piece of yew dating evidence exists at Tandridge. The base of the crypt was built in Saxon times and they had to build stone vaulting over the yew tree's roots that stands over 7.6 metres (25 feet) from the church. This proves the tree was fully grown a thousand years ago! Tandridge gives remarkable proof of the yew tree's long life and also the respect shown by the Saxon builders for their tree.

The name Tandridge can mean 'the red

tree on the hill', a perfect description for a remarkable tree. Other churchyard yews of note in Surrey are at Alfold, Charlwood, Dunsfold and Little Bookham. Outside of churchyards, big trees are at Old Enton (in a field), Peper Harrow and Woldingham, Newlands Corner and a big female tree at Ketfold's Farm.

The most famous yews are the *Druid's Grove* at Norbury Park. George Meredith wrote in 1869 'anyone walking under them should remember that they were saplings when Jesus Christ came to earth'. Brailey, in his *History of Surrey* (1850) wrote: 'Many of these yews are of great age and venerable aspect, and of a girth seldom equalled.' John Lowe's *The Yew Trees of Great Britain and Ireland* documented the Druid's Grove in 1897. It would seem that some of the oldest trees were planted to form a rough avenue. There are also many scattered trees growing in fairly dense undergrowth, along with box.

The great storm of 1987 and the further storm in 1990 had a detrimental effect on the grove. Trees were uprooted and much damage was caused to the crowns of the yews. The trees have largely been left alone with little tidying up, deliberately, to see what happens in regrowth.

Much debate has surrounded the origin of the Druid's Grove but it is clear the trees are extremely old and the name they take goes back into the mists of time and may well be connected with the Celtic Druids of pre-Christian times.

LONDON

The *Royal Botanic Gardens at Kew* is the most famous collection of plants in the world. It is more though than merely a collection. Kew has a wide-ranging role to research, protect and ensure better management of the Earth's environment by increasing our knowledge and understanding of the plant kingdom. To quote their words 'the basis of life on Earth'. Their mission also states 'whenever possible, the Royal Botanic Gardens, Kew will endeavour to reduce and reverse the rate of destruction of the world's plant species and their habitats'.

These lofty and worthwhile ideals owe their origins to the first unofficial director of Kew, Sir Joseph Banks. It was under his direction that collectors were sent out all over the world in pursuit of plants of economic, scientific or horticultural interest.

The garden estate consists mainly of two separate estates which originally belonged to the Royal family. George III's mother Augusta laid out 9 acres as a botanic garden in 1759. On Augusta's death in 1772 George III combined his grandfather's estate of Richmond with Kew, and Banks started his work. In 1840 the gardens were handed to the state for upkeep and development and in 1841 Sir William Hooker became the first official director.

Kew now covers in excess of 120 hectares (300 acres) and contains over 40,000 different types of plants. It also manages Wakehurst Place, near Ardingly, Sussex. This is a woodland garden in the High Weald which is a must for plant enthusiasts.

In 1983 the Royal Botanic Gardens became a corporate body with charitable status and a Board of Trustees. It is primarily funded by government grant but also by support from its own Foundation and the valuable work put in by the Friends of The Royal Botanic Gardens, Kew.

Kew has unequalled collections of many genera including oaks, ashes, limes, catalpas and zelkovas. A day's visit would not do justice to this wonderful place. You would need to return to see more.

Amongst the great collections at Kew are many record-breaking trees. There are far too many to mention all of them here but the trees below give a taste of what can be found.

The leaning Pagoda tree (*Sophora japonica*) is a native of China introduced into Britain in 1753. The surviving tree at Kew is one of the first five to have arrived in this country. Originally taken to the Duke of Argyll's estate at Whitton it was replanted in Kew in 1762. This tree located near the new Princess of Wales's House is one of the original trees contained in Princess Augusta's garden.

Nearby is the evergreen Turner's oak (*Quercus* x *turneri*) a hybrid between the native common oak and the evergreen Holm oak. This impressive tree is one of Britain's biggest

Turner's oak at the Royal Botanic Gardens, Kew

and in mild winters shows off its shiny green leaves right through to spring.

Also in the same vicinity is one of Kew's oldest trees a ginkgo from China dating from 1762, planted less than 40 years after their first introduction into Europe. On the lawn near the ginkgo is another old tree from the original garden, the locust tree (*Robinia pseudoacacia*).

To the east of the Waterlily House on a big open lawn known as Seven Sisters stands one of Kew's greatest and most remarkable trees. The huge chestnut-leafed oak (*Quercus castaneifolia*) is by far the largest in Britain and is Kew's biggest tree by bulk. This tree was grown from seed imported in 1843 from the Caucasus and has made remarkable growth since its planting date in 1846.

This rare tree derives its name from its un-oak-like leaves. As the name suggests they resemble the leaf of a sweet chestnut rather than that of our common oak. The tree is related to the Turkey oak. The Kew tree measures over 30 metres (98 feet) tall with a girth of almost 7 metres (23 feet) round, making it an impressive tree by any standards. A seedling from this was planted on the Museum Lawn in 1953 and has developed into another fine chestnut-leafed oak.

In the oak collection, beyond the Rhododendron Dell on Mount Pleasant Hill, stand many uncommon and rare trees including one of Britain's biggest pin oaks (*Quercus palustris*). From north-eastern and central United States the pin oak has delicate, deeply cut foliage and is noted for the scarlet autumn colour of its leaves.

Kew cannot be described in a few words but it holds a unique position in the history of plant hunting, in the work it has, and continues, to carry out, and in our knowledge and management of the earth's plant life.

Across the Thames from Kew and visible from the river bank near Mount Pleasant, *Syon Park* is another great park full of rare trees. It is much smaller than Kew but botanically its history is much older. The park is recognised as a Grade I landscape and is one of Britain's oldest parks. It was started in the 1430s by Bridgehine Nuns. From then until now it has continually developed with major changes in the 1540s, mid-eighteenth century and early nineteenth century. The nuns of the fifteenth century collected plants and trees and planted them in their original twelve hectares (thirty-acre) garden and orchard.

Syon was described as 'the first Botanic Garden' in the 1540s and before the end of that century the ninth Earl of Northumberland acquired the lease and later the freehold of the park from Queen Elizabeth I and his descendants live there to the present day. From his rooms in the Tower of London, where he was imprisoned following the gunpowder plot, the ninth Earl sent out his plans for the improvement of the park. Eventually the Tudor terraces and walls were removed to create a more open landscape setting. This was created by the first Duke of Northumberland who engaged 'Capability' Brown to design the new park. Brown turned the river into a feature lake.

Now the estate holds more than 3,000 trees, 40 per cent of which exceed 100 years old and 187 of those are over 200 years old, a few of which will be survivors of Brown's original planting. Syon is particularly noted today for its collection of big and rare oaks, maples, catalpas, swamp cypresses and very impressive big zelkovas. Record breaking broadleaf trees abound at Syon.

In the terrible storm of 1987 Syon, like Kew, lost many trees. Again, 1990 saw further storm damage and an extensive replanting programme was started and has continued up till the present day.

Within London are many parks and squares that contain fine trees. Battersea Park has notable whitebeams, narrow-leafed and weeping ash, Chinese privet and a record hybrid strawberry tree. It also is home to *Grace Darling's oak*. This is a turkey oak planted by Sir John Crastor before the Second World War to the memory of the heroine of a famous rescue in 1838. She had rowed with her father from the Longstone Lighthouse on the Northumberland coast to rescue the survivors of a shipwreck.

The story captured the hearts of the nation and Grace Darling's name is known to this day. She died of tuberculosis only four years after her famous heroics. Trees were planted at various ports around Britain under the direction of the Grace Darling League. The League raised money for the lifeboats around Britain's coast. The Battersea Park tree was planted one hundred years after the Northumberland coast rescue.

St James's Park offers one of the largest fig trees in Britain. Another can be seen at Dean's Yard, Westminster. Kensington Gardens can boast Britain's tallest manna ash. The slow-growing evergreen box has one of its champions in West London, at Gunnersbury Park.

The tree with the closest associations with London is the plane that takes its name from the city London Plane. The traditional squares and streets are the places to see this handsome tree with its flaking light-grey bark (e.g. Lincoln Inn Fields). In recent years the disease Anthracnose has taken away some of its reputation for withstanding anything thrown its way from road salt to smog and general city pollution. The London plane is a hybrid between the Oriental plane and the American plane. It is, of course, not restricted to London and is grown throughout Europe, particularly France. The tallest in Britain grows at Bryanston School, Dorset and the most magnificent, one of Britain's greatest trees, is at the Bishop's Palace, Ely, a tree featured in other pages of this book.

London hosts the tree with the most macabre past of any – the *Tyburn oak*. It was used as a gibbet for over 600 years until 1783 but became unsafe and was replaced by man-made structures. Offenders from petty thieves to murderers were hanged in batches on specific days. Six or more at a time were jeered and spat at by crowds who gathered for the 'entertainment'. The tragic associations of Tyburn became too much for the locals in that part of Middlesex. The village

was given a new name derived from the parish church of St Mary's. Ty-burn became Mary-bourne. Later it was further altered to Mary-le-bourne, when French names became fashionable.

Another famous oak gave a London suburb its name. At One Tree Hill, Camberwell, stood the *Honour oak* which, until relatively recently, still existed in remnant form. The original name for the tree was 'The Oake of Honour', the name given it by Queen Elizabeth I. The history of the tree and why it was so named is now blurred, but the oak must have had some special past for it to be named by a monarch.

The connections between Queen Elizabeth and individual trees are many. *Queen Elizabeth's oak*, dead since 1870, stands as a mere shell in Greenwich Park, London. The Queen supposedly rested below the tree and in later years she recalled the oak's 'cool darkness'. The *Hatfield oak* and *Northiam oak*, mentioned elsewhere in this book, also had a connection with the Queen.

Half Moon Lane in London SE 15 had, and may still have, the remains of the *Camerwell elm*, which is an extremely old tree dating it is said from the fourteenth century. In 1875 a drawing of the tree appeared in *Ye Parish of Camerwell* by William Harnett Blanch.

Within the northern ring of the M25 Epping Forest covers 2,500 hectares (6,000 acres). Although 800 of these are grassland, it is still a large chunk of woodland centred on High Beach, west of Loughton. It occupies a ridge between the Lee and Roding Valleys and is famous for its hornbeams, lopped for centuries by the commoners of surrounding parishes. There are as many beeches as hornbeams scattered evenly throughout the woodland cover. The hornbeams come close to dominance near the Loughton side of the forest. The weirdly shaped old trees are the product of centuries of hard work and use although the lack of any major cutting back in later times has created a dense shade where very little grows. 'Named' trees such as the *King's oak* near the Conservation Centre, the *Fairmead oak* and many others have largely gone or become sad relics but the forest still has a special atmosphere.

Its nearby population use the forest extensively and major routes can be used to walk the area, such as Centenary Walk and Three Forests Way. However, to get a real feel of the place it is necessary to get off the main routes. This is possible as access is free everywhere.

BUCKINGHAMSHIRE

The main tree of the Chilterns is undoubtedly the beech, and Burnham in Buckinghamshire is the most celebrated patch of woodland for seeing the old beeches growing on the chalkland soils.

Just north of Slough, *Burnham Beeches* was once owned by Burnham Abbey and it remained in private ownership until 1880 when the old Corporation of London bought the area for use as public recreation land. The old weirdly shaped pollarded trees have repeatedly reproduced branches over the years from their slowly decaying trunks, so creating their distinctive shapes. The material collected from the beeches was either used in the local furniture trade or as firewood.

There has always been debate as to the origins of Burnham Beeches. One school of thought claims they were planted during enclosures by local landowners to stop commoners from grazing sheep over the land. Another theory is that the trees are truly native, as with all the beechwoods of the Chilterns, and have been selectively managed by the landowners over the last few centuries.

They have certainly been managed as wood pasture, that is, livestock being allowed to graze below the scattered pollarded trees. They are regarded as one of the foremost examples of this form of land management in Britain. As a result of this the area holds National Nature Reserve status. Recently experiments have been carried out to rein-

Burnham Beeches, Bucks – atmospheric at any time of the year

troduce the old wood pasture regimes and certain areas are fenced whilst grazing and pollarding are practised again.

As is widely known, the old pollard oaks and beeches are hosts to many insects and fungi and are micro nature reserves in their own right. Much valuable work is being carried out at Burnham with comprehensive record keeping and data evaluation adding to our woodland and tree knowledge.

At one stage before the First World War all the old trees were condemned and plans were laid to replant all the woodland areas. Fortunately it never happened and even when it was used as a military transport park in the Second World War almost all the 1,600 old trees survived.

The age of the old trees has been calculated as being between 250 and 400 years. They were believed to have been first pollarded at about 35 years old about 300 years ago. They were then re-pollarded at an average of 12–15 years ceasing approximately 120 years ago apart from some limited continuance. The decline in the pollarding practice coincides with the widespread and cheap use of coal as a fuel source. Queen Victoria liked the Burnham beechwood fuel so much she had the charcoal transported to Balmoral especially for her own use.

There are many artistic connections with Burnham including Mendelssohn's fondness for the woods where he walked and gained inspiration for his music. The poet Thomas Gray often stayed at the Grove, Burnham and walked the woods. It was at nearby Stoke Poges he wrote of the churchyard yews in his most famous work *Elegy*.

As well as the beeches there are many old trees in the woods, particularly oaks, and marked on the location maps down the 'drives' are named, trees such as the *Druids oak, His Majesty's* and the curious *Jenny Lind* tree – a huge old beech. The main access roads into the woods are Morton Drive, Pumpkin Hill, Lord Mayor's Drive and Park Lane.

Burnham Beeches is enjoyed by thousands every year who appreciate the peace and tranquillity amongst the old trees. When visiting the woods, even on the coldest or wettest of winter days, it is easy to see a walker, a jogger or a driver going to Burnham for their recreational time. For those who take the time to explore the deeper paths there are still secret places amongst the old grey decaying giants of Burnham.

Gayhurst, a small hamlet on the River Ouse in Buckinghamshire, is noted for its part in the Guy Fawkes Gunpowder Plot. The Elizabethan Manor was given to Sir Francis Drake by Queen Elizabeth I. Drake did not particularly want the manor so he sold it the very next day to William Mulsho. The buildings were refashioned and the parkland developed and planted with specimen trees. Mary Mulsho married Everard Digby who became involved in the Gunpowder Plot and it was from Gayhurst

Gayhurst walnut – record common walnut in historic parkland

Old ash tree at Gayhurst, Bucks

that he was taken to the Tower of London.

In latter years the house has been partly used as a school. On the north side of the drive just inside the parkland stands the huge *Gayhurst walnut*. This tree of considerable age is one of the largest and probably one of the oldest common walnuts in Britain. Its main feature is the beautiful, heavily fissured, pale-grey trunk that is over 6 metres (20 feet) round. The outer branches of the tree have in recent years been cut back. The walnut is now approximately 20 metres (66 feet) in height.

Opposite, on the southern side of the drive, is another tree of note, an ancient ash of incredible shape. Although no record breaker, the old pollard must be one of the best old ashes in the county and a tree worthy of seeing in its own right, never mind its illustrious neighbour. It brings to mind the rural poet John Clare in his sonnet:

> old huge ash dotterel wasted to a shell
> whose vigorous head still grew and flour-
> ished well
> where ten might sit upon the battered
> floor
> and still look round discovering room for
> more.

BEDFORDSHIRE

Between Bedford and Sandy is the village of Mogerhanger. 'The Park' is a Georgian house set in 6 hectares (15 acres) of parkland with big trees around the buildings. The property is now owned by Harvest Vision, a Christian group who are developing the whole complex as a Prayer Retreat and Training Centre. The hall has an interesting and varied history. It was originally owned by the Thornton family who were members of the Clapham Sect, the evangelical group who played a significant part in the nineteenth century revival in Britain. They campaigned successfully for the abolition of slavery and other social reforms.

During the 1914–18 war 'The Park' was used as a hospital for wounded servicemen. It later became a TB isolation hospital and

Mogerhanger — The Park has big trees including an early Copper beech

then an orthopaedic hospital. It was eventually closed in 1987 and was unoccupied from then until 1994.

The grounds are gradually being restored and the specimen trees to be found include a good Tree of Heaven (*Alianthus altissima*) and rare Cucumber tree (*Magnolia acuminati*) and of particular note a copper beech (*Fagus sylvatica v. purpurea*) which is a giant of its type and is Britain's largest. Its graft line drips like fat over the common beech rootstock.

Woburn Park in Bedfordshire has many fine oaks, the most famous of which is the *Abbots oak* that owes its reputation to the story of its grim past as that of a hanging or 'dool' tree. The Abbot and Prior of Woburn, the Vicar of Puddington and others were supposedly hanged on the tree under orders from Henry VIII. In his book *Church History of England*, Dodds states that the Abbot, a Roger Hobbs, took the courageous

ABOVE: *Abbot's oak, Woburn Park – grim reminder from time of Henry VIII*
BELOW: *Great oak of Woburn – 900-year-old relic*

step of not compromising his conscience for a rich pension as many had done, but had denied the king's supremacy over his marriage to Anne Boleyn. For his defiance against Henry he and others equally critical of the king were hanged on an oak tree in front of the monastery. As was the custom he was drawn by sledge to the place of execution after his trial for high treason at Woburn.

The *Abbot's oak* is in fact one of the smaller oaks in the magnificent Woburn Park. Its age is put between 400 and 600 years old. That is old but compared to the *Great oak* of Woburn, which has an age estimated at 900 years, it is a comparative newcomer. This common oak is close to the main drive through the park near to the Head Deerkeeper's house and its diameter when measured in 1992 was 2.96 metres (9.7 feet). According to the county records it is the largest and probably the oldest known tree in Bedfordshire. There are many other huge old oaks at Woburn mainly the common oak (*Quercus robur*) but a very large sessile oak also grows in the parkland. To give some idea of Woburn's importance to Bedfordshire's tree heritage, of the top

twenty largest trees nine grow at Woburn.

According to David Alderman, Woburn had in the early 1800s one of the best plant collections of anywhere worldwide. Willows, pines, heathers and grasses grew in comprehensive collections. The climate of eastern England with its cold dry winds and frost inhibited growth and killed off many species. Also the storm of 1915 blew down many more of the bigger trees. The Park still remains though a fascinating and interesting place where truly old and big parkland trees can be enjoyed at any time of the year. Of the exotic trees a Chinese zelkova, a giant redwood and an impressive Hungarian oak of national stature can also be seen there. There are also some magnificent cedars.

HERTFORDSHIRE

One of Hertfordshire's finest trees is the *Great oak* at Panshanger located off the B1000 between Hertingfordbury and Welwyn. It grows on what was the Earl Cowper's estate of Panshanger Park.

In 1789 the naturalist Gilbert White,

Magnificent spreading cedar at Woburn – storm damage has begun to affect the tree's crown

author of *The Natural History of Selbourne*, went from Hampshire to see the tree and was impressed with its form. An even more famous visitor was Sir Winston Churchill who remarked that it was the 'finest and most stately oak growing in south-east England'. The County Council placed a tree preservation order on the tree in 1953 and near the original tree a young oak, grown from an acorn of the original, was planted by Sir Winston.

In 1814 a T. Medland created a painting of the tree and showed it in full vigour. Jacob George Strutt sketched the tree for his book *Sylva Britannica* (Portrait of Forest Trees) published in 1822, and he remarked after sketching the oak:

the waving lightness of its feathered branches, dipping down, towards its stem, to the very ground, the straightness of its trunk and the redundancy of its foliage, all give it a character opposite to that of antiquity. Nulli penetrabilis astro – Impervious to the Day.

It measured 6 metres (20 feet) in circumference at 1 metre (3 feet) from the ground. When measured in 1993 the fine oak measured 7.4 metres (24 feet) circumference at 1.5 metres (5 feet) and to quote Jim Paterson 'just putting the tape round its vast bole has been one of life's great pleasures'. According to Jim Paterson the tree was about 200 years old in 1719 due to the timber content. It is now at the optimum height of 20 metres (65 feet) and is probably 475–500 years old. With luck, and being left to grow in freedom from disturbance, it may reach 750–800 years. A truly excellent tree.

Hertfordshire still has a few famous marker trees. In the grounds of Haileybury College, near Hertford, is *Quitchell's oak* standing on Quitch Hill. A plaque reads: 'This tree was recorded in 1634 as the boundary corner of St Margaret's parish (formerly Thele)'. Another tree in the grounds is the *Dumb-Bell oak*, so named because of its peculiarly shaped trunk.

A big, spreading, distinctive looking oak in the grounds goes by the name of the *Lightning oak* referring to its having been struck in 1898. It appeared dead at the time and was considered for felling the following year. However, it recovered and a plaque was placed on the bole of the tree in 1904: '*Saepe Jovis telo Quercus ad usta virat – Ovid*' (Often the oak by Jove's bolt flourishes). By 1966, fresh bark completely covered the plaque and a new one was placed on the tree.

Another oak on the boundary between St Margaret's and Great Amwell parishes has a ring sunk deeply in its trunk. Local tradition has it that Dick Turpin the highwayman tethered his horse to the ring while awaiting the arrival of coaches on the London–Hertford road.

South-east of Mogerhanger and Biggleswade, the village of Ashwell in Hertfordshire derives its name from the River Cam appearing from the ground as a great spring beneath the roots of an ash tree. The present tree is a successor to the original that gave the village its name. The Anglo-Saxons named the village a 'well' which was another name for a spring. In Ireland there are many associations between ash trees and holy wells.

Hatfield House near the town of that name, has a park that is the largest in the county. The remains of an old oak tree, under which Princess Elizabeth was reputably sitting when news was brought of her accession to the throne after the death of Mary Tudor, are still preserved.

In the churchyard of Tewin in Hertfordshire lies the tomb of Lady Ann Grimstone who died in 1713. Before her death she wrote that if trees grew from her grave it would prove the truth of the Resurrection. Today her tombstone is split in two by the growth of ash and sycamore trees.

At Much Hadham Rectory in Hertfordshire grows the biggest and probably the earliest black walnut in Britain. A very impressive, hugely spreading tree, it grows on the long lawn at the back of the house. The tree was once even larger but tree surgery has reduced the overall size. The remains of far earlier tree work are also evident. Further on by the west side of the lawn, a giant horse chestnut, one of Britain's biggest, grows very tall and stately. Younger trees also dot the extensive lawn area. The 'old rectory' dates from the early seventeenth century and is in private ownership. Anyone wishing to see the Much Hadham walnut would firstly have to seek permission from the owners.

Much Hadham village is one of the most attractive in Hertfordshire. Its long main street is filled with buildings of fine quality. Near the church is the Palace, for 800 years the country residence of the Bishops of London. It was probably the early Bishops who influenced the growing of ornamental trees in the vicinity because of their extensive travels and palace guests from the new world.

A copper beech, drawn by Adrian Hill in

*Black walnut at Much Hadham Rectory, Herts – a
hugely spreading tree of great historical interest*

Grimstone oak	Surrey	14.63m.	(48ft.)
Hempstead oak	Essex	16m.	(53ft.)
		3ft.at	(36ft.)
Merton oak	Norfolk	19.20m.	(63ft.)
Cowthorpe oak	Yorks	23.75m.	(78ft.)

1934, grows near Much Hadham Hall,
which is probably the village's most splendid
mansion.

ESSEX

J.C. Loudon listed notable oaks in his work
of 1838. He selected trees in which the
boles were of 9 metres (30 feet) or upwards
in circumference. According to Loudon,
the largest five measured at ground level
were:

Salcey oak	Northants	14m.	(46ft.)

The *Hempstead Oak* was the foremost of
Essex's oaks. A drawing was featured in the
Gentleman's Magazine of 1802. The Essex
directory of 1848 stated that 'Arthur Young
mentions two, immense pollarded oaks in a
field near Great Dawkins Farm House at
Hempstead.' The venerable old trees were
already in decline by then, and by 1894 they
lay prostrate in the field.

Another famous Essex oak was the *Fairlop oak* in the Hainault district of Waltham Forest. Much was written about this Epping Forest tree. Beneath its shade, which covered an area of 91 metres (300 feet) in circumference, an annual Fair was held on 2 July each year. No booth was allowed to be erected beyond the extent of its boughs. The print from the *European Magazine* of 1802 shows the great tree, but it is clearly in decline.

Many stories are linked to the tree. Its name is derived from a Mr Day, who procured a large limb from this, his favourite tree, out of which he made a coffin for his own interment. It was judged that the act did not injure the tree but was a 'fair-lop'! The *Fairlop oak* was cut down before 1820. The pulpit and reading desk in the church of St Pancras were constructed from its remains.

Other famous Essex oaks were the *Fairmead oak*, *Cuckoo oak*, *Pulpit oak*, *Danbury oaks*, and the *Great oak* still standing at Barrington Hall, Hatfield, *Broad oak*. The *Great Yeldham oak* has only recently gone.

Another huge, native tree is the pollard field maple at Downham churchyard. One of England's biggest. An unusual layering horse chestnut is found at Langleys, Great Waltham.

To the east of Bishops Stortford and the M11, and now almost within the roar of Stansted Airport's jets, lies the National Trust property of Hatfield Forest. This important forest, which should not be confused with Hatfield Park in Hertfordshire, has retained its ancient character through many generations of landowners.

The Houblon family created one of the lakes and it was they who were credited with planting the horse chestnuts, at least one of which is known for its grandeur. The real features though are the great pollard and coppice hornbeams scattered about the open chases. These wonderful trees are well worth a trip to see as they constitute a rare surviving example of a medieval Royal hunting forest. The pollard thorns are also a feature. The whole forest was designated a National Nature Reserve in 1994 and, unusually, parking is allowed on the chases amongst the old trees.

Standing by the Shell House is an old oak with an iron ring on its trunk. The ring of the *Lantern oak* held a light that was used for parties around the Shell House and lakeside area. On the far side of the house stands a huge oak often used as a picnic spot because of its welcome shade on a warm day.

OXFORDSHIRE

Loudon wrote the history of the Cedar of Lebanon in Britain up to 1838. The single source of the cedar was supposed to be Mount Libanus, but in 1514 there were only twenty-six trees at this site. Sir Joseph Hooker gave an account of the tree in Asia Minor in 1862. It was known by repute through biblical references and seventeenth century herbalists. It was present in Britain in the mid-seventeenth century.

The *Childrey cedar*, standing in the former rectory garden near Wantage, Oxford was, according to unbroken tradition, planted shortly after 1642 by Edward Pococke, who had brought seeds back from the Lebanon. C.J. Cornish described its history in *Country Life* magazine in May 1903. Loudon, Elwes and Henry refer to others, but as with the Childrey tree, none have verified planting dates. The cedars at Wilton, Wiltshire may well have been amongst the first planted.

Writing in his *Forest Scenery* of 1791, William Gilpin gave the following description of the *Magdalen* or *Great oak* of Oxford:

Close by the gate of the water walk of Magdalen College, it perhaps stood there as a sapling when Alfred the Great founded the University.

Assessing the tree's age he stated:

This tree, however, can almost produce historical evidence for the age it boasts. About 500 years after the time of Alfred, William of Waynfleet expressly ordered his college [Magdalen] to be founded near the 'Great oak'.

Hornbeams in Hatfield Forest

He went on to describe damage to the oak in Charles II's reign due to the building of the college. The tree eventually fell in 1788. A magnificent chair was fashioned from the bole and given to the president of the college. So part of the great Magdalen oak remains to this day as a link with the University's origins. Standing in the grounds of the college is the tree that replaced the oak, the London plane (planted 1801).

The initials 'HD' and 'TD 1784' are carved on an old oak growing in a field at Shipton-under-Wychwood, Oxfordshire.

The initials belong to Harry and Tom Dunsdon, eighteenth-century robbers hanged in Gloucester. Their bodies were hung on the *Gibbet oak* until they rotted, as a warning to other would-be robbers and highwaymen to see what fate awaited them if caught committing similar crimes. Similar 'Gallows' or 'Gibbett' oaks at one time dotted the English landscape.

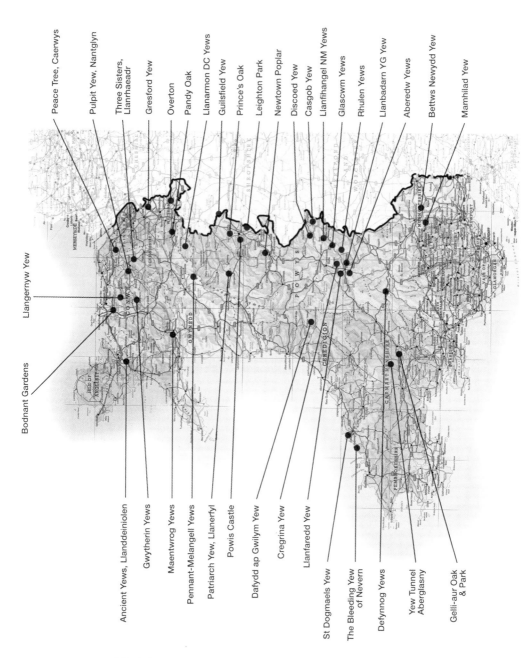

Peace Tree, Caerwys
Pulpit Yew, Nantglyn
Three Sisters, Llanrhaeadr
Gresford Yew
Overton
Pandy Oak
Llanarmon DC Yews
Guilsfield Yew
Prince's Oak
Leighton Park
Newtown Poplar
Discoed Yew
Casgob Yew
Llanfihangel NM Yews
Glascwm Yews
Rhulen Yews
Llanbadarn YG Yew
Aberedw Yews
Bettws Newydd Yew
Mamhilad Yew

Llangernyw Yew

Bodnant Gardens

Ancient Yews, Llanddeiniolen
Gwytherin Yews
Maentwrog Yews
Pennant-Melangell Yews
Patriarch Yew, Llanerfyl
Powis Castle
Dafydd ap Gwilym Yew
Cregrina Yew
Llanfaredd Yew
St Dogmaels Yew
The Bleeding Yew of Nevern
Defynnog Yews
Yew Tunnel Aberglasny
Gelli-aur Oak & Park

© Bartholomew 1996. Reproduced with permission of Harper Collins Cartographic. MM-1297-78.

Wales

The River Wye and its steep-sided gorge forms the border at the south-east of a country whose heart is dominated by high peaks and plateaux. Below the Brecon Beacons there is a green ribbon of land leading into the farmlands of the Vale of Glamorgan. Farther west, Pembrokeshire has magnificent cliff scenery, quiet bays, and the cathedral named after St David, the patron saint for Wales. There are few yew trees in this 'little England', but elsewhere the country is truly the land of the ancient yew.

Cardigan Bay curves in a sweep, with rivers from the Cambrian mountains emptying into the sea along the coastline. Cader Idris lies north of the Plynlimon plateau and, further north, moody Snowdonia looks over the much frequented mountain passes as they lead to the coast.

The Isle of Ynys Mon (Anglesey), the last refuge of the Druids, has a coastline of true quality and to the east of the Snowdon range that great Welsh river, the Conwy, flows through a beautiful valley which is flanked on its eastern side by a garden containing trees of international renown. Less frequented villages and towns lie towards the borderlands and in the old kingdom of Powys, a romantic castle built on a rock looks down on an historic landscape and garden full of magnificent trees.

The River Dee lends itself to another section of the border with England where ruined castles recall the struggles of Welsh heroes against the English. In the valleys, near the borders, some great oaks grow and ancient settlements built on pre-historic sites are reminders of a great Celtic past.

When looking at trees associated with Wales, the tree that comes to mind above all others is the ancient churchyard yew.

Although reputedly the largest and oldest is in Scotland at Fortingall, with other 'giants' being found in southern England and several Midland counties, the number of big, old yews in Welsh churchyards links the tree very closely with the Principality.

The picture conjured up is of raised, circular churchyards along country lanes, or hills overlooking wild landscapes, and there are the huge, dark yews, looking as if they had been there for ever. The mystery that makes them even more intriguing, is that there is no real concensus of why they are there.

In pre-Christian times, yews were planted on or near burial sites. Was it to indicate an available supply of water? Recent research by water diviners gives some confirmation to this old theory. The yew was the original 'magic wand' and the wood of yew was preferred by diviners in earlier times to that of hazel. Circles too were thought to possess supernatural properties (no corners for evil spirits to enter), so the forming of circles and yew trees were thought to keep out evil.

The *Book of Llandaff* (twelfth century), stated that sanctuary would be available for 'those who sought it, between the yew tree and the Church door'. Edward I in 1307, decreed that groups of yew trees should be planted in all churchyards in the land to provide some protection to the fabric of the church from high winds and gales. It is also believed that the trees were planted in churchyards to provide suitable wood for bows. There may be some truth in the theory, although there is no good documentary evidence to support it. The main supply of suitable bowmaking wood was from the Iberian peninsular, and the bowmen with the best reputation in Wales were from the south of the country and they preferred elm rather than yew.

The association of the evergreen yew

with church and religion has many forms. The habit of placing a sprig of yew in the grave of a deceased to symbolise everlasting life still carries on in parts of Wales. I have witnessed this in recent years in a Welsh country churchyard. On Ash Wednesday, another custom was to use the ash from burned yew twigs to smear on the forehead to show penitence.

The use of yew foliage as decoration, for example during the Advent and Christmas seasons to symbolise everlasting life, is a custom still widely retained.

The poisonous nature of the tree also contributed to its mystique. In fact, the flesh of the berries from the female tree is harmless and is readily eaten by birds for autumn and winter feed. The seed itself though is highly poisonous as is most other parts of the tree.

The fruit fascinated early peoples, and the symbolism of females and fertility is closely associated with the appearance of the berry.

This book cannot fully explore the yew tree nor cover all of the ancient yews of Wales. There are still very old trees waiting to be discovered. I have only recently found several very old veterans. The oldest are not necessarily the biggest, and very decayed trees can be partly hidden away and covered by earth and ivy.

There are nevertheless, other ancient trees dotted about Wales, although they are not as old as the churchyard yews. The following are some from throughout Wales.

PEMBROKESHIRE

South-west between the Preseli Hills and the sea is the churchyard at *Nevern* (Nanhyfer), first established by the Irish Christian missionary Brynach. Incorporated into the church of today are the two fifth-century gravestones, now used as windowsills. An avenue of eight yew trees leads from the gate to the south porch. The second tree on the right from the gate is the *Bleeding yew of Nevern*. It is so named because of a wound, caused by a branch that was removed last century, which never heals. A

Bleeding yew of Nevern – grows close to a tenth-century Celtic cross

red substance, coloured by the dark red of the yew wood, oozes from the tree. The churchyard at Nevern has many attractions. The tenth-century Celtic cross is reputedly the finest in Wales, there are fascinating gravestones, and outside and up from the churchyard is the Pilgrims Cross, a wayside shrine used by the pilgrims from the north on their way to St David's in the far west.

CARMARTHENSHIRE

One of Wales's best ornamental tree collections lies close to the Tywi Valley, south-west of Llandeilo by the Black Mountain. *Gelli-aur* (The Golden Grove) was once an enormous park and it still covers a large piece of rural Carmarthenshire. Not far from the great Regency house, now an agricultural college, is the old arboretum. Here are some fine and very big old trees. A big group of holm oaks (*Quercus ilex*) can be viewed from one of the ridgeway paths, along with views out over the surrounding

When Merlin's oak shall tumble down
Then shall fall Carmarthen town

According to mythology, the sorcerer Merlin issued these words. Merlin also predicted that the town would become flooded on Lammas Day, and so for many years, much of the population of Carmarthen would desert the town on that day. Over time the practice ceased, but the oak still received the ultimate respect. Even when Merlin's oak died, it was preserved in concrete and protected by railings.

Eventually, due to road improvements and town expansion, it was removed and the remains are now housed in the local museum. Carmarthen is reputed to have been Merlin's birthplace. At the battle of Agincourt, his emblem was on the banner

Gelli-aur oak – old veteran near impressive Golden Grove arboretum, south-west of Llandeilo

landscapes. Huge conifers of note include record pines, firs, and thuja's and the *Gelli-aur oak*, a weird, and fantastic old relic on the garden edge. Recent restoration work at nearby *Aberglasny* has now revealed the incredible yew tunnel. Fused branches are a feature of this amazing medieval find.

Further west down the A40 and lower Tywi Valley the famous Welsh town of Carmarthen cherished a superstition concerning an old oak that stood for many centuries, in the highway on the Abergwili road:

Yew Tunnel, Aberglasny – remarkable find in restored grounds

FIG. 36.—ANCIENT RESUSCITATED YEW AT BETTWS NEWYDD.

ABOVE: Gardeners Chronicle *1890 print of Bettws Newydd yew*
BELOW: *Internal stem clearly visible on present day yew at Bettws Newydd*

borne by the fighting men from Carmarthenshire, whose heroic archery probably won the day for Henry V.

MONMOUTHSHIRE

North of the town of Usk in Gwent, a yew tree featured in the *Gardeners Chronicle* of the 1890s looks just the same one hundred years on. The *Bettws Newydd yew* has an internal stem of large proportions, a living proof of the continuity and ability of the yew to have 'near perpetual' life.

John Lowe's classic book, *The Yew Trees of Great Britain and Ireland* (1897), features several trees in Wales, including the one at *Mamhilad* near Pontypool in the churchyard of Saint Ilfyd. In 1840 when measured by Loudon it was 8.9 metres (29.3 feet), then

Dafydd ap Gwilym yew at Strata Florida Abbey

now, within its hollow, the tree contains a simple stone with his name on it. It is interesting, looking at photographs from the 1940s, to note the absence of the stones that are now built up around the base of the yew.

Another reference to Strata Florida is in 1895 when remeasured by Rev. Cook it was 9 metres (29.8 feet). Now, 100 years later, it is 9.4 metres (31 feet), although the main trunk is now appearing to split. Here, once again, internal stems are very evident. This old settlement stands on a hill northeast of the industrial town.

CEREDIGION

A few miles from Cardigan are the ruins of the twelfth-century Abbey at Saint Dogmaels. The Abbey was in fact established over 500 years ago after the church of the first Christian missionaries in the sixth century. An original stone inscribed in Ogham script commemorates Sagranus, son of Curiotamus. It is one of the best preserved early stones in Wales. Between the Abbey and the church stands an old yew surrounded by a high wall, an unusual sight in this historic place.

The romantic and beautiful place that is home to the ruins of Strata Florida Abbey in Dyfed was once the centre of a huge estate covering this region. The Cistercian monks had a powerful and highly organised community that operated from the abbey. In the adjacent graveyard lies the grave of one of Wales's most celebrated poets, Dafydd ap Gwilym. In the fourteenth century the monks planted a yew tree on his grave, and

Majestic Douglas fir in parkland at Powis Castle

from Leland, who observed that when he visited Wales, in the reign of Henry VIII: 'there was thirty-nine vast Ewgh trees in the churchyard belonging to Strathfleur Abbey'. In 1890, three of the thirty-nine remained, and the largest of those was in two parts, with a passage through the centre. It must have been quite a sight! Now, one hundred years on, only Dafydd ap Gwilym's tree remains.

POWYS

Just into Wales near Loton Park, Alberbury, is the locality of the *Prince's oak*. The name of the district is derived from the tree associated with the Prince of Wales (later King George IV).

In September 1806, the Prince and the Duke of Clarence were staying with Sir Robert Leighton at Loton Hall. Sir Robert suggested that the Prince might ride a few hundred yards across the border, so visiting the country of which he had recently been

RIGHT:
Powis oak with castle in background

made Prince. Accepting the offer, the Prince crossed the border and noticed a majestic oak by the roadside. He picked some sprigs of foliage from the tree and, placing them in his hat, rode back to Loton Park, proclaiming that he had been to Wales and to prove it had Welsh oak in his hat! From then on the tree was referred to as the *Prince's oak* and the locality assumed that name. The oak is still healthy and stands on top of a bank near a minor road junction. A brick wall and railings have been put around the tree and a brass plaque can be found in the wall.

Perched high on a sandstone rock above the seventeenth-century garden terraces, Powis Castle looks down on the historic landscape and the footpath to Welshpool. The original castle was built in the thirteenth century by Welsh princes and has been owned and altered by generations of the Herbert and Clive families since.

The terraced garden is most distinctive, laid out as it is in the grand Italian style. The great clipped yew buttresses are a remarkable feature and many fine trees grow in the garden and also in the woodland garden that skirts the ridge to the west. An old cork oak can be found down one of the paths.

Outside the gardens in the deer park are some great trees. In and around Gwen Morgan's wood are Britain's largest ponderosa pines (*Pinus ponderosa*), a beautiful pine with 'silver' plated bark, once described by Alan Mitchell as 'easily the finest known'. Close by stands one of Britain's tallest trees, a very straight and majestic Douglas fir (*Pseudo tsuga menziesii*). Gwen Morgan's oak is a giant pollard sessile oak of great age. It has recently undergone tree surgery to remove weight from the main limbs. This was carried out in order to alleviate strain on the very hollow main trunk. Other big old oaks abound including a record breaker out on the estate.

The other notable oak is the *Powis oak*

Gwen Morgan's oak – old sessile oak pollard

Black poplar, Newtown – beside River Severn

lent stand of sequoias. One fallen tree is now sending out a line of young redwoods, the coast redwood being one of the few conifers capable of coppicing.

Wherever the native black poplar grows into an open crowned, mature tree, it attracts admiration. Throughout the River Severn valley, the occasional specimen can be found, never far away from water.

When it grows near to the centre of a town, it is altogether more unusual, and the well-known black poplar at Newtown, Powys, is in that category. The *Newtown poplar* is of some considerable age and certainly pre-dates the municipal car park that now surrounds it. The River Severn embankment, built to control flooding, rises above the tree to the north, and considering all the drainage alterations, it is surprising that the old tree survives. Originally, it would have grown on altogether wetter and less disturbed land. When travelling along the A483 in central Wales, this landmark tree of Newtown is unmistakable.

Giant redwood, Leighton – branches from fallen tree growing into trees themselves

growing on a knoll on the south side of the castle. If ever there was a tree that was the epitome of an old parkland oak it is this tree. There are huge whitebeams and lucombe oaks which stand out with their evergreen leaves if visited on a sunny winter's day. Yet more big trees in the form of lime avenues and big beeches are outside the main park enclosure towards the Newtown road. Further out again on the estate other treasures are hidden from general view.

Leighton Park near the Welshpool border, the infamous leyland cypress was accidentally grown in 1888 as a hybrid between the Chamaecyparis and Cupressus species. This fast-growing conifer has been commonly used as a hedging plant over the past twenty years. Its vigorous growth of over three metres (10 feet) in five years can be seen as both an advantage and a disadvantage! Within the woods at Leighton is an excel-

Pennant-Melangell, four ancient yews encircle the pre-Christian churchyard

At Glascwm on the Gladestry road from Cregrina, the early Christian Celts set up a religious 'llan' in the village. This was the centre that controlled Rhulen, which later became a 'satellite settlement'. Again, at Glascwm, old yews dot the churchyard, as they do at Llanfihangel-nant-Melan, a village to the north, where eight surviving yews ring the pre-Christian churchyard dedicated to Saint Michael. Other huge ancient yews worth seeing in this area are in Radnor forest, west of Presteigne. Discoed and nearby Casgob. The Casgob churchyard was a site of habitation in the Bronze Age, which at that time was protected by a high earth rampart.

Further south-west, beyond Brecon, along the Usk valley is the small village of Defynnog. This is home to several ancient yews, one with a record girth. As with Gwytherin and Llangerneyw in the north, the site contains a pre-Christian stone.

Across the Snowdonia National Park, Bala, and the Berwyn mountains, the head of the Tanat Valley, approached from Llangynog, holds the 'secret place' of Pennant-Melangell. A scatter of buildings, including a retreat for the sick, are found near the circular churchyard.

Four ancient yews surround the small church, which has been beautifully restored over the past decade. The shrine of Melangell is located within. The legend of Melangell is derived from the seventeenth-century transcript *Life of the Saints*:

One day a prince Brochwell was hunting, and his hounds disturbed a hare which took refuge in a thicket. The hare then hid under the skirts of the virgin Melangell as she prayed. The hounds fled howling, the huntsman's horn became frozen to his mouth. Melangell informed the prince that she had come to the place seeking refuge. The prince granted the valley to her, and from then she founded a religious community.

Tradition states that there was a nunnery at Pennant. The shrine became a place of pilgrimage for those seeking religious fulfilment and cures for ailments. The stone shrine was thrown out of the church in the seventeenth century. Eventually it was restored, and put to stand in the chancel, behind the altar, in the late 1980s. It is the earliest known surviving Romanesque shrine in northern Europe.

In 1987, a film crew who were making a programme on the life of Ann Griffiths, the nineteenth-century Welsh hymn writer, severely damaged the grassland under one of the yew trees. They had wanted to film a burial scene with a wintry background. The April weather was unobliging, so the crew decided to fake snow using industrial salt. This was scattered on the branches and ground.

After filming, the salt was unfortunately washed into the turf and the foliage of the tree became burnt. Great concern was expressed about whether the tree would survive. The damaged grass was reinstated by using old turf from a local source. Looking at it in 1994, the tree appears to have completely recovered.

Another unusual feature of Pennant is the layered branch of the yew to the south of the churchyard. The site at Pennant is in fact pre-Christian and the surrounding yew trees must be of a great age. Pennant is peaceful and indeed very special.

South of Pennant and Lake Vyrnwy is the main road linking England and the West coast of Wales. One of the villages mid-way between the Mallwyd junction (ancient yews in Mallwyd churchyard) and Welshpool is Llanerfyl. The *Patriarch yew* stands close to the church of Saint Erfyl. It is an enormous and strangely shaped ancient tree. The trunk is split into four huge, twisted parts, one branch male and the others female. The tree, of which there is no other in Wales of such shape, was honoured by the Welsh poet Evan Breeze. Some years ago, an early Christian grave was discovered beneath the yew. At the back of the church a stone has the following inscription: 'Here lies in this grave Rustece, daughter of Paterninus, aged thirteen years. May she rest in peace.'

Just north of Welshpool is Guilsfield, Cegidfa in Welsh. By the gate into the large

Patriarch yew, Llanerfyl, a grotesquely-shaped ancient yew

Rhulen – ring of ancient yews in remote Radnor churchyard

churchyard is a gravestone which is adorned by a skull and crossbones. In 1707, a man died at the age of 90 and the inscription tells the tale of how, as a boy, he helped his father to plant the tree that now stands behind his grave. To think that this yew is from the seventeenth century only confirms the great age of the ancient relics.

In the upper Wye Valley near Builth Wells, is one of Wales and Britain's largest yew trees in the churchyard of Llanfaredd.

It is decayed on one side, but is still a fine tree. There are tumuli on top of the hill and a spring just to the east of the church.

In 1944, a visitor to the church recorded that the cross and candlesticks were made of yew wood. The Radnor hills to the east of the Wye contain several gems.

At Aberedw, social history reveals that the churchyard was once used, as most were, for games, dancing and merrymaking. Musicians played from the tiered rows of benches in the porch and dancing took place between the two big yews.

Up the Edwr Valley, another ancient tree stands by the gate leading to the church of Saint Padarn at Llanbadarn-y-garreg.

Further on, down the narrowest of lanes into the wildest of Radnor landscapes, is the tiny settlement of Rhulen (Rhiwlen). On top of the Bronze Age mound is the simple, late Norman church with its unique recessed door and altar surround. Against the east wall of the church are the remains of a yew that crashed in a storm in the mid-1980s. This tree prevented any extension to the chancel in the fourteenth century. Around the perimeter of the mounded churchyard are extremely old and battered yews. This site, described by Donald Gregory as having 'some mysterious alchemy', is indeed worthy of finding in this beautiful and relatively unknown part of Wales.

A few miles north stands the *Cregrina yew* in a churchyard upon one of Alfred Watkins 'ley lines'. His book, *The Old Straight Track*, has been somewhat discredited over recent years, but it is still a fascinating study of the Herefordshire/Radnorshire countryside.

GWYNEDD

Several miles inland from Port Dinorwic,

Gwynedd, on the North Wales coast, is Llanddeiniolen where three huge old yews may be seen in the sombre, eerie church-yard.

East of Porthmadog and Portmeirion is the old village of Maentwrog in the Vale of Ffestiniog. Within the churchyard, next to the south porch, the 'stone of Twrog' stands. Probably an early Christian missionary, Twrog is believed to have died in 610. In all probability this site was a Bronze Age settlement. Now the massive ancient yew trees protect the site from the elements.

CONWY

One of the greatest gardens in the British Isles is found in Gwynedd, North Wales. Turning south off the Llandudno Junction to the Betws-y-coed road at Tal-y-Cafn you reach the National Trust garden of Bodnant. Overlooking the valley of the River Conwy with magnificent views of Snowdonia to the south-west, the 32 hectare (80-acre) garden spreads across a glen through which a small

river flows towards the Conwy. In late May and early June the Laburnum Tunnel is a spectacular and world-famous feature. The golden walk being a major Bodnant attrac-tion. The hybrid strawberry tree (*Arbutus xandrachnoides*) is Britain's finest specimen seen growing on the top terrace in front of the house. The red peeling bark is a most attractive feature.

A notable ancient yew can be found at the aptly named Llangernyw to the east of the Vale of Conwy on the Llanrwst to Abergele road. The huge yew is somewhat ruined by the oil tank placed within the hollow bole, one of the worst examples of an old tree treated in a shabby manner. The most intriguing sight in the churchyard are the standing stones, one with a distinctive mark. It is a classic example of an ancient site that has been christianised.

South of Llangernyw, on a far wilder road (B5384) but next to the same River Elwy as the previous churchyard, is Gwytherin.

Here, on a banked site, great old yews

Gwytherin – Bronze Age stones and ancient yews

grow, and a line of standing stones from the Bronze Age or earlier testify to the site's Celtic past. One of the stones was converted to a tombstone with an inscription in the fifth century. Over ten years ago, fire partly destroyed the yew on the east side of the churchyard enclosure, but the place is well worth visiting despite its remote position.

DENBIGHSHIRE

At Llanrhaeadr, near Ruthin, a property known as 'The Three Sisters' is home to one of the original three sweet chestnuts which by tradition date from around 1640. One tree is now merely a stump; a second tree is a dead, windblown skeleton; the third tree, although having a hollow and badly charred interior, is still very much alive. R.T. Wheeler inspected and measured the trees in April 1984, and confirmed that the still living tree has a girth exceeding 12 metres (41 feet). Two earlier references describe them as: 'fine chestnut trees, one of which is near 24ft in circumference'. Pennant, *Tours*

in Wales, 1781; and 'after nearly 300 years one has nearly disappeared, but two remain'. W.A. Evans, *Three Leafy Sisters*, early 18th century.

The *Three Sisters* at one time grew in the parkland surrounding the large old farmhouse at Bachymbyd, located further down the lane. They now stand in the garden of the newer house close to the A525 Denbigh–Ruthin road. When compared to other old chestnuts, the age of the survivor would seem to be at least 350 years old.

Directly to the east as the crow flies, but north then south-east by road, is the village of *Nantglyn* (located several miles south-west of Denbigh, north of Llyn Brenig). Here is the ultimate sacred yew tree, for within the hollow trunk of the 8 metre girth tree has been constructed stone steps and a pulpit for outdoor services. The tree is probably not benefitting from the old structure within it,

The Three Sisters – the remaining sweet chestnut near Ruthin

Pulpit yew, Nantglyn — with stone steps leading to the heart of the tree

but if ever there was a case for linking the shelter of the spreading yew branches and preaching, then this is surely it. (To further substantiate the link, at La Haye de Routot, Normandy, France, there is an enormous hollow yew that houses a tiny chapel.)

FLINTSHIRE

In the attractive North Wales village of Caerwys, south of Holywell and the A55, an official eisteddfod was ordered by Queen Elizabeth I in 1568. The event itself goes back well before the sixteenth century as a more informal affair, and as far back as the twelfth century there is evidence of a gathering in the village. From 1568, trade certificates were issued to minstrels and craftsmen, and the contestants in the eisteddfod would sit in the town square composing their songs and poems.

The *Caerwys* or *Peace tree* was the focal point of the square and across from this was the Town Hall where the Bards competed.

The event went into decline over the centuries, but was revived in 1819. The old tree, believed to be a sycamore, was deemed dangerous and eventually felled. The

Peace tree, Caerwys

sycamore that stands in the square today is part of a monument to the village and its history. The tree was planted by the Earl of Plymouth in March 1968 to replace the *Peace tree* that dated from 1919.

WREXHAM

West of the Shropshire borderlands, near Chirk, lies the Ceiriog Valley, the opening of which is spanned by the magnificent aqueduct built by Thomas Telford. At the natural end of the valley is the tiny hamlet of

Llanarmon Dyffryn Ceiriog, with its two hotels 'The West Arms' and 'The Hand'. The churchyard contains an unusual raised mound and very old yews with particularly good fluted trunks. The whole area is a delight for exploring, with Britain's highest waterfall at Llanrhaeadr-ym-Mochnant just a few miles to the south.

In the Ceiriog Valley, is the locality of Pontfadog, home of the *Pandy oak*. It grows next to an old farmhouse off the lanes above the north side of the village. The tree looks over the lovely, peaceful valley, and is one of Britain's, and certainly Wales's, largest oaks with a girth of over 12 metres (39 feet). Inevitably an old pollard, the tree has many holes, burrs, broken limbs etc. but has also a healthy crown of newer growth. Mr Morris, who lives in the farmhouse, is very proud of the tree, and rightly so.

The Pandy oak stands in the beautiful Ceiriog Valley

To the east near the English border, is Gresford's large (locked) churchyard. The celebrated male *Gresford yew*, a recorded tree in 1813, 1836 and 1878 stands gloomily behind iron railings.

By tradition, one of the Wales' seven wonders are the yews in Overton-on-Dee churchyard, a pleasant village near Wrexham. They are not as old as many trees, and recent tree surgery has detracted from their appearance. They are, nevertheless, worth visiting if nearby.

Wales can justifiably claim to be the land of the ancient yew tree, for when travelling across the whole country, you are never far away from one of the old living links with the past.

The Pandy oak with the proud owner

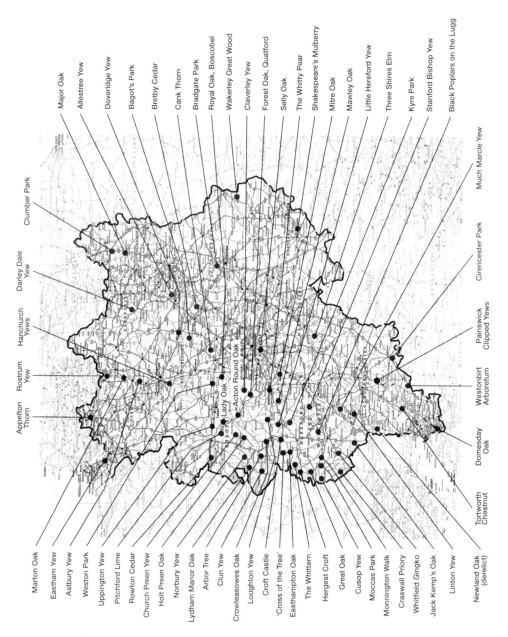

Major Oak
Allestree Yew
Doveridge Yew
Bagot's Park
Bretby Cedar
Cank Thorn
Bradgate Park
Royal Oak, Boscobel
Wakerley Great Wood
Claverley Yew
Forest Oak, Quatford
Selly Oak
The Whitty Pear
Shakespeare's Mulberry
Mitre Oak
Mawley Oak
Little Hereford Yew
Three Shires Elm
Kyre Park
Stanford Bishop Yew
Black Poplars on the Lugg

Clumber Park
Darley Dale Yew
Hanchurch Yews
Rostrum Yew
Appelton Thorn

Much Marcle Yew
Cirencester Park
Painswick Clipped Yews
Westonbirt Arboretum
Domesday Oak
Tortworth Chestnut

Lady Oak
Acton Round Oak

Marton Oak
Eastham Yew
Astbury Yew
Weston Park
Uppington Yew
Pitchford Lime
Rowton Cedar
Church Preen Yew
Holt Preen Oak
Norbury Yew
Lydham Manor Oak
Arbor Tree
Clun Yew
Crowleasowes Oak
Loughton Yew
Croft Castle
'Cross of the Tree'
Easthampton Oak
The Whittern
Hergest Croft
Great Oak
Cusop Yew
Moccas Park
Monnington Walk
Craswall Priory
Whitfield Gingko
Jack Kemp's Oak
Linton Yew
Newland Oak (derelict)

© Bartholomew 1996. Reproduced with permission of Harper Collins Cartographic. MM-1297-78.

Central Shires of England

The appropriately named locality of Four Oaks, near Meriden, lies between the cities of Birmingham and Coventry and is reputedly the centre of England. The surrounding countryside of fertile farmland has the River Avon meandering through what can be described as the heart of the country. This land was once dominated by the 'Warwickshire weed' or English elm to give it its true name, now alas no longer showing its towering shapes across the landscape. The elm, though, still remains in the hedgerows and may yet again have its time.

The Avon passes by Warwick castle and its historic landscape, and then flows quietly through Stratford and the Vale of Evesham, and on to join the Severn at Tewkesbury. That river enters England in Shropshire, a county so rich in tree heritage, then it loops the town of Shrewsbury and cuts through the Ironbridge Gorge before continuing towards Bridgnorth and Worcester.

Farmland full of hedgerow trees and small woodlands roll out to the Welsh border, with magical places such as the Golden Valley hiding their tree treasures below the Black Mountains. Old, untouched deer parks, full of ancient timber are part of Herefordshire's tree legacy.

On the south-western fringe of the Shires the Malverns rise, a small ribbon of hills behind the flattest of lands. The orchards and hopfields are fewer now, but still have an atmosphere all of their own. Beyond the Avon and Severn, old country towns are embraced by the limestone uplands of the Cotswolds. This attractive land contains many old estates where great trees stand in full glory. Here an ambitious landowner had the foresight to plan and plant one of the world's greatest arboreta.

In the north-west of the central shires, the Cheshire plain is dotted with black and white buildings, an oak that was England's biggest and an historic thorn. A world famous telescope looks out to the stars over a fine young arboretum. The plain slopes gently towards the estuary of the river Dee and eastwards to the Derbyshire Dales and Peak District. Famous country houses in Derbyshire are surrounded by great landscapes containing notable trees. The hilltops are crowned with clumps of ash, beech and sycamore, as the land finally falls toward the cities of Derby and Nottingham.

The recreational area of Cannock Chase in Staffordshire lies south-west of the Peak District, where tree husbandry and folklore exist beside the great house and park of Shugborough.

In the east, Nottinghamshire is forever associated with Sherwood Forest, and still has remnants of that once great woodland, and in The Dukeries is a park with the longest double lime avenue in Europe. The county also has an apple tree with a name known throughout the world.

Further south, Leicestershire and its rolling field patterns are broken by the upland area of Charnwood, a heathland with an old forest and ancient trees. In Northamptonshire, fine hedgerows, estates, and new landscapes around the county town, finally give way to the counties surrounding the great London metropolis.

GLOUCESTERSHIRE

In Tortworth village, in the county of Gloucestershire, close to the church and standing behind an iron railing, is the huge *Tortworth chestnut*. The tree is really a small woodland or coppice in its own right. The main trunk is a huge, gnarled, twisted bole with large cavities, there is evidence of old fires and broken limbs everywhere. From the

Tortworth chestnut, ancient survivor

'original' come great secondary trees and branches curve over to touch the ground and layer in the leaf litter.

The tree is impossible to measure accurately for there are so many bits of new growth and cavities in the main trunk. The plaque on the gate reads:

> This tree supposed to be Six hundred
> Years old 1st January 1800,
> May Man Still Guard thy
> Venerable Form,
> From the Rude Blasts, and Tempestuous
> Storm,
> Still mayest thou Flourish through
> Succeeding time,
> And Last, Long Last, the Wonder
> of the Clime.

There are several references to the tree in past centuries, the word 'tort' may refer to the tree being a place where courts were held and laws enforced. In the *Gentleman's Magazine* of 1762 the following extract reads:

> I submit the following calculations of the age of a celebrated chestnut tree, which, in all probability is the oldest if not the largest tree in England, being 52 feet. round, to be transmitted by your means to posterity.

This eminent tree is the property of the Rt. Hon. Lord Daveat Tortworth, alias Tamworth, Gloucestershire.

> I may, with reason, fix its rising from the nut in the region of King Egbert AD800. From this date, to attain to such maturity and magnitude as to be a signal tree for a boundary or landmark, called byway of distinction the Great Chestnut Tree at Tamworth, in the reign of King Stephen. I cannot allow less than 335 years which brings it down to the first year of King Stephen AD1135.

In 1763 a Mr Collinson wrote the following:

> The extraordinary size and antiquity of the chestnut tree at Tortworth, now the seat of the Lord Ducie, mentioned in your faithful register, excited my curiosity to see it, and I have been for some years trying to procure a drawing of it from its noble owner, but without success. I have at last met with an ingenious young man, John Player of Stoke, who at my request has attempted to give a sketch of it, as well as the nature of its situation between three walls would admit.

He goes on to say:

> Five feet from the ground it measures 50 feet round and the largest part of the tree is living and very fruitful having on it a great quantity of nuts, seemingly like the true Spanish kind. As the nuts fall their growth is encouraged by the weeds that are under it. Many young trees are come up and surround the old one.

Tortworth chestnut – (drawing by A Howard)

The Tortworth chestnut is obviously very old and may well be in excess of 600 years. The sweet chestnut was probably brought to England by the Romans and was largely used for coppicing purposes. The Tortworth tree is a wonderful sight and the mixture of growth ages adds to its interest. On the other side of the church from the chestnut is a magnificent silver lime (*Tilia tomentosa*) which is the largest of its kind in Britain.

Throughout southern Britain, there are other examples of huge sweet or Spanish chestnuts but none with quite the ground coverage as the Tortworth tree. Other examples of old chestnuts are the very large one at Canford School, near Poole, Dorset. It has the strange nickname *Mungay oak* and has fire damage inside the bole. Nearby, in the woodland area is the remains of a very old coppiced chestnut. At Howlets Park, Kent is another huge old tree, and the avenue at Croft Castle, Herefordshire is mentioned elsewhere in the book.

Close to the city of Bristol, at Ashton Court, the *Domesday oak* has received much

Record Silver lime, Tortworth church

attention through the centuries, including a radio programme in the 1970s that used the old tree as a symbol of continuity in a changing world. As with so many of the old specimen oaks, much ironwork, props and other paraphernalia were put on the tree during the Victorian period.

The churchyard in the lovely Cotswold village of Painswick is home to a remarkable collection of clipped yews. Reputedly ninety-nine of them stand statuesque around the Church of St Mary the Virgin.

The yews used to be clipped in early September, close to 8 September, which is the feast of the Nativity of Our Lady. The following Sunday was known as 'Clipping Sunday'. The parishioners would walk in procession around the church and then link hands to circle the church. After the circle they would listen to the sermon at the steps leading to the tower.

Painswick clipped yews, – late spring sunset

Until 1956 the largest oak in Britain was the *Newland oak* in Gloucestershire. It measured 14 metres (46 feet) and grew in a field on the edge of the Forest of Dean on the east side of the Wye. The remains of the tree can still be seen, and a young tree grown from an acorn of the old *Newland oak* now stands amongst the debris of the still fenced tree.

Photographs of the old tree are still in existence. From these it can be seen that the oak was indeed a monster!

One of the world's finest tree collections is at Westonbirt near Tetbury, Gloucestershire. Here over 4,000 different trees and shrubs from all over the temperate world grow in the 243 hectares (600 acres) that make up the arboretum.

There are over 18,000 specimen trees and many of these are the oldest and largest examples in Britain. The collection also includes rare, endangered and historically important trees.

The history of Westonbirt is fascinating. At the age of 21, Captain Robert Holford started to plan an extension to the grounds of his father's estate. Ten years later, when he inherited the property, he had laid the foundations for one of the world's most outstanding collections. The Holford family had, for generations, been leading London judges, but Robert's great interest was trees and shrubs.

Like many wealthy landowners, he commissioned plant hunters to bring back examples of rare and hitherto unknown trees from all over the temperate world.

He began to plant in the area called Saville Glade. Then in 1855, he designed a series of radiating rides, including the famous Holford Ride. Between 1850 and 1875, he planted the first Acer Glade and Colour circle. He later moved on to the then wild area of Silk Wood. Robert's son George inherited his father's enthusiasm, and together they created Waste, Broad and Willesley Drives.

After Robert's death in 1892, George continued his work and when he also died in 1926, his nephew Lord Morley succeeded to the estate. The mansion, across the Tetbury road, was sold, but the arboretum was retained. Under the guidance of the curator W.J. Mitchell, Westonbirt's reputation went from strength to strength.

However, in 1956, five years after Lord Morley's death, Westonbirt passed to the Crown in lieu of death duties, and then on to the Forestry Commission. The rest is recent history.

There are too many outstanding trees at Westonbirt to list them all here, but well-known features include: the group of incense cedars planted in 1910 in Holford Ride; the Holford pine, peculiar to Westonbirt, in Marley Drive; a big Caucasian wingnut by the gate from the main drive onto the Downs, the large American red oak; and the many rare and beautiful birches and hickories growing in the old arboretum. In Silk Wood, off Willesley Drive, the pencil-slim group of Serbian spruce (*Picea omorika*) are outstanding. Close by, a Brewer's weeping spruce is well worth seeing as is a silver pendant lime (*Tilia tomentosa* 'Petiolaris') on Willesley Drive, and a very straight boled Dutch elm (*Ulmus hollandica*).

Further into the wild woodland are trees from a different age. A great ring of small leaved limes, grown from the same rootstock, were first coppiced many, many centuries ago and the process repeated through successive generations. This 'tree' pre-dates the present arboretum by a thousand years.

Westonbirt is a truly magnificent place in the autumn, when it receives its greatest number of visitors, but each season brings out a different facet of this exciting and beautiful place.

The mellow old market town of Cirencester is built over the Roman town of Corinium, which was second only to London in size. Dominating the Market Place is the Church of St John the Baptist, the largest parish church in Gloucestershire. The view from the tower peers over the

Westonbirt Arboretum – sugar maple in the autumn

great yew hedge surrounding Lord Bathurst's home at Cirencester Park, right next to the town. The park was laid out in the early eighteenth century by the poet Alexander Pope and the first Earl of Bathurst. The house is not open to the public but the huge 1,200 hectares (3,000 acre) park is, and it contains a wealth of great open crowned trees culminating in its superb chestnut avenue.

HEREFORD AND WORCESTER
In the lovely, little known county of Herefordshire are many fine trees. The county is particularly good for oaks. In hedgerows around the county great big old trees and well-formed young trees are growing.

Croft Castle – sweet chestnut avenue

At Easthampton Farm, near Shobdon stands the *Easthampton oak*, one of the largest sessile oaks in Britain with a girth of over 10 metres (33 feet) in 1994 and standing over 25 metres (82 feet) tall. The bole is hollow but the tree stands majestically on the brow of the hill in a field opposite the farmhouse overlooking the rolling Herefordshire countryside. The tree belongs to nearby Shobdon Court and the estate is owned by chicken farmer and tree enthusiast Colonel Corbett who, now in his eighties, is developing a private arboretum in his wonderful grounds. His project was started twenty years ago and is being added to annually. The Colonel's maternal family were the Holfords, who started Westonbirt Arboretum. A few miles from Shobdon can be found Croft Castle. Here at Croft are good avenues of both young and old oaks and limes. The castle has a history going back to the medieval period and there is evidence in the surrounding parkland of the original landscape. None more dramatic than the

Easthampton oak – majestic tree near Shobdon

extraordinary avenues of huge old gnarled sweet chestnuts. These are very atmospheric and a must for anyone finding themselves near Croft. Part of one of the avenues has now been fenced off by the National Trust because some of the chestnuts have experienced severe dieback, thought to be associated with the cattle that previously were allowed below them. Let's hope the protective regime works for it is a splendid place to be. The oldest chestnuts are generally recognised to be in excess of 350 years old.

Ancient timber – Croft Castle

If you visit Croft, walk to the far end of the avenue of chestnuts and there you will come across a small collection of very old contorted thorns and crab-apples. Croft Castle grounds also contain Britain's largest girthed sessile oak, once forgotten and only recently rediscovered in a seldom visited part of the old estate. The big oak in the field to the west of the castle is *Sir William's oak*, one of the oldest on the estate.

A mile west off the main Hereford–Kington road (A4111) at Eardisley is the small locality of *Great Oak*, so named because of the giant oak standing at the centre of the collection of houses that make up the hamlet. Over fifty years ago the crown was broken off in high gales. Extensive tree surgery to lessen the crown weight has helped to preserve the tree and it now has a healthy young crown atop its huge hollow trunk. It measured 9 metres (29.5 feet) in the summer of 1994.

Speculation as to the history of the tree refers to possibly a gospel oak or court tree. Little more is known other than it has been there well beyond present human memory.

Just in Herefordshire, on the eastern side of the Black Mountains, is the ruined Priory of Craswall. The Priory was built by the rare order of Grandmontine 1225–1441 in this beautiful remote part of the borderlands. The Priory has had archaelogical work carried out to it over the last ten years by the enthusiastic Craswall Grandmontine society.

At least once a year a pilgrimage takes place across the hills to the Priory from the Golden Valley.

'Great Oak' near Eardisley

At the corners of the old walls, the roots of planted old yew trees have become entangled in the masonry, so acting as a preserver of the ruins since the other walls have collapsed. Weird shapes with tentacle-like roots and fallen yews still flourishing can be found amongst the debris. Speculating on the age of the yews they would appear to be 500–600 years old, so fitting in with maybe the latter days of the Grandmontine Order.

Across a field an old sweet chestnut grows, probably associated with the priory for this is definitely not sweet chestnut country. The whole site is worthy of further research for the association of tree and building is a fascinating one.

Down the lanes into Hay-on-Wye the old yew at Cusop churchyard stands less than half a mile from refreshment and many book shops. Just over the county boundary in north Herefordshire, along the A456 near Tenbury Wells, is the village of the appropriately named Little Hereford. An old yew stands in the churchyard not far off the main road. This tree is of great age, probably dating from at least the Norman period.

Further south and not far from each other are two wonderful old Herefordshire churchyard yews. At Much Marcle, south-west of the black and white timbered town of Ledbury, is the *Much Marcle yew*. This magnificent, fully crowned tree is situated on the south side of the church. The tree is completely hollow and within its trunk a wooden seat in three sections has been cleverly constructed. The seat can accommodate seven people. The tree's crown is supported by an iron frame, put there in Victorian times. The churchyard, church and yew are well worth visiting.

South of Much Marcle and the M50, and to the west of Newent, is the locality that is home to the *Linton yew*. The tree has a girth exceeding 10 metres (33 feet) and its main feature is a classic internal stem. It stands to the north-west of the church.

This is one of the hidden trees of Herefordshire, not known to many.

In the beautiful rolling borderland

Branches of the Much Marcle yew are held by a giant frame

Ancient Linton churchyard yew – internal stem

Date	Girth	Height
1924	3.22m. (10ft. 7ins.)	
1947	3.48m. (11ft. 5ins.)	
1963	3.80m. (12ft. 5ins.)	20.73m. (68ft.)
1973	3.96m. (13ft. 0ins.)	23m. (75ft.)
1984	4.20m. (13ft. 9ins.)	20.12m. (66ft.)
1995	4.39m. (14ft. 5ins.)	20.42m. (67ft.)

This male ginkgo is a beautiful tree with a thick, grey, heavily ridged bole and big handsome crown. The foliage, so much unlike any other tree, varies in shape and size depending on age. The walled garden in which the tree now stands, close to the 'temple' conservatory, was built after the ginkgo was planted. The protection created by the walls may well have helped the tree to the big size it now enjoys as Britain's biggest girthed Maidenhair tree. Close by, a 100-year-old tunnel of old apple varieties takes you back to a different age of gardening.

between Herefordshire and Wales is a gem. Whitfield House is at the end of a long drive through impressive parkland from the Hereford–Abergavenny road at Wormbridge. This is close to The Golden Valley and Abbey Dore Priory. The old walled garden, which is a short walk from the house at Whitfield, contains one of Britain's finest maidenhair trees (*Ginkgo biloba*) referred to as a 'living fossil' by Darwin. It is indeed a unique tree. It is the only living representative of the ginkgo family of plants. All the others have become extinct. Since ancient times the ginkgo has been cultivated around Chinese and Japanese temples, for in those countries it was deemed sacred. It arrived in Europe at Utrecht in 1730. In Britain it has been cultivated for a little over 200 years.

The *Whitfield ginkgo* was planted under the direction of Lady Catherine Stanhope soon after 1775, probably 1778. In 1785 Sir Hungerford Hoskins mentioned it as 'rare and worthy of notice'. In 1868 the famous Woolhope Club visited the tree. At that time it was 2.2 metres (7.15 feet) in the girth and 15.4 metres (50.5 feet) high. Since then it has an excellent history of measurements over the last eighty years:

Whitfield Ginkgo – Britain's best, grows in an old kitchen garden

Across the Welsh border at Glasbury, another huge tree probably planted about the same time, and introduced to these parts by the same people, grows in a different manner. It has three main trunks that branch out at ground level.

In the hills to the west, the private estate of Kentchurch Court, north-west of Garway Hill, has some outstanding trees. The deer park has largely been untouched since medieval times and has an atmosphere locked in time. Giant field maples and thorns dot the hillside. Huge sweet chestnuts and *Jack Kemp's oak* look out over the Black Mountains to the west. Jack Kemp was a local poet who regularly sat in the tree composing poetry. The oak is one of England's biggest and no other could grow in such splendid surroundings. Several great yews also grow in this magnificent place.

The largest of these trees has a girth exceeding 9.15 metres (30 feet) and is one of the largest yews found outside a churchyard in Britain.

In Munsley churchyard is a yew with a girth of 8.2 metres (27 feet) and standing on a small mount in the churchyard at Stanford Bishop is a yew with a girth of over 6.7 metres (22 feet). This tree has legendary associations with St Augustine, who it is said positioned his chair under the tree in Roman times. Dr James Johnston discovered a very old and worn chair in the church in the Victorian period. Certain features of the wooden chair, such as the oak pegs and the box lid seat hinged with round pieces of wood, indicated the possibility of seventh century origins. The chair was eventually acquired by Canterbury Cathedral and debate as to its origin still continues today. Stanford Bishop is a small village in the hop growing area of eastern Herefordshire. It lies south of Bromyard, close to the attractive River Frome.

At Monnington-on-Wye, north of

Jack Kemp's oak – the poet sat in this romantic veteran

*Monnington Walk – the long walk between yews
and Scots pines*

Wormbridge, the Court was once the home
of Roger Monnington who married Owen
Glendower's daughter Margaret. Her rebel
father sought refuge here and is supposed to
have taken flight back to Wales via Brobury
Scar, a distinctive and well-known outcrop
high above the River Wye to the west. The
mile-long Monnington Walk, made famous
by Kilvert's diaries, leads to the scar and is
one of Britain's oldest, still complete avenues
of Scots pines and yews. It was planted to
mark the election of William Tomkyns as
MP for Weobley in 1628. The avenue is very
unusual and worth walking from either the
Monnington or Brobury end.

At Brobury Scar, on the sandstone
outcrop, are other old Scots pines, sweet
chestnuts and old beeches with their bark
covered in 'initial' carvings. It is a fine place
to wander through the dramatic hanging
woods that look down to the Wye and across
the fertile valley on the southern side of the
river. At the Scar are traces of an ancient
camp.

Just upstream on the southern bank lies
the much renowned Moccas Park. One of

the finest examples in the country of a
medieval deer park, it is surrounded by a
pale, traditional oak fence. Behind the fence
the great old oaks can be seen dotted across
the parkland up to rising ground to the
south. An agreement between the owners
and English Nature allows sensitive management of the park, which is designated a
National Nature Reserve. Reverend Francis
Kilvert wrote the following description of
Moccas's trees in his celebrated diary in
1876:

*grey, gnarled, deformed, hunch backed,
misshapen, old men,
that stand waiting and watching
century after century
biding God's time
with both feet in the grave
and yet tiring down
and seeing out generation after generation.*

Many of the old oaks had names and
today the dead and rotting wood in the park
are ideal conditions for many species of
beetle of which some are only found at
Moccas. Fungi and lichens also thrive
making Moccas one of the richest parkland
sites in Britain.

Not unnaturally, there is no access without prior authority and that can be applied for via English Nature in South Shropshire.

The rest of Moccas Park lies to the north of the B4352 stretching down to the river. Further along that road, Bredwardine has some huge oaks in its roadside hedgerows. One colossus grows about a mile on the western side of the village. There are others and near the church towards the river the old orchard land contains some venerable old fruit trees. Britain's biggest wild pear (*Pyrus communis*) grows at Bredwardine.

At Lingen there is a ring of chestnuts around the churchyard, and down the lane to the east a crossroads is shaded by a big old oak tree. The locality has the magical name 'Cross of the Tree' and nearby, by a stream leading to the Lugg, is *Mistletoe oak*. Did an oak grow here with mistletoe? Revered by the Druids it is nevertheless almost unknown for an oak to be host to mistletoe today. It is good to think one once grew in this beautiful part of Herefordshire.

Black poplars on the banks of the River Lugg

'Cross of the Tree' – rural Herefordshire at its best

Following the River Lugg beyond Leominster on its way winding southwards, it eventually passes Moreton-on-Lugg. On the banks of the slow flowing river grow willows and alders, and north of Moreton across the fields, grow two great big black poplars. These are two of Herefordshire's biggest and their heavy branches dip down towards the water as if trying to touch it. They can be seen close to by following the footpaths across the fields from the lane towards Marden.

The European larch is a tall and stately tree and becomes pyramidal in shape when given space in which to grow. The trunk becomes stout if the tree is allowed to grow. The bark is pink to dull red and brown in colour and deeply fissured in old trees. It came to Britain from the Alps early in the seventeenth century.

During the last quarter of the eighteenth century, some people, encouraged by the Society of Arts, began extensive planting of this tree with a view to obtaining useful timber. Earlier than this, however, in 1728 the Duke of Atholl began cultivating larch on a big scale. Some very early larches grow in Scotland.

One peculiarity with some early planted trees is a very distinctive 'potted' appearance. These are referred to as 'Pedestal' larches. A theory exists that these trees were brought to this country as early examples of containerised trees and were grown on in pots before their very limited distribution.

At Pothill, Auchterarder, Perthshire is an example that is 18 metres (59 feet) high with a 150 cm.(59 in) diameter at 2 metres (6.5 feet) in 1985, but the finest pedestal larch is the beautiful tree growing at 'The Whittern' near Lyonshall in Herefordshire.

It measured 20 metres (66 feet) by 256 cm. (101 in) diameter at 1.5 metres (5 feet) in 1963 and 21 metres (69 feet) by 170 cm. (67 in) diameter at 2 metres (6.5 feet) in 1990. The huge twisted wrapped over 'pedestal' is like nothing else. The planting date of the tree is put at 1736 and nearby stands a lovely young larch, a self-seeder from the big old parent tree. In April when fresh green shoots clothe this deciduous conifer and the red flowers are just conspicuous, it is a sight to behold, growing as it does on the edge of lawn overlooking the rolling Herefordshire countryside.

Across the lawn, a contemporary of the larch, a Cedar of Lebanon stands with a storm damaged crown. At the front of the house another tree from the same era, a beech with low layering branches, dominates the ground. Other impressive trees are all around.

Early spring morning and an old Cedar of Lebanon at 'The Whittern'

The beautiful pedestal larch at 'The Whittern'

Near Ledbury is one of the great nineteenth century pinetums at Eastnor Castle, planted between 1840 and 1880 by the second and third Earls Somer, although some initial, limited planting was carried out before that date. The site is hilly and well wooded, and lends itself ideally for a 'natural' planting style.

Between Kington and that marvellous part of Offa's Dyke, Hergest Ridge, is Hergest Croft. There are really two separate gardens at Hergest: one around the house and the other half a mile away in a wood. Both have been made in this century and both have important collections. Hergest Croft is one of the finest private collections of trees in Britain. The famous plant collecting Banks family still run this gem of a place near the Welsh border.

Deep in the wonderful Wyre Forest near Bewdley grows the *Whitty pear*, a member of the Sorbus family of trees. This tree was first recorded in the forest in 1678 by Alderman Edmund Pitts. In 1855 a flowering branch of the tree was exhibited at the Worcestershire Naturalists Club. Grafts had been taken by them from the original tree. It was just as well, for by 1862 the original *Whitty pear* (*Sorbus domestica*) had been burnt. Further up the River Severn at Arley Castle, two trees existed that were grown, it was claimed, from seeds of the Wyre Forest tree, but these have now gone.

In 1913 another tree, also grown from the seed of the original, was planted near to the spot in the forest where the first tree grew. That tree, close to one of the main footpaths, is now over 10 metres (33 feet) tall. A simple sign marks its position, otherwise it would be difficult for the layman to find. There is another school of thought which claims that the tree now standing in the Wyre Forest was grown from a graft and not from a seed. The species occurs naturally in southern Europe but not in Britain, so how the original tree came to be in the Wyre Forest is an intriguing mystery. The *Whitty pear* is similar to the mountain ash or rowan but has larger fruit and the surface of the bark is

Whitty pear – deep in the Wyre Forest

more broken and fissured.

One of the Worcestershire's most renowned trees is the *Mitre oak* at Crossney Green, Hartlebury. Now little more than shell with young growth shooting out of the cut limbs, it sits rather incongruously next to the busy A449 dual carriageway between Kidderminster and Worcester.

It is likely that the oak was planted in later centuries on one of the old boundaries of the Hartlebury Manor which was originally granted to the Bishops of Worcester by King Mercia in AD 670. Measured in 1958 at 7.3 metres (24 feet) girth and a height of 21 metres (70 feet) it later received extensive tree surgery after a woman was struck by a falling branch. A lot of local correspondence and debate ensued and the state of the tree was discussed at length. It was eventually left with a protective fence erected around the tree.

The name of the tree is derived from a Bishop's headgear, and in his writings Bede refers to an oak near the borders of England and Wales where bishops met. There is no reference, however, to where that tree stood. The *Mitre oak* has received much publicity over the years, so much so that a large inn a few hundred yards away bears its name. Poems have been written about it including the one published by the former Vicar of Dudley, Dr Booker. A few miles from the *Mitre oak* another boundary tree, the *Rock oak* stood, which may have been the oak referred to by Bede.

Four miles south of Tenbury Wells on the B4214 Bromyard road lies Kyre Park, (pronounced Kear). There has probably been a settlement at Kyre since the ninth century. A castle was built in the twelfth or thirteenth century and the present house is built around its shell. (The house is not open to the public.) In 1754, the present shrubbery was laid out and some of the earliest features still survive. It is now in an ambitious state of restoration.

The shrubbery walk, which starts near the house, covers over 12 hectares (29 acres) and within it are five lakes, waterfalls, a hermitage, a Norman dovecote and a Jacobean tithe barn. On the walk, the most famous tree to be viewed is the *Parted yew*, included in John Lowe's classic work *The Yew Trees of Great Britain and Ireland* (1897). There has been much debate over the years as to whether the *Parted yew* is one tree or two.

John Lowe was honorary physician to the Prince of Wales, and was fascinated with the age of yew trees. He conducted a study into that subject. Although not visiting Kyre Park, he was sent details of the two yews by the owner Mrs Baldwyn Childe. One of the trees has now gone without trace, but the other was described as follows: 'In the Shrubbery stands a very old tree, split in two parts, the portion on the lower ground has fallen partly over, and so slipped away from the upper half.' He also wrote: 'Kyre Park contains many fine and notable trees of oak, beech etc.'

The *Parted yew* still grows vigorously, but inspection reveals that it is probably two trees which grew close together, with one eventually falling, and then, as yews do, regrowing. The upright tree is female, the leaning tree male. Although it is possible to have branches of different sex on the same tree, it is uncommon. Both of the trees are of some considerable age. When visiting the park at Kyre, one sees many old yews and also a huge amount of regeneration. The islands in the lakes are full of yew, which may be native to these woods or may have been seedlings from medieval plantings.

The other yew mentioned by Mrs Baldwyn Childe was the *Court Leet yew*, which she located 'outside the wood patch grove'. One hundred years ago, some fine trees grew at Kyre, amongst which were huge zelkovas, recorded by the Woolhope Club, and some of England's finest oaks.

Much has now gone, but just down from the house, on the north side towards the shrubbery, is a monster fern leafed beech (*Fagus sylvatica* 'Asplenifolia'). This giant was 15 metres (50 feet) high and had a girth of 3.35 metres (11 feet) in 1907. From very early photographs it can be seen that the beech was a big spreading tree 100 years ago. Considering that the fern leaved beech was first grown in Britain in about 1820, the *Kyre beech* must have been one of the first planted and is certainly the biggest recorded in Britain by some margin.

Not greatly tall at 22 metres (72 feet), which is typical of the type, this tree's outstanding feature is the spread of the branches, which cover over 33 metres (108 feet) of the surrounding ground. Its girth in 1995 was 5.63 metres (18 feet) at 1 metre and 6 metres (20 feet) at 1.5 metres.

Also in the shrubbery is a fine stand of hornbeam, and an Atlas cedar of noble proportions.

The huge spreading fern-leafed beech at Kyre Park

Fern-leaf beech with owner

SHROPSHIRE

On the junction of the B4202 and the Cleobury Road on the Shropshire side of the Wyre Forest grows the *Mawley oak*, a good example of a landmark tree. It originally marked the meeting of two woodland tracks on the outskirts of the Wyre Forest several centuries ago. The shrinking of the forest boundaries means the tree is now strictly outside the forest area.

Wyre Forest naturalist Norman Hickin states in his excellent book *The Natural History of an English Forest* that he inspected the tree in October 1968. The girth was then 7.2 metres (23.5 feet) giving a diameter of 2.3 metres (7.5 feet). There was, he calculated, 1,185 sq. metres (1,417 sq. yards) of ground covered by foliage (one tenth of a hectare – quarter of an acre). He estimated the height at 26 metres (86 feet). The bark housed a wren's nest. A huge main limb broke out of the tree in the 1970s. The cessation of pollarding the tree has meant that huge weight is contained in the overcrowded crown. It is only a matter of time before more timber falls from this venerable old tree.

Nearby is Mawley Hall and Estate, with one of Shropshire's largest larches in the grounds. The Wyre Forest area is indeed an excellent place to visit for those who like walking under and near trees.

In mainland Europe, particularly Germany, are found some very old large leaved limes. They are often in the centre of villages, or close to human occupation. Squares in medieval towns are also places to see them. It is known that some of these trees are in excess of 700 years old. In England, big old limes are not so commonly associated with buildings. An exception is in the Shropshire village of Pitchford, near Acton Burnell. Here the *Pitchford lime* grows in the grounds of Pitchford Hall, a superb Tudor building constructed for the Ottley family around 1560, although there is evidence of an earlier structure. The tree stands on high ground to the south-west of the house.

The old estate map of 1692 shows 'the tree with the house in it'. This makes the lime at least 400 years old, as it would seem obvious that the tree at that time must have been fairly large in order to accommodate the tree house. The lime is the largest large leaved lime in Britain with a girth in excess of 7 metres

(23 feet). The tree house, now a black and white timbered structure, was renovated in the 1970s, and within the spreading branches of the tree, great clumps of mistletoe grow. The young Queen Victoria stayed at Pitchford in 1832 and in her diary of that year, she relates her experience of going up to the tree house via its staircase. The tree and house are unique in Britain and it is undoubtedly one of the world's greatest tree houses.

An early print of the Pitchford lime – 'the tree with the house in it'

A famous old tree that grows near Quatford, south of Bridgnorth, on the east of the River Severn, is the *Forest oak*. In 1082, Roger Montgomery, a relation of William the Conqueror, and one of the major Norman lords of the region, married his second wife Adelissa. When Lady Adelissa was sailing to England to join her new husband, the ship on which she was sailing ran into a terrible storm. The passengers believed that the ship would go down and everyone would perish. During the storm, a monk who was travelling with Adelissa, fell asleep. In his sleep he dreamed that a woman appeared and said to him:

if thy lady would wish to save herself and her attendants from the present danger, let her take a vow to God, and faithfully promise to build a church in honour of the Blessed Mary Magdalene, on the spot where she would first happen to meet her husband, the earl, in

England; especially where groweth a hollow oak tree, and where wild swine have shelter.

When the monk related his dream to Adelissa, she vowed to carry out the building of the church. The storm abated and they continued their journey. Riding through the Morfe forest on top of the sandstone escarpment at Quatford, on the edge of the earl's hunting grounds and close to a big old oak tree, Adelissa met Roger out hunting boar. The promise was kept and the church was built on top of the sandstone hill, across open land from the oak tree. The legend is depicted in some twentieth-century stained glass windows on the south side of the church.

The Forest oak, Quatford – old print depicting the legend

111

THE LADY OAK, CRESSAGE.

Lady oak, Cressage – earlier this century

Lady oak, Cressage – the old shell leans on the young oak

One tree that may well have survived from the original, huge Forest of Shropshire is the *Lady oak* of Cressage. The remains of the tree are now no more than a big hulk of bark leaning against a younger oak, either grown from an acorn dropped from the mother tree or deliberately planted as a replacement. Once upon a time, the *Lady oak* would have been a notable landmark to travellers between Bridgnorth and Shrewsbury. The remains now stand marooned in an open field, between the disused Severn Valley railway line and the A458. The original road that passed below the tree was realigned when the railway was built in 1861. Not far from the oak is a cross marking the now demolished Saxon church of St Samson. The tree was carelessly set on fire on the 25 June 1814, reputedly by gypsies, who regularly camped by the tree. The oak was regularly referred to after that date and in the *Gardeners Chronicle* article in 1877, H. Eversheds mentioned the fire damage to the tree. It was still bearing acorns in 1950 and finally died in the severe frosts of 1982. For a tree that was termed 'nearly demolished' in 1814, it did well to hang on for another 170 years!

In the thirteenth and fourteenth centuries, it was the practice to bestow religious names on well-known objects. Several other Lady oaks existed in this area. Another story relating to the *Lady oak*, Cressage is about the satirist Jonathan Swift (1667–1745), writer of *Gulliver's Travels*, who once sheltered below the tree in a summer storm on his way to Shrewsbury. Also sheltering were a young rough-looking couple who said they were eloping. They were looking for a clergyman to marry them. The cleric Swift married them there and then without a witness and wrote this poem about the incident:

Under an oak in stormy weather
I joined this rogue and whore together
Let none but the God who
makes the thunder
E'r put this whore and rogue asunder

Between Acton Round and Monkhall an old track that once went through the medieval Shirlett Forest goes beside the huge old hulk of the pollarded sessile oak, the *Acton Round oak*. It is one of the country's largest, with a girth of over 8.8 metres (29 feet). Shirlett is derived from 'share of the shire' meaning that the woodland was once a part of the original Royal Shropshire Forest of Norman times. Individual trees are mentioned in the forestry 'perambulation' of 1300. These boundary marker trees such as *Ravenshok* (Ravens oak) and *Fendehok* (Fiends oak) of Shirlett are a fascinating glimpse of forest of old. In 1256 other references to boundary trees mentions the boundary tree *Ronsak*, which stood upon the King's Highway between Weston and Wenlock. Also another large (*grosum*) oak tree stood upon Corve towards the West.

Whether the *Acton Round oak* is 'Ronsak' is hard to determine. Can it really be over 800 years old? It would seem unlikely but seeing it now, growing on this beautiful ridge looking over the rolling Shropshire countryside, one feels it has seen many, many centuries.

One of Britain's largest girthed oaks grows on the brow of a small hill in the rolling hill country near Bishop's Castle in South Shropshire. The *Lydham Manor oak* is a huge, burred, lichen and moss covered giant. In fact a small nature reserve in its own rights. Growing from the bole are other trees such as holly and elder. The practice of pollarding having ceased, it is possible the tree experienced a rapid increase in girth as a result. In 1946 the tree was measured by Gardner as 10.36 metres (34 feet). In 1984 it was a little under 12 metres (39 feet). A remarkable increase of 1.6 metres (5.25 feet) in thirty years. At its present rate of growth

Lydham Manor oak – a classic old pollard of majestic size

Lydham Manor oak – grows in beautiful south Shropshire countryside

it may well eventually become Britain's largest girthed oak. The *Majesty oak* in Fredville Park, Kent is the only big oak with comparable growth rates.

The *Lydham oak* has a similar size and appearance as *Billy Wilkins'* in Melbury Park, Dorset. The tree today looks very healthy and set for many more years yet. The age is estimated at slightly younger than *Billy Wilkins'*, probably 600–700 years old.

This lovely area is excellent tree growing land. Next to the driveway leading up the hill towards the Manor House is another impressive oak of 9 metres (30 feet) in the girth. This tree has a clean trunk apart from a split caused by excessive branch weight, due in part to the neglect of traditional management practices. A cable has now been inserted in an effort to keep the crown intact. In the very warm drought conditions of August 1989 a large limb suddenly dropped from this tree. Was the tree shedding leaves to avoid excessive transpiration?

Lydham Manor has two exceptional walnut trees. It also has Shropshire's record fern leafed beech. It must be stressed that the park is private and permission must be sought from the Sykes family to look at their marvellous trees.

Standing in front of Crowleasowes Farm, Bitterley, near Ludlow, Shropshire, on the edge of the original medieval Clee Forest, is the *Crowleasowes oak*. It has a girth in excess of 11 metres (36 feet). Inevitably it is a hollow pollard oak but, unlike most, its branches have been regularly cropped. Attached to its trunk are bits of Victorian ironwork.

Two references from 1889 are as follows. Oliver Baker talks of 'an oak of gigantic girth' in 'Ludlow Town and neighbourhood', and Thornhill-Timmins writing in *Nooks and Corners of Shropshire* describes a tree on his approach to the farm 'an oak with gigantic girth but hollow within, flings its vast limbs athwart the greensward before the entrance way'. The farmhouse at Crowleasowes is a superb Jacobean period building in front of which, near the tree, stands a restored cider press.

Growing directly above a spring near Holt Farm, Plaish in central Shropshire is yet another giant pollard oak. The *Holt Preen oak* has a girth exceeding 8 metres (26 feet) but its most unusual feature is the water that issues from beneath its roots. Until after the Second World War this natural spring supplied the village of Plaish with drinking water. A large stone trough has been built close to the tree and around it there is a stone wall believed to have been built at the same time as the sixteenth-century farmhouse.

The spring water is piped to large underground stone chambers hidden in the field. One chamber houses a pumping engine, the other a water wheel. The wheel and engine are now unused and were finally replaced by an electric pump. The village was only in recent years put on mains water supply

Holt Preen oak, a spring flows from within the tree

One of England's most notable trees is the *Royal oak* at Boscobel, Shropshire. This tree is internationally famous and is visited by thousands of people every year. The hundreds of public houses named 'The Royal Oak' throughout England are named after the tree at Boscobel. The familiar inn sign depicting the oak and crown within its spreading branches originates from the day the future Charles II hid in an oak tree to escape Parliamentary

troops. The incident took place after Charles had unsuccessfully fought the battle of Worcester and he and his followers fled north to escape capture.

Dressed in rural clothing, Charles arrived at White Ladies Priory close to Boscobel House on 4 September 1651. Charles and his companion, Richard Pennderel, hid amongst the trees in Spring Coppice, near Boscobel House.

The following day Charles and Richard walked nine miles to Madeley (now in Telford) with the intention of crossing the River Severn at the ferry below Madeley Bank, but they found the river crossings to be well guarded, so they spent the day in a barn owned by a Catholic sympathiser named Wolf. That night they returned to Boscobel.

On Saturday 6 September 1651, Charles and Major Careless, who was staying at the house, decided to spend the day in a large oak tree in Spring Coppice to avoid capture. The account of the events were written down by Samuel Pepys after Charles had dictated them to him in 1680. When nightfall came they said they would risk sleeping in the house because of the uncomfortable time in the tree. The following two days Charles tried to relax and spend time in the garden and arbor on the mount, still evident in the garden today. After his rest he made his way via Bristol to Shoreham and sailed to France.

The oak in which Charles hid was located about 150 yards south-west of the house in Spring Coppice. After Charles's triumphant return from France on 29 May 1660, which initiated the Reformation, the story of the future King and the oak spread and many travellers visited the tree and took away all sorts of souvenirs. A brick wall was built as protection for the tree but the plundering continued so that by 1700 not much of the old tree remained.

Seats, toys, models and cigar and snuff boxes were made from the oak and traveller John Evelyn commented that the tree was not only dead but nearly gone by 1706.

In 1712 William Stakeley wrote about a sapling growing by the older tree. He assumed it was from an acorn from the original oak.

In the eighteenth century accounts begin to emerge of two trees, one dead and one alive. Local evidence shows that the old stump was dug up and the roots were manufactured into trophies. The Victorians created the myth that the second tree was in fact the one Charles hid in. They changed the plaques to fit their version of the story!

The site of the present tree indicates an age of approximately 250–300 years old, which fits in with the second tree theory. There is now a younger tree grown from an acorn from the second tree standing not far away. The original tree, from the descriptions given, was an old thick trunked, recently pollarded oak that was growing in a fairly dense copse. Today's *Royal oak* stands alone in a field, the woodland gone and is surrounded by iron railings put up in 1817.

There are several stories of oaks grown from Boscobel acorns thriving today, including Charles II himself planting several in St James's Park, London. Numerous paintings, broadsheets, poems and medals have all added fame to the story of the *Royal oak*. To complete the story, Charles II, on his triumphant return to England from France on 29 May 1660, named the date Oak-apple Day and decreed celebrations should commence. Oak-apple Day was widely celebrated well into the twentieth century.

Close to the old main road between Telford and Shrewsbury, not far from the Roman city, is the quiet village of Uppington. An ancient hollow yew, with a girth exceeding 8.8 metres (29 feet) grows near the old church. A Roman altar, found buried in the churchyard, now stands near the tree.

The most famous black poplar in Shropshire and probably England was the *Arbor tree* of Aston-on-Clun. The tree stood on raised ground by a small bridge near the centre of the village. Throughout the year the old hollow poplar was decorated with multi-coloured flags attached to long torch poles. The poles were nailed to its trunk.

Every year on or about 29 May, Oak-apple Day, the tree was re-dressed with new flags and a celebration took place. This takes the form of a re-enactment of an historic wedding and procession to the tree. Local children dressed in costume meet the 'bride and groom', who used to approach in a pony and trap. Dancing takes place by the tree and sprigs of oak are borne by the participants. The village fête is held in a nearby field. At one time cuttings taken from the tree were given out to new village brides. The remarkable thing about the Arbor Day at Aston is that the ancient practice has survived. The ritual has its roots in early pagan fertility rites.

Arbor tree – the old poplar has gone but an offspring continues the story

The *Arbor tree* used to be known as *'The Bride's tree'*. This was derived from St Bridget or the even earlier 'Brid', the Celtic fertility goddess. It is known that the Celts would hang clothing on a special tree to ensure fertility, and the practice, a form of votive offering, is worldwide. Tree dressing continues in rural Ireland and in recent years the practice has been revived. The earliest written records of the *Arbor tree* are from the 29 May 1786 when on that date John Marston from Oaker married Mary Carter from Sibdon. They had four children and are both buried at Hopesay Church. The family tombstone can be seen near the church porch.

As already mentioned the date of 29 May has much significance. On that date in 1660 Charles II returned to England from France on his birthday to restore not only the monarchy but also the old festivals and customs. Oak-apple Day was the spring festival and oak-apples were paraded and worn by the festives on 29 May. These original pagan festivals were frowned upon and purged during the fifteenth and sixteenth centuries and also during Cromwell's rule. The tree dressing probably continued from 1660 until 1786 and the Marston wedding. The practice then continued with the help of the Oaker Estate.

Sadly, in September 1995, during high winds and heavy rain, and after an unusually dry summer, the *Arbor tree* fell. The demise of the tree received widespread media coverage and debate. Many people went to the village to view the 'remains' and to take souvenirs. Cuttings were taken, and the resulting young trees will stir many memories of the original. As one villager said: 'a forest will grow from the old tree'. A young *Arbor tree* was planted in its parent's place on 16 December 1995 as the villagers are determined to continue the tradition. The following lines are from the poem *Ballad of The Arbor Tree*: by Tom Beardsley

In Aston Clun stands a tree,
A Poplar dressed like a ship at sea,
Lonely link with an age long past,
Of Arbor trees I am the last.
Beardsley, (1956)

The border counties of Shropshire and Herefordshire are closely linked with Wales. The early peoples inhabiting these lands had the same customs and traditions and these neighbouring counties have some notable yew trees.

The great *Claverley yew*, in East Shropshire, near Bridgnorth, is over 8 metres (26 feet) in the girth and stands to the east of the church. It is now almost completely hollow. The churchyard in which it stands is the focal point for this delightful village. The site looks very pre-Christian on a mound with an embankment and standing near a brook. Restoration work on the church early in the twentieth century revealed pagan burials from below the floor of the church. This would indicate the burials were from around the fourth century, therefore of Roman and British date. The now popular estimate for the age of this tree is around 1,500 years old.

The well-documented, celebrated *Church Preen yew* is probably Shropshire's most well-known yew, but it is certainly not the biggest and probably not the oldest. In the *History of Church Preen* by Arthur Sparrow, many details of the tree's size are recorded. The earliest measurement is from 1780 and at 1.2 metres (4 feet) above ground it was 5.8 metres (19 feet) in the girth. In 1833 it was 6.7 metres (22 feet) and in 1897 it measured 6.8 metres (22.3 feet). In June 1983 it had increased slightly to 6.9 metres (22.6 feet). In just eighty-six years it had put on 10 cm (4 inches) in girth. The tree stands next to the tiny chapel in this beautiful part of rural Shropshire, not far from Wenlock Edge. An iron band placed around the tree a century ago was carefully replaced in 1994 to allow the tree to expand. This work was undertaken by the Trevor-Jones's, who have enhanced their most special garden at Preen Manor over the last decade.

Within their grounds is another excellent yew by the pool, and many more new plantings. Twenty-one people stood within its very hollow trunk in 1897. The French botanist and traveller de Candolle estimated the tree to be about 1,400 years old in 1831

Church Preen yew – January snow and the great old tree

and Dr John Lowe thought it between 750 and 1,000 years old in 1897. The writer Fletcher Lowe in 1890 described the tree as 'the beautiful old female yew tree laced with myriads of fruit on which innumerable birds were feasting'.

In south Shropshire, other ancient yews can be found. At Hope Bagot, near the Clee Hill, of the several trees that border the lane to the church, the oldest is a female with a girth over 7 metres (23 feet). Directly below the tree, in the bank, is a holywell. A spring is also located across the lane.

Younger trees used to line an old track leading towards the Clee Hill. This landscape feature is fairly common in Shropshire and Herefordshire, but unfortunately in this case the trees have been felled. Possibly the oldest in Shropshire is the *Clun yew* in the south-west of the county. Its remaining pieces

measure over 10.5 metres (34.5 feet). It is very decayed, and local amateur historian and local character, Tom Beardsley, excavated around the base of the tree in May 1946. He found old pieces of the original trunk. It is probable that the *Clun yew* is of extreme age and is equal in age to some of the greats of Wales.

The male *Norbury yew* near Bishop's Castle grows on the south side of the church and is in good condition. The churchyard is known to date from the Saxon period and the wall built around the yew dates from before 1790. The tree measured at base 10.7 metres (35 feet) in 1983.

Two huge yews one male, one female, grow in a field opposite the present church at Middleton Scriven, South Shropshire. The mystery is, why do they grow in a field away from the church? At Ashford Carbonel, south of Ludlow, no less than five huge yews surround the church. The largest of the trees measures over 8.2 metres (27 feet).

In a remote village near the Brown Clee Hill in south Shropshire the *Loughton yew*, a female tree with a girth exceeding 9 metres (29 feet), was subject to an interesting survey in 1986. A sample of the wood was carbon dated at Cambridge University as 550 years old (plus or minus 50 years) making the sample dated AD 1435. The sample was taken from midway in the hollow bole so it is safe to assume the tree exceeds 1,000 years. The earliest chapel at Loughton is recorded as 1291 so it is intriguing to wonder what preceded the structure, if anything.

Of the exotic trees in Shropshire the *Rowton Castle cedar* is a must for anyone travelling the Shrewsbury to Welshpool road. It dominates the mock castle it stands next to.

CHESHIRE

A tree grown from a cutting from the *Glastonbury thorn* forms the story associated with the village of Appleton Thorn, near Warrington in Cheshire. At the cross roads in the centre of the village, between the church and the 'Thorn' public house, grows the tree. The sign by the tree reads:

Cedar of Lebanon, Rowton Castle – a tree with a 30-metre (98-foot) spreading crown

This thorn tree is an offshoot from the famous Glastonbury thorn in Somerset. A thorn tree has stood here since the 12th Century when, according to local historians, the original tree was planted by a Norman knight Adam de Dutton. He was returning from the Crusades in 1178 when he made a pilgrimage to the Abbey bringing an offshoot of the famous thorn back with him to plant on this site as a thanks-giving for his safe return. Over the centuries the custom of 'Bawning the Thorn' grew up.

'Bawning' means decorating the tree with flowers and ribbons. This is done to the singing of the *Bawning Song*, written by R.E. Egerton-Warburton, a local Cheshire poet of the nineteenth century, after which, village children dance around the tree. The present ceremony was revived in 1973 and is held annually on the third Saturday in June. The tree is decorated by local children and items placed on the tree are made by

Appleton thorn – decorated each June by local children

themselves, their families and local schools.

On approaching the proud village, the sign shows, with the depiction of the thorn on the emblem, the origins of the village name. So many place names are derived from trees but only a few still have the living links with their past as does the *Appleton thorn*.

The giant *Marton oak* near Congleton, Cheshire is now split into four large pieces. It is very hollow and is a genuine ancient oak. The remaining parts still support a healthy crop of leaves and the squat nature of the tree probably means that it can live for a long time yet. It was reported as a 'lost' tree in the 1980s but it is still well and truly alive and flourishing. It is said that it once acted as a shelter for an old bull and it was obviously a focal point of the farm and its buildings in past centuries. It now stands in private grounds off the appropriately named Oak Lane, Marton village, on the road from Congleton to Alderley Edge.

Marton oak - one of England's greatest old oaks

Within its shell a miniature black and white cottage now stands giving the big old tree a giant scale. The *Marton oak* was once, when more complete, one of England's biggest oaks measuring over 13.7 metres (45 feet) girth at 1.5 metres (5 feet) in the middle of the nineteenth century. Its largest limb was over 3.5 metres (11 feet) round. According to David Bethel in his book *Portrait of Cheshire* (1979) it was fenced into a triangular enclosure by the local Women's Institute. This fencing has now disappeared.

On 21 July 1923, Sidney Wicks, who was a tutor at the Manchester YMCA, took a party of students to Greendale Farm in Mottram St Andrew for a picnic. He was taking classes in the art of Public Speaking. While at Greendale Farm he was inspired to form a club which he called the 'Rostrum':

for those who desire to advance themselves in the mastery of the Art of Public Speaking, with Freedom of Speech, Loyalty to Truth, Clarity of Thought and Love of the English Language.

Under the spreading yew tree in the garden at Greendale they took a pledge to uphold the ideals of the movement. Every year on the nearest Saturday to 21 July the members made a pilgrimage to the tree for a renewal of their pledges and to bring in new members. Two of the original were Australians and they took the movement back to Australia. Seven years later, on 21 July 1930, the Australian Movement was founded in Sydney. There, they used an angophora tree as the focal point of the ceremony. The movement has now spread to many cities and the membership has reached 2,000.

The tenant at Greendale gave wood from the yew to make gavels at the meetings. He also joined the Rostrum Movement. Sprigs of yew were used in the pledge ceremony until the 1950s and pieces of the original yew have been presented to members in Australia to keep the links intact. Sidney Wicks said: 'The yew tree is legendary in Australia and Mottram St Andrew an honoured name. The village little knows how famous it is'.

The village is now in the rich commuter belt south of the Manchester conurbation. Nearby is the picture-book Cheshire village of Prestbury.

The Rostrum Movement no longer meets annually at Greendale Farm but the Movement continues, and the yew tree symbol is still proudly held in both northern and southern hemispheres.

On the Wirral peninsula, traditionally part of Cheshire, but now under Merseyside administration, the *Eastham Churchyard yew* was, amazingly, written about as an old tree in 1150. The tree fits the description in the parish records, when the monks of St Werburgh were asked to 'have care of ye olde yew'.

In Britain there are few such early written references to individual trees. The *Eastham yew* has an estimated age of beyond 1,500 years.

Near Congleton is the pretty village of Astbury with its distinctive church with separate tower. In the churchyard are the remaining portions of the *Astbury yew* thought to date from Saxon times and now merely a shell of the original. On viewing it today, it seems incredible that it still lives, for the broken and sinewy remains lean almost prostrate across the churchyard path.

Astbury yew – South Cheshire, incredible relic from Saxon days

STAFFORDSHIRE

The county of Staffordshire once had four large forests until the industrial era devastated the wooded landscape. Some of the larger houses and estates were the original royal hunting lodges.

Eyton, writing on the Domesday survey of Staffordshire, mentions the county and its fame for excellent sycamore trees. The wetlands that surrounded Burslem were covered in alders and willows according to the Domesday survey and were probably used for coppice as a cropping regime and were managed for their produce.

Near the village of Abbot's Bromley, famed for its horn dance, is Bagot's Park now owned by a private company and no longer run by the Bagot family. In the old park used to grow the well known *Beggar's oak*, one of the largest of Staffordshire oaks.

There were also other named trees such as the *Bagot's Walking Stick*, a tall tree with few branches, the *Cliff oak*, The *King oak* and the *Venison oak*.

The *King oak* was felled for use in the construction of the famous Cunard ship the *Queen Mary*. The *Beggar's oak* got its name from the tale that the Bagot family had a curse put on them by an old gypsy woman who had been refused money by those of the Bagot family while she was resting beneath the tree. The oak was also the meeting place of all the local deer poachers, thieves and vagabonds who held wild revels around the tree each year. Alas few of the great trees at Bagot remain as much of the land has been cleared, apart from the Bagot Wood itself. The other grand tree of Bagot was the massive *Bagot beech*, a layered beech tree that was photographed in 1912 and then again in 1951 showing the great drooping branches. It is in this part of the country that the naturalist and broadcaster Phil Drabble lives and works and has intimate knowledge of this beautiful part of Staffordshire.

Immediately to the south of Shugborough by Milford Common on rising ground is the beginning of Cannock Chase Country Park.

It is largely owned by Staffordshire County Council and now covers over 1,200 hectares (3,000 acres), which makes it one of England's largest country parks. Originally a hunting ground created by William the Conqueror, it was known as the King's Forest of Cannock. In 1290 the rights passed to the Bishop of Lichfield and the Bishop's Chase of Cannock was created. After many changes of fortune and use, including two large military camps during the 1914–18 war, the third Earl of Lichfield gifted over 800 hectares (2,000 acres) of the north-west part of the Chase to the County Council in 1957.

At Broadhurst Green the Commonwealth and German cemeteries are sombre reminders of those from all parts who died in the wars. Across the road from the cemeteries is a fairly insignificant but historically interesting tree called the *Cank thorn*. The thorn commemorates a boundary tree, first recorded over 600 years ago. The original tree marked the boundary of Berkswich and Brocton parish with the parishes of Colwich and of Cannock. Now it is the point at which the open heathland joins with Forestry Commission woodlands. References to the *Cank*, or *Kank*, or *Canok thorn* occur as early as the fourteenth century. Another fascinating reference from 29 May 1671 reads:

thence to Horsemere pool, thence to Cannock Thorne where a Gospell being read we went by Sherbrooke to Haywood park gate, where is a Gospell place

It has several other references and was clearly used for the 'beating of the bounds' on Ascension Day each year.

Edees, a local man, wrote in 1948 that to his knowledge a thorn was growing there in 1888. He identified the thorn as a North American species of thorn. As to why an American thorn came to this spot is a mystery.

What is clear is that in 1965 the very unhealthy state of the *Cank thorn* was causing local concern. Tree surgery took place with dead wood removed, and cuttings and seed

Cank thorn – present-day replacement for the original boundary thorn

were used for propagation purposes. Then, in 1971, a large flail, cutting the verge, hit the old tree and wrecked it. On inspection the remains of an old iron guard were found. The seeds and cuttings had failed, but unknown to all, a forestry worker had taken a rooted sucker and planted it out in his garden at Portal Pool. This new thorn was planted alongside the old stump in March 1972. The thorn of today is quite healthy, and is either the cockspur thorn or the broadleaf cockspur thorn (*Crateagus prunifolia*) of obscure, probably hybrid, origin. It has conspicuous white flowers in June and has beautiful, eventually deep red, late autumn colour. The remains of the old protective fence surrounds the present low growing tree. It is left so as to avoid the fate of its predecessor!

The *Stafford oak* stood at Tixall Park until 1881, when it was burnt beyond repair by a fire mysteriously lit in its hollow trunk.

In the compact but fine cathedral city of Lichfield, Dr Johnson spent the early and late part of his life. A huge lakeside tree known as *Johnson's willow* grew on the Stowe reservoir embankment until 1830. Dr Johnson rarely visited Lichfield without paying a visit to the tree.

Standing as it did in sight of the triple spired cathedral, he persuaded Dr Jones, a close friend, to describe it in the *Gentleman's Magazine* of June 1785. A picture of the willow appeared in the publication with the title 'View near Lichfield; including a most remarkably large willow tree'. Several willows propagated from the original tree have continued the connection and, on the banks of the pleasant Stowe Pool, a survivor from *Johnson's willow* can still be used as shade on a hot summer day.

Near Trentham is Hanchurch where a strange collection of yew trees surround a rough square piece of land of about a third of a hectare (an acre) in size. It is generally believed that a church once stood at the centre of the space. There is no trace of a structure today, but it may well have been a wooden church that was burnt down many, many centuries ago. By local tradition, the yew trees are over a 1,000 years old.

Weston Park, ancestral home of the Earls of Bradford, on the Staffordshire–Shropshire border, had, until the 1980s, one of Britain's greatest Oriental planes growing on the lawns by the house. It eventually succumbed to irretrievable storm damage.

Only photographs and drawings are testimony to its size and stature. However, much remains in the park, with other old planes, oaks, an impressive layered sweet chestnut, nothofagus, and the rare sassafras. The park was designed by 'Capability' Brown.

DERBYSHIRE

In the village of Darley Dale in the Peak District, north-west of the Derbyshire town of Matlock, in the churchyard of St Helen's is the well-known and well-documented female *Darley Dale yew*. The tree has been measured and written about since 1817.

In 1888, Mr Paget Bowman cut pieces of

Darley Dale yew – a churchyard yew of some fame

wood from the outer bark to count the annual rings. He counted 33 to 66 per 25 mm (one inch) radius (1.46 average). The cut wood can be clearly seen today behind the iron fence that surrounds the tree.

The girth of the tree was 10 metres (32.7 feet) when measured in 1970 at 1.5 metres (5 feet) from ground level. The plaque near the tree has the following extraordinary words:

[Probable Age 2000 years]
But whatever may be its precise age, there can be little doubt that this grand old tree has given shelter:
To the early Britons when planning the construction of the dwellings which they erected not many yards west of the trunk;
To Romans who built up their funeral pyres for their slain companions first clear of the branches;
To the Saxons, converted, perchance to the true faith by the preaching of Bishop Diuma beneath its pleasant shade;
To the Norman masons carving their quaint sculptures to form the first stone house of prayer;
and to the host Christian worshippers who from that day to this have been borne under the hoary limbs in woman's arms, to the baptismal font, and then in on men's shoulders to their last sleeping place in the soil that gave it birth.

The other distinguishing feature of this yew are the dipping lower branches layering into the soil and fresh branchlets growing upright from those points. The site of the *Darley Dale yew* is probably pre-Christian as many indications point to early occupation. There are some fascinating primitively inscribed stones standing in the church porch and within the churchyard.

Also in West Derbyshire, near the River Dove a few miles from Uttoxeter, the village churchyard of Doveridge has a venerable old yew to the south of the church. This tree has variously been described as the oldest in England and the best in Britain. Neither is true but the yew has a girth of exceeding 6 metres (20 feet) and is worth seeing when in this rural part of Derbyshire.

Close to Burton-on-Trent inside the Derbyshire border at Bretby, an old cedar has its main branches chained and braced to prevent any major part of the tree breaking off or collapsing.

The reason for this is that the tree was once in the ownership of the Caernarvon family and the family believed that if a major branch fell, bad luck would shortly follow.

A large limb was supposed to have fallen just before the death of Lord Caernarvon after his discovery of the tomb of Tutankhamun.

Allestree, north of the city of Derby, supposedly takes its name from a Saxon king who commanded a wide territory around those parts. The 'tree' in the place name probably refers to the ancient *Allestree yew* growing in the churchyard. This tree has an estimated age exceeding 1,000 years.

NOTTINGHAMSHIRE

Sherwood Forest in Nottinghamshire will be forever linked with the Robin Hood legend. The remaining forest of today is really pockets of Corsican and Scots pines covering approximately sixty-five square kilometres (twenty-five sq. miles) of heathland between Nottingham and Worksop.

A flavour of the original forest can be sampled at the Sherwood Forest Country Park, near Edwinstowe.

Here in 200 hectares (500 acres) many walks have been created or refurbished by the county council. Old stunted oaks, many dead, scrub birch and occasional holly and yew grow on the poor soil. The oak regeneration is good within the fenced areas.

A short walk from the visitor centre is the tree known as the *Major oak*, one of the largest of the surviving oaks.

The tree takes its name from Major Hayman Rooke who lived nearby in the early 1800s. The original name was the *Cockpen tree*, so called because game cocks were kept in this part of the forest, and the hollow tree was used as a shelter and roosting spot.

In the past there were many other well-known trees in the forest. Their evocative names were, the *Centre tree*, the *Shambles oak* or *Robin Hood's Larder*, the *Duke's Walking Stick*, the *Two Porters*, the *Remarkable*, and the *Greendale oak*. This once had a much larger girth than the *Major oak*, and reportedly had a coach and six driven through its hollow base for a bet in the 1720s!

The *Major oak* is one of the most famous trees in England and has close associations

Major oak, Sherwood Forest — probably England's most famous oak

with Robin Hood. Some of the links can be attributed to Lord Tennyson who visited the area with his son before the production of *The Foresters*. A passage of the play reads:

Robin Hood: *Where lies that cask of wine whereof we plundered the Norman Prelate?*

Little John: *In that oak where twelve can stand inside nor touch each other.*
[A reference surely to the Major oak.]

The tree is now visited by thousands each year. Some years ago it was fenced to protect the base of the tree from compaction caused by all those feet. This had caused, it was thought, the dieback of the crown.

Since the fencing, bark mulch has been distributed under the crown spread and extensive tree surgery has been carried out, including huge props under the out-stretched limbs. Is it all really necessary?

Beyond the fence, the now urban-looking scene includes ice cream vans, seating, signs and all the trappings of the modern age. Any visitor from abroad searching the Robin Hood legend must leave thinking they have visited a 'muddled' theme park.

Further away from the car parks 'The Birklands' gives a glimpse of the true 'blasted' trees of Sherwood. The heathland is scattered with half dead, characterful, old oaks that are worth walking amongst. The continuity of forest cover here has endowed this place with an internationally renowned invertebrate population. Visit in the autumn to see the oaks and bracken in all their splendour.

A probably more rewarding experience than the Sherwood visitor centre can be found, nearer to Worksop at Clumber Park. In the area known as The Dukeries, the park is managed by the National Trust and covers over 4,000 acres of drives, walks, lakes, park-land and woodland. The house has gone but 'Capability' Brown designed the park, and the tree highlight of the park is Duke's Drive, a 3.2 kilometre (2-mile), 200-year-old double lime avenue that was set at the instigation of the Duke of Newcastle in the 1770s. This must be considered one of the ultimate examples of a lime avenue anywhere.

WARWICKSHIRE

South-west of Warwick and Stratford-upon-Avon, the attractive village of Pebworth, in the Vale of Evesham, once had a famous elm dominating the village green.

The *Three Shires elm*, marked on the old Ordnance Survey maps, overhung three counties and three parishes; Cleeve Prior, Worcestershire; Salford Prior, Warwickshire; and Pebworth, Glou-cestershire.

By 1958 the old original elm had gone, and the OS map showed the site as Three Shire elms, describing the place where the regener-ation (from the root system of the fallen tree) grew. That new growth has continued despite the ravages of elm disease, and Pebworth and surrounding countryside has hedgerows full of elm. Older villagers still recall the great tree on the green, which was well known and could be seen for miles around.

WEST MIDLANDS

Closer to Birmingham, Three Shires Oak Road at Smethwick recalls another tree whose branches spread, this time stretching into the counties of Staffordshire, Shropshire and Worcestershire. In 1908, Smethwick Corporation felled the tree in the interests of safety and for a road widening scheme.

The well-known Birmingham locality of Selly Oak took its name from the giant oak that used to stand at the junction of the main street and appropriately named Oak Tree Lane.

The old tree's trunk took up a consider-able part of the pavement and was destined for removal in a 1908 road widening scheme. Huge local opposition to the felling of the tree saved it, but eventually the pressure for house building and the advancing age of the oak, brought its doom. When it was felled, there was again great uproar from the locals and from people who used it as a prominent landmark. The great butt of the fallen tree was ironically placed in 'Selly Oak Park'.

LEICESTERSHIRE

In Leicestershire's upland area of Charnwood, the variety of soil types must have given the forest its range of native trees.

In Swithland Woods, north of the city of Leicester, the remnants of an ancient forest can be seen. This is a true mixed woodland, with a rich ground cover, whose origins can be traced back to the wildwoods of 2,000 years ago. The wood was preserved in 1931 by donations from the Leicester Rotarians.

The dramatic heathland of Charnwood that overlooks Swithland and the recent Cropston Reservoir, also has the gem Bradgate Park.

It covers 400 hectares (1,000 acres), six miles from the centre of Leicester, and was started by Thomas Grey in about 1490 and finished by his son, the grandfather of Lady Jane Grey. The park incorporates a lot of the Charnwood Forest area, with bracken-covered hills, granite outcrops and some superb ancient timber. Amidst the old oaks are the remains of later ornamental plantings.

The main entrance to the park is from the village of Newton Linford.

Old relic oaks in Bradgate Park, Leicestershire

NORTHAMPTONSHIRE

The old Rockingham Forest is still just recognisable by a scattering of green patches to the west of Oundle and at Wakerley Great Wood, near the river Welland, between Corby and Stamford, one of the renowned *Fox trees* still survives.

This great beech, with huge root buttresses stands at the approach to the Forestry picnic site. The *Fox trees* were dedicated to keepers of Rockingham Forest for prowess in killing foxes.

A mulberry tree with a fascinating history grows on a lawn in the park adjacent to Abingdon church, a district of Northampton.

The actor David Garrick planted the

Shakespeare's mulberry – in fact an offshoot planted by David Garrick in 1778

mulberry as a rooted cutting taken from the original *Shakespeare's mulberry* at Stratford-on-Avon in 1778. William Shakespeare planted the original in his garden and even after Sir John Clopton rebuilt the house in 1702, the tree was jealously preserved. That changed in 1756, however, when the new owner, a parson, tired of sightseers viewing the tree so decided to cut it down to rid himself of the problem. Cuttings were taken and David Garrick, one of the playwright's interpreters, forged the link with the great man through to today by planting this offshoot of *Shakespeare's mulberry*.

Ketts Oak
and Browick Hall

Coltishall Poplar

Hethel Old Thorn

Huntingfield Oak

Haughley Oak

Great Glenham

Thorpe Morieux

Chelsworth Poplar

Gospel Oak, Polstead

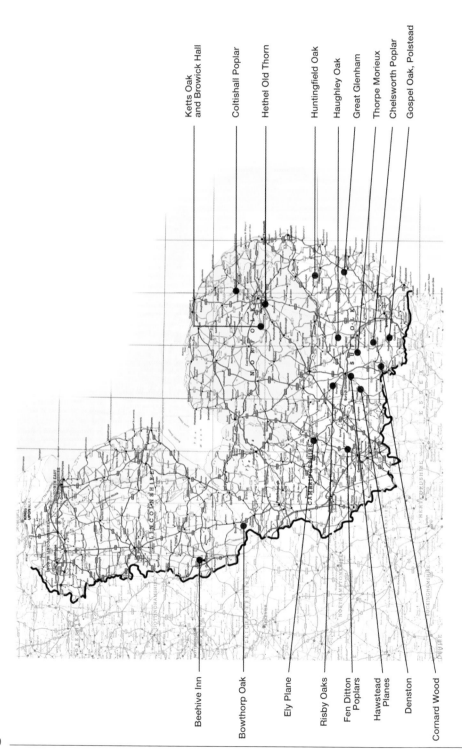

Beehive Inn

Bowthorp Oak

Ely Plane

Risby Oaks

Fen Ditton Poplars

Hawstead Planes

Denston

Cornard Wood

Eastern England

The flatness of the Fens creates horizons that seem to stretch to infinity, and the eastern sky takes on a mood all of its own. There are no sunsets more glowing than those that reach out over the Fenland landscape. One of Britain's biggest oaks grows within Lincolnshire, and in Castor Hanglands near Peterborough are ancient pollard thorns that have few equals. In the real fenland, high embankments carry the roads above the rivers and channels that make their direct way towards The Wash. Tall church towers, seen for miles around, are often surrounded by the only big trees of the village. On the Isle of Ely, an historic plane tree spreads magnificently over the lawn of the Bishop's Palace by the great cathedral.

Farther east are gentle hills, forests, heathlands and the Stour valley, so beloved by the painter John Constable, who made famous the treescape of this lovely area on the Suffolk–Essex border. Constable's inspiration, Thomas Gainsborough, depicted the trees of his local wood, Cornard near Sudbury, in his paintings. This whole eastern region is rich in ancient trees, and great pollards stand in wood pastures, in parks, on farms and in woodlands.

East Anglia's capital is really the cathedral city of Norwich, which is surrounded by fertile land and has one of the greatest thorns in England growing not far away. To the east, the Norfolk Broads is the landscape of water and willows.

North of Norwich and The Wash, the land rises to the chalk uplands of the Lincolnshire Wolds and the Lincoln Edge. In a gap in the ridge, made by the River Witham, stands the city of Lincoln, with one of England's loveliest cathedrals. Its three slender towers look over a rich patchwork landscape that spreads towards Horncastle and beyond.

LINCOLNSHIRE

An older and more impressive old pollard than the *Major oak* in Nottingham is to be found north of Stamford in Lincolnshire. This tree is located at Bowthorp Park Farm near Witham-on-the-Hill. The *Bowthorp oak* (*Quercus robur*) is one of the country's largest with a girth of 11.9 metres (39 feet diameter in 1994). The hollow tree is in a field behind

Bowthorp oak – one of the country's largest and most celebrated veterans

Beehive Inn – an old postcard showing the hive in the beech tree

the farmhouse and is in excellent health (1994). The Blanchard family are justifiably very proud of the old oak. It is by far the largest oak in the East Midlands. In 1768, it was reported to be 'in the same state of decay since the memory of the older inhabitants and their ancestors'. At that time a floor, door and benches were fitted and the crown was used as a pigeon house. It was boasted that twenty people could dine within the tree! The original opening has since narrowed, and the bole, according to Mr Armstrong early in the nineteenth century, was over 11 metres (37 feet). That being the case, the tree is estimated to be in excess of 1,000 years old.

The Beehive Inn in Castle Gate, Grantham, is unique in that its 'sign' is really a living beech tree, which has a hive located in one of its main forks. When the beech is in flower, the 'occupants' have little distance to travel to collect their nectar! The tree has featured in many photographs and also in a well-known local postcard, sold in the 1970s.

CAMBRIDGESHIRE

In the flatlands of Cambridgeshire stands the Isle of Ely with its magnificent cathedral. The original monastery was founded in 673 by St Etheldredra, a saxon queen from East Anglia. Her shrine is in front of the High Altar. The present building was started in 1083 and is a striking sight across the strange landscape surrounding the town. Across the lawns in front of the cathedral stands the Bishop's Palace, now a Sue Ryder home. The palace garden at the rear of the house contains several large plane trees.

The tree standing on the lawn is by far the largest and one glance will tell you it is a very special tree.

The *Ely plane* is a London plane, a hybrid between the Oriental and American planes, probably originating in the south of France in the 1650s.

This Ely tree was the first planted in Britain along with one at Barnes, London in about 1680 and is now a magnificent specimen and a wonderful link with the seventeenth century.

The plane measures 35 metres (115 feet) high, has a girth of over 8.4 metres (27.5 feet),

The Ely plane – one of the earliest London planes to be planted

and its huge spreading branches are well over 30 metres (98 feet). The bright green huge leaves are 20 cm. (8 ins) wide and the flaking grey bark, which leaves red, white and yellow patches, makes for an eye-catching sight in both winter and summer. The Palace garden is only open to the public on Thursdays.

Hethel Old thorn, Norfolk – an old print

NORFOLK

South of Norwich, east of Wymondham, is the locality of Hethel, famous as the home of Lotus cars. It is also the home of the *Hethel Old thorn*, which stands in a field near to the lovely churchyard and within a small reserve managed by the Norfolk Naturalist's Trust since 1960. The thorn is by local tradition the site where peasants met during a revolt against King John. This would mean the tree should be at least 700 years old, which on seeing it stretches the imagination somewhat.

The thorn has been measured over many years. Grigor examined it in 1841 and found a trunk with a girth 3.7 metres (12.1 feet) and branch spread of 9.5 metres (31 feet). Some villagers can still remember dancing by the tree, so it is likely that the thorn has more connections with May Day celebrations than to King John and is probably a Boundary tree.

In 1755, it measured 2.8 metres (9 feet) at 1.3 metres (4 feet) from the ground, so in ninety years it put on 0.9 metres (3 feet) in girth. Remarkable growth but not one that equates with traditional age. The tree was listed in the 1841 *Register of Remarkable Trees in the County of Norfolk.*

Hethel Old thorn – grows near the church at Hethel

SUFFOLK

There are only six species of the plane tree family worldwide. They are all large and long-lived trees. The first to be introduced to Britain was the Oriental plane from Asia Minor and south-east Europe, brought here in about 1550. The giant spreading tree at Corsham Court is one of the most impressive, the great plane at Weston Park, Staffordshire has now sadly blown down, but three relatively unknown but magnificent Oriental planes grow at Hawstead Place Farm, south of Bury St Edmunds.

The *Hawstead planes*, growing in a field some way below the farmhouse, were planted in 1578 by Sir Robert Drury to mark the visit of queen Elizabeth I to Hawstead. The original moated manor house no longer remains but the island and cobbled moat do, as well as the statue of 'The Green Man' erected for the Queen's visit with her entourage of 'nine hundred'! The statue was repaired and remounted at the 400th anniversary in 1978. Three new trees (these are the hybrid London planes) were also planted in that year by villagers as part

Chelsworth poplar, Suffolk – growing near the River Brett

OPPOSITE: *Hawstead planes, Suffolk – growing in a field and connected to a visit by Elizabeth I*

of the commemorative celebrations. The magnificent old trees must have been amongst the first planted in England, and they are still going strong in the latter stages of the twentieth century. Hawstead is a private place and viewing is strictly by appointment with the eminent 'green', farmer Ben Powell.

Suffolk boasts one of the largest native black poplars in Britain at the picturesque village of Chelsworth next to the River Brett. The black poplar is one of our rarest and most distinctive trees. It can reach over 30 metres (98 feet) in height and has huge heavy arching branches which often touch the ground. The bole and boughs are covered in bosses, the bark is deeply ridged and the name derives from its dark, almost black appearance from a distance. The male trees, which have scarlet catkins in early spring, are much more common than the females, which have green catkins. The tree reproduces rarely by natural means. The flood plains, rivers and stream margins by which it grows indicate it may well have relied heavily on flood water to carry branches that rooted downstream as means of propagation.

Black poplars are frequently recorded in the sixteenth and seventeenth century but from around 1800 the records have diminished. The surviving trees, which have been subject to surveys recently, are mainly old trees.

Chelsworth lies in that beautiful part of Suffolk between Sudbury and Stowmarket and the tree is downstream from the narrow bridge. Several footpaths can be found on either side of the River Brett around the village. The Chelsworth poplar is an unusually straight growing tree.

Well known to oarsmen are the black poplars at Fen Ditton near the city of Cambridge and further north in Norfolk, at Coltishall Mead is a fine black poplar made famous by Lonsdale Ragg's drawing in 1938.

The wood pasture and the pollard oak are a feature of the old landscapes of East Anglia. The huge oak growing in the field at Thorpe Morieux, a few miles north-west of Chelsworth, is a relic of the old landscape. Great Glenham and Denston, also in Suffolk, have good examples of old oaks along with Browick Hall, near Wymondham in Norfolk. A sixteenth century map of Risby, near Bury St Edmunds, shows pollard oaks in a field as distinct from woodland. Those trees, of which there were many, still stand as they did in the 1500s.

Also in Suffolk but further north-east towards Southwold is the great *Queen's oak* at Huntingfield. This is the last remnant of the medieval Huntingfield Park. It has been known about and recorded for over 200 years and it was once considered one of the biggest oaks in England. Interestingly it is now smaller than it was two centuries ago and like the *Meavy oak* in Devon, it has had phases of dieback and regrowth. A description of the *Queen's oak*, named after Queen Elizabeth's visit to the park in the sixteenth century, by a Mr Baker of nearby Heringham Hall in 1836, says:

it is between 1,000 and 1,100 years old according to a historical document in my possession. At this time some parts of the tree are in great vigour, having healthy arms 10ft in circumference, and even larger. The boughs cover a space 78 yards but the trunk has since gone to decay, it being quite hollow.

Huntingfield Hall which stood 'within two bow shots' of the tree was apparently built around six massive oaks which supported the roof. In 1772 the roots had decayed so much that the structure had to be 'shored up' by new timber and masonry. The Hall has now been completely demolished due to the decaying nature of the building.

Another great Suffolk oak is the *Haughley oak* at New Bells Farm, north of Stowmarket. Measured by the great Essex tree recorder Maynard Grenville in 1953 it was over 10.7 metres (35 feet) in the girth at breast height. Jim Paterson recorded it at 10.97 metres (36 feet) in 1987.

On the 26 June 1936 Lonsdale Ragg spent the day drawing the old relic *Gospel oak* in Polstead Park, Suffolk. By 1956 it had almost completely collapsed, succeeded by an offspring oak nearby and a holly that grows amongst the remains of the once mighty trunk. The annual ceremony of gospel reading below the tree still takes place each July.

There were many oaks in England with the name 'Gospel' attached to them, a reminder of the time when these oaks stood on the parish boundaries and were used in the ceremony of 'beating the bounds'.

The Polstead oak grew just outside the churchyard, near a gate leading towards Polstead Hall. Today the remains of the oak decay slowly, never touched since the day it finally fell. The young oak grows well beside it and the holly thrives. The *Gospel oak* was probably in excess of 800 years old.

Next to the beautiful flint church of Polstead stood the Red Barn where over a century ago Maria Marten's body was found after mysteriously disappearing from her home in the village. The murder and subsequent trial made national news all those years ago.

Sudbury, on the River Stour, was the birthplace of one of England's greatest painters, Thomas Gainsborough, in 1727. Within the garden of his home, now open to the public, is an old mulberry tree which dates from Gainsborough's youth. Cornard Wood, known as 'Gainsborough's Forest' is found just outside Sudbury. It was here that the painter worked in the mid-eighteenth century gaining his reputation for landscape paintings. The details of individual trees in the forest can be seen via his work in the National Gallery, London.

Remains of the Gospel oak at Polstead Park

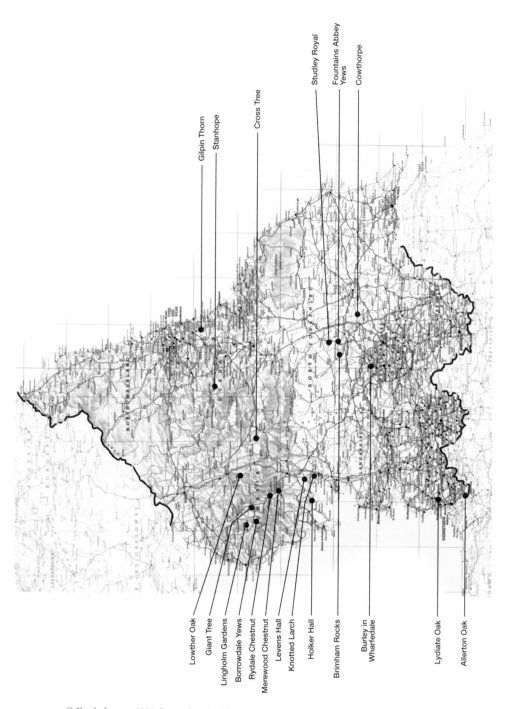

Gilpin Thorn
Stanhope
Cross Tree
Studley Royal
Fountains Abbey Yews
Cowthorpe

Lowther Oak
Giant Tree
Lingholm Gardens
Borrowdale Yews
Rydale Chestnut
Merewood Chestnut
Levens Hall
Knotted Larch
Holker Hall
Brimham Rocks
Burley in Wharfedale
Lydiate Oak
Allerton Oak

© Bartholomew 1996. Reproduced with permission of Harper Collins Cartographic. MM-1297-78.

North Country

The Humber makes its way to the North Sea between the wolds of Lincolnshire, and Yorkshire, where rich farmland rises above sheltered valleys. The old city of York stands at the gateway to two great National Parks, the Yorkshire Dales and the North York Moors. Between them the Vale of York has historic towns, abbeys and castles. Here the tree heritage is rich with such gems as Fountains Abbey, Studley Royal and, further east, the most impressive Castle Howard. Not all is old, for at Thorp Perrow one of Britain's best young arboreta grows at the edge of the dales at Bedale.

Far across the Pennines lies the Lancashire plain and its holiday coast. Inland are the secluded but treasured landscapes of the Forest of Pendle and the Forest of Bowland. To the north, the land sweeps past Morecambe Bay to Cumbria and the Lake District. Cumbria has much to offer the tree explorer, including the famous *Borrowdale yews*, *Holker's lime* and the *Giant tree* by Thirlmere.

Further north-east, the Eden valley drops from the high Pennines towards the coast near Carlisle, where Hadrian's Wall begins crossing eastwards to the North Sea.

The River Tyne divides the valleys and moors of Teesdale and Weardale in Durham from Northumberland's impressive coastline. Inland there are historic houses and gardens where England's most famous landscape designer Lancelot 'Capability' Brown started his career. Tree-lined roads lead over the green dales of the National Park towards the huge Border Forest that surrounds Britain's largest man-made lake at Kielder Water.

YORKSHIRE

The impressive ruins of one of the greatest abbeys in England stand in the lovely valley of the River Skell, 6.5 kilometres (4 miles) south-west of Ripon. There is still much to see, mainly due to William Aislabie, the former owner of adjoining Studley Royal, who acquired Fountains Abbey in 1768.

The early beginnings of the abbey form a humble story. The prior and several monks at St Mary's Abbey, York disapproved of the laxity which they claimed had overtaken their establishment and with the considerable help of Archbishop Thurston left to start anew after riots in 1132. The thirteen dissident monks made their way up the Skell Valley from Ripon to the site given to them by the Archbishop. The site was a wilderness and under a large elm tree in the middle of the vale they built a shelter of thatch and straw. According to Dr John Burton in his book *Monasticon Eboracense* (1758): 'It is supposed that they soon changed the shelter of their elm for that of seven yew trees'. These yews grew south-west of the Celarium. This history was taken from the words of Hugh of Kirkstall who recorded the story in the middle of the thirteenth century at the Abbot of Fountains' request.

The traveller John Leland recorded that the great elm was still there in 1540 and as late as the eighteenth century the rotted stump of the *Fountains' elm* was recorded 475 metres (1,500 feet) east of the abbey on the north bank of the River Skell.

According to George Strutt in the 1820s the yews were badly treated and neglected. The largest of the seven trees had already come down in 1658 and was estimated by its annual ring count as over 1,000 years old. Today little remains of the original trees but relatively old and young yews grow all around the Fountains Abbey site. Cascading down the rock face are the great branches of old yews that grow on the cliff. These wild trees are a great feature of the valley. Other trees are dotted down the valley and by the

Fountains Abbey – wild yews cascading down the walls of this romantic monastic ruin

series of canals and pools fed by the River Skell, often frequented by kingfishers and other birds, are flanked by woods, ornamental trees and quaint buildings such as The Temple of Flame, Octagon Tower and Surprise View. The National Trust has sensitively restored the Studley Royal Gardens since taking over the estate in 1983 and it is now a major attraction along with Fountains Abbey, which is cared for by English Heritage.

Three notable conifers near the water are a wellingtonia by the footpath at 'Quebec', a very tall spruce opposite Temple of Piety at Drum Fall and an excellent Scots pine growing on a lawn near the northern ticket office. Of the many deciduous trees a big copper beech overlooks the Half Moon Pond and a strangely shaped 'humpback' hornbeam grows at Quebec.

The Studley Deer Park has excellent big parkland trees. Twisted sweet chestnuts, field maples, oaks, beeches and one of England's biggest geans (wild cherry) grows here. John Aislabie, former Chancellor of the Exchequer, devoted much of his enforced retirement time after the 'South Sea Bubble' in the early eighteenth century to the Deer Park as well as the garden. Although the park was already established he added the avenues plantings. There is an imposing avenue of limes, with an outer avenue of sweet chestnuts on the main drive framing a view of Ripon Cathedral. An avenue of oak ran eastwards from the house (now gone) and a further avenue of limes ran north–south of the main drive. For those with a real taste for parkland trees this whole area is well worth walking, allowing plenty of time to stop and contemplate the unique landscape history of this little part of Yorkshire.

The final piece of the jigsaw was put into place when William Aislabie purchased Fountains Abbey from his neighbour, so bringing the whole scheme brilliantly together. In 1992 a new Visitor Centre was

river to the east are two yews of great age. One of these trees has layering branches rooted into the river bank. Along with natural regeneration the National Trust have also planted many young yews along the paths bordering the valley side. A spreading sycamore of immense size grows on the southern bank of the river.

Studley Royal which adjoins and merges into the Fountains Abbey site is regarded as the best remaining water-garden in England. Laid out in the flat bottom of the narrow valley the garden at the northern end blends into the Studley Deer Park. The

RIGHT:
Studley Royal – tall spruce and Temple of Piety

The Lime Avenue that leads you towards Ripon Cathedral, Deer Park, Studley Royal

opened by the National Trust on high ground north of Fountains Abbey.

Nidderdale is one of Yorkshire's smaller dales. On its way down from the Pennines, but before reaching the plain of York below Knaresborough, the dale curves around a rocky plateau above the village of Summerbridge. Above the valley and visible for many miles around, Brimham Rocks reach over 300 metres (980 feet) above sea level. The National Trust now own 154 hectares (380 acres) of this moorland of which the main feature is the collection of grotesque rock formations. The rocks are millstone grit, carved into their fantastic shapes over thousands of years by sheets of ice, winds and frosts. Many of the rocks have names related to their shape. Examples being Pivot Rock, Druid's Writing Desk, The Cannon, Chimney Rock, Baboon, Sphynx, Eagle and Camel.

On the 'Turtle Rock' below the Brimham House Visitor Centre grow two

Brimham Rocks – a rowan clinging to life is silhouetted against a late summer's evening sky

amazing trees. A silver birch clings to a ledge on a higher part of the rock. The silhouette of the tree creates a beautiful picture reminiscent of delicate oriental art. The larger lower tree, but still just as incredible, is a rowan. Again this tree grows straight out of the rock at an impossible angle. The roots of the trees travel the rock surface searching for cracks and crannies where some form of substance can be found to feed the weather-beaten crowns. On a nearby rock an oak grows in likewise fashion. Towards the Watchdog and set beside a path is a large isolated rock from which another oak grows. One of the largest at Brimham, the roots of this tree travel eventually to sandy soil beside the rock. In 1995 a large section of this tree fell, exposing the amazing root area of the rest. This collapse was probably due to the exceptionally warm dry summer of that year and its effect on the rock and tree structure.

Many paths lead out from the car park area. Most of the famous rocks are located from here up to the house approximately 600 metres (650 yards) away. Away from the main area quieter but still rocky paths lead over Brimham. The views in all directions are superb.

In the 1970s in Burley-in-Wharfedale, a favourite landmark was lost when the sycamore known as the *Pudding tree* was deemed unsafe and felled by tree surgeons. The tree stood by the Malt Shovel Hotel and the tree took its name from the custom of dispensing puddings from below the tree every seven years at the quaintly named 'Great Pudding' Festival. The original tree was an elm and a replacement sycamore was planted in the late 1870s to carry on the tradition.

No mention of Yorkshire's trees can be completed without noting the legendary *Cowthorpe oak* that grew north-east of Wetherby.

For Evelyn's *Sylva*, Dr Hunter produced a plate of the oak and stated that 'when compared to this, all other oaks are but children of the wood'. At 0.9 metre (3 feet) from the base, the measurement of girth was 'sixteen yards' and at ground 'twenty-six yards'. Its height in its 'ruinous state of 1776' was 85 feet.

MERSEYSIDE

At Lydiate in north Merseyside is a public house built around an old oak tree. Part of the oak still supports the roof of the 'Scots Piper' pub. The original name of the inn was the Royal Oak, but it was renamed after one of Bonnie Prince Charlie's troops, who was wounded in battle, took refuge at the establishment and was nursed back to health by the Moorcroft family. That family were licensees for 500 years until 1945, when they sold the pub to a brewery. The *Lydiate oak* is likely to remain as an integral part of the building for many centuries yet.

In the eastern suburbs of Liverpool still stands the famous old *Allerton oak*, once a boundary and court tree.

CUMBRIA

At Arnside Knott, on National Trust land to the east of Grange-over-Sands, stands a most unusual piece of timber called *The Knotted larch*. At one time at this spot stood two pairs of knotted larch trees. These trees were tied together at 2 metres (6.6 feet) from the ground. The legendary story tells of two lovers who tied the trees as a mark of their love for one another. Two of several stories researched by Amy Bradshaw tell of a solicitor from Kendal and his bride visiting the site on their honeymoon in 1862 and the other story concerns the daughter of Lord Harrison and her friend falling for the sons of a local farmer. They were forbidden to marry so they 'entwined' the young larches as an everlasting memorial to their shared love. The story goes that as long as Lord Harrison's house at Arnside Tower stood the trees would live. Unfortunately in the first decade of this century the tower collapsed and the larches began to die, till eventually only the strange contorted shape now seen was left as the memorial to the lovers of long ago. An old photograph of the trees taken in 1905 is now with the John Marsh Photo Archives.

A few miles north of Grange-over-Sands

is Holker Hall, the gardens of which date back to the 1720s. Sir Thomas Lowther and Lady Elizabeth Cavendish were instrumental in laying out the gardens and deer park from that date. The gardens contain some notable specimen trees including monkey puzzle, ginkgo, Hungarian oak, weeping holly, and cutleafed beech. The most impressive tree though is *The Holker lime*, a common lime that stands near a path with its huge over-hanging massed branches forming a most impressive canopy. The trunk of the tree makes it Britain's largest girthed common lime. It must have been one of the original plantings at Holker or predate the main creation of the early eighteenth century park.

On private land off the Windermere–Ambleside road, opposite the Brockhole National Park Centre, can be found a big old coppiced sweet chestnut. The eight trunks that make up the *Merewood chestnut* have now developed into big spreading stems in their own right. They have been estimated to be about ninety years old, so revealing valuable history into the discontinuance of the coppicing practice in this woodland. More local information is available on the wood-land and its various management practices and produce. The chestnut can be visited by gaining permission from the present owners located at nearby Merewood Lodge.

Another huge and mightily impressive chestnut on private grounds lies to the north of Ambleside at Rydal Hall near beautiful Rydal Water. The girth of the heavily burred and gnarled *Rydale chestnut* is in excess of 11 metres (36 feet) and speculation as to why it grows where it does points to a building existing here prior to 1600. The chestnuts from this tree may well have been a food source in the Middle Ages. Again permission may be granted to see the tree from the owners of Rydal Hall and Gardens.

The Cross tree of Great Ormside lies to the east of the M6 and south-east of Appleby. Turning east at Burrell's, off the B6260, the village of Great Ormside is near the River Eden. The sycamore was planted into the space once occupied by the Market Cross.

The cross was destroyed during the Civil War and only the steps remained as a reminder of the once flourishing cheese and butter market that took place around this focal point near the church.

At Little Ormside a cedar of Lebanon, brought from that country as a seedling by General Whitehead, can be seen in the garden. He is believed to have kept the young tree in the brim of his hat on his journey. He was allowed a pint of fresh water a day as an allowance and he carefully and

The Cross tree, Great Ormside, Cumbria – 300-year-old sycamore planted where the village cross once stood in 1693

unselfishly shared his water with the young cedar. An inspiring story of a tree lover of the first degree.

The *Lowther oak* of Lowther Castle, south of Penrith, stands close to the public road through the castle grounds heading towards Askham. Lowther folklore decrees that if the branch of the oak touches the ground bad luck will befall the Lonsdale family of Lowther. Hence the small props that keep a wickedly bent main branch from touching the earth. The drive through the park is a fine one surrounding the 'fairy tale' castle.

On the western side of Derwentwater, a few miles from Keswick, Lingholm Gardens is home to an enormous Norway spruce, one of Britain's biggest. The spruce stands at over 44 metres (144 feet) tall with a girth exceeding 4 metres (13 feet). The gardens at Lingholm have been in existence since before 1900 but Colonel George Kemp's

The Lowther oak - ancient folklore decrees that the branches should not touch the ground

development at the turn of the twentieth century is largely responsible for today's scene at Lingholm.

On the side of Thirlmere, growing on the old Armboth Estate is a conifer planted in 1821 and now named *The Giant tree*. Accurate records of the tree have been kept and in 1994 it had grown to 43 metres (140 feet) in height with a girth of 5.8 metres (19 feet). The conifer is a silver fir and is well worth the walk up the path from the parking area near Armboth. A sign points the direction towards the impressive fir. This part of the estate was sold to the Manchester Water Works in 1882 as the ground plan for the Thirlmere Reservoir was put into operation to supply the growing city of Manchester. Close by the *Giant tree*, a ring of beech trees mark the spot where cockfighting was carried out until officially outlawed in the middle of the nineteenth century.

Yew trees play a prominent part in this book and the Lake District is an area where the yew grows as a wild tree and has many associations with the district. William Wordsworth made the *Borrowdale yews* famous in his evocative writings of 1803,

Poems of the Imagination:
  Are those fraternal four of Borrowdale
  Joined in one solemn and capacious grove:
  Huge trunks and each particular trunk a
  growth
  Of intertwisted fibres serpentine

The winter storms of 1883–4 damaged the grove and blew down one of the bigger trees. The old hulk still remains as a reminder of that storm. There may be found older yews but the dramatic location of the Borrowdale trees gives them a particular quality of timelessness and the constant battle of natural structures against the elements. The *Borrowdale yews* can be found near Seathwaite, south of Keswick, above the river on the west side of the valley.

Other well-known yews in Cumbria are the *Lorton yew*, also referred to by Wordsworth, and the now fenced-off ruin of the *Yewdale Monarch* at High Yewdale Farm near Tilberthwaite. The *Patterdale yew* was a famous old tree photographed in the late nineteenth century that has now been lost and there is the legend of an ancient yew at Aldingham, supposedly planted by St Cuthbert when he came over from Ireland to spread christianity to the north-west of England.

An old hollow oak growing at Irton Hall is known as the *King oak* and according to tradition Henry VI stayed by the tree because the locals refused him shelter.

At Levens Hall the yew topiary work is renowned as a classical example of this form of high fashion in horticulture. The beech hedge in the same grounds is one of the oldest in Britain going back over 300 years.

There is also a mile-long avenue of oaks.

On the opposite side of the A6 road there is an impressive park that is historically fascinating as it shows stirrings towards a more natural landscape design style. The park extends across the valley and gorge of the River Kent. Trees in clumps and lines seem to have been planted expressly to enhance this delightful piece of country, though the park appears to have been laid out very early in the eighteenth century before the landscape movement really got going. The original architects of both garden and park were the owners of Levens Hall, Col. James Graham and his gardener, Guillaume Beaumo, a Frenchman trained at Versailles. The work appears to have been done between about 1690 and 1720.

One can see that in Cumbria amongst the magnificent lakeland scenery another rich vein of culture exists, that of the trees of the region.

DURHAM
In the town of Houghton-le-Spring between Durham and Sunderland there is a thorn, known locally as the *Gilpin thorn* growing in the Rectory grounds. The name of the tree is taken from Bernard Gilpin, Rector of the Parish from 1557 to 1584. Gilpin was known as the Apostle of the North for his great work in the north-east as a champion of the poor. The original thorn was grown from a cutting taken by Gilpin from the famous *Glastonbury thorn*. His tree died in the 1970s and was replaced by a further cutting.

At Stanhope, Durham, in the gap in the churchyard wall, is a recognisable and very big fossilised tree stump, estimated at over 250 million years old. The fossil was found in a nearby quarry and erected, for display purposes, close to the churchyard.

RIGHT:
The Giant tree, Thirlmere – one of the original plantings in the winter of 1820 on the Armboth Estate. The silver fir now reaches over 43 metres (140 feet) tall

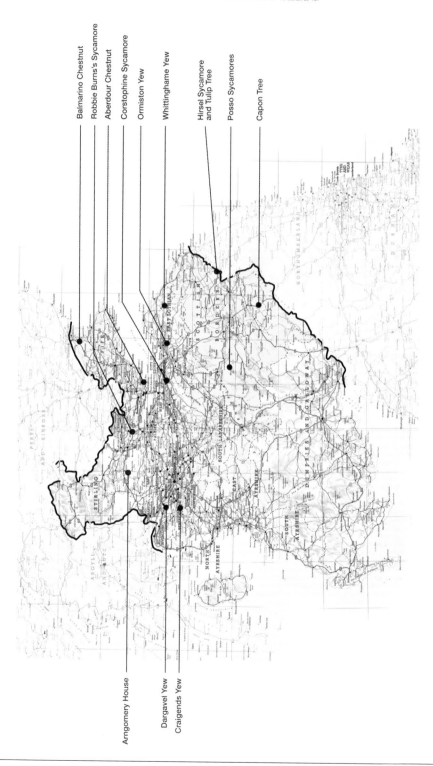

Balmarino Chestnut

Robbie Burns's Sycamore

Aberdour Chestnut

Corstophine Sycamore

Ormiston Yew

Whittinghame Yew

Hirsel Sycamore
and Tulip Tree

Posso Sycamores

Capon Tree

Argomery House

Dargavel Yew

Craigends Yew

Scottish Lowlands

The River Tweed today forms the eastern end of a border that at one time in history moved back and forth as the Scots and the English contested the land surrounding the boundary. The moorland, beyond Coldstream and the great trees of The Hirsel, still bears many scars of a turbulent past. Ruined abbeys and castles, and the *Capon tree* of the Jed forest are all part of this historic land. Great trees grow in the Borders such as the original upright beech at Dawyk, and giant sycamores at Posso. Many travellers pass by on their way north, never sampling the delights on offer.

To the west, beyond the southern uplands, is the rugged outline of the Galloway Forest. Beyond, the Rhinns of Galloway, a strange hammerhead of land washed by the Gulf Stream, has a temperate climate, with subtropical trees growing in gardens near the coast.

Near Lanark, the Clyde breaks over spectacular waterfalls and downstream, west of the great city of Glasgow, are several notable trees. Southern Scotland's other great river, the Forth, is bordered by many sites with important tree collections. The capital city of Edinburgh still has elegant avenues of elms and a tree with strange leaves and a tragic tale! In east Lothian are yews with stories of intrigue and plotting on a grand scale.

Across the Forth, the region of Fife juts out into the North Sea and on its northern shoreline, on the Firth of Tay, stands one of Scotland's oldest chestnuts at the melancholy Balmerino Abbey.

Capon tree, Jedburgh, Borders

BORDERS

In the Border region, on the main A68 south of Jedburgh, is an ancient oak, reputedly the last survivor of the Jed Forest. It is known as the *Capon tree*, the name reputedly derived from the Capuchin monks who sheltered beneath its branches as they journeyed on their pilgrimage to the nearby Abbey in Jedburgh. The tree is hollow with long, low branches. It has wooden supports and has the look of a very old pollard. It grows on the banks of the River Jed and, close by, behind the protective fence, is a young oak grown from an acorn from the ancient tree. (To see the tree it is best to park off the main road by the bridge, and then to take the short walk back to the gate.)

On Jedburgh's Festival day in July, when 'The Callant' leads his mounted cavalcade on the last historic ride, he visits Ferniehirst Castle the home of the Kerrs. The cavalcade returns home by the *Capon tree*, where it stops for refreshment just as the monks did those many centuries ago.

Hirsel sycamore – commemorates the Battle of Flodden

The Border Games take place the following day and are started by the firing of a cannon in the Market Place at 6 am.

Jedburgh, because of its position near the Borders, has the history typical of a frontier town. It was the land of the Border Reivers, where 'Jethart's Justice' meant 'hang first, try later'. Jethart is a local name for the Borough of Jedburgh. The town's other claim to tree fame is that of the *Jethart pear*, from when Jedburgh was famed for its fruit. In the garden of the house where Mary Queen of Scots stayed, are several ancient pear trees, and a more recent commemorative planting by Queen Mary of England. In the Abbey grounds is a collection of recently planted pear trees from all over the British Isles.

RIGHT:
Posso sycamore – a true giant in a remote valley on the Borders

The enormity of the root buttress is only realised when you stand near the Posso sycamore

North-east of Jedburgh, beyond Kelso, is Coldstream and the Hirsel Estate. Within this Country Park are some fine trees. No finer sycamore can be seen than the *Hirsel sycamore*, a huge spreading tree with evidence of old chains and newer cables in the crown. It was supposedly planted in 1513 to commemorate the Battle of Flodden Field in Northumberland. This battle was between King Henry VIII's troops, led by the Earl of Surrey under instruction from Queen Catherine, and James IV of Scotland, aided by the French. James was killed at the Battle. The tree stands at the south-east corner, just outside the walled garden and close to the path of the River Leet.

In 1994, it measured 6.5 metres (21 feet) at 1.5 metres (5 feet) from the ground. Whether it is in fact over 400 years old I should think is a matter of some debate. Also standing near the Leet until it fell a few years ago, was a huge, 500-year-old sweet chestnut.

At the centre of the walled garden is the *Hirsel tulip tree*, measured once at 24 metres (78 feet) in height and 7 metres (23 feet) in the girth. J.C. Loudon writes of the tree in 1838: 'a low tree, planted 100 years, but only 13 feet high with a trunk 4 feet in diameter'. Recent severe surgery has brought the tree down to the height of 10 metres (33 feet), but it has responded well despite being very hollow.

It certainly looks a very old tree, and in 1994 measured 7.5 metres (25 feet) at 1.5 metres (5 feet). Its positioning at the centre of the walled garden is intriguing and it is one of the biggest girthed tulip trees in Britain. The walled garden is now a privately-run tree nursery. Hirsel was the home of the former Prime Minister, Sir Alec Douglas Home, a man with a fascinating career in politics.

In a loop of the River Tweed, Dryburgh Abbey, 16 kilometres (10 miles) west of Kelso, is one of four twelfth century Border abbeys founded in the reign of David I. It was built in 1150 and is regarded as the most beautiful of the Border ruins. It, along with the other abbeys, was ravaged by the English until the mid-sixteenth century when left finally broken. Dryburgh's greatest fame is that it contains the tomb of Sir Walter Scott and also Earl Haig, the First World War leader. Impressive cedars of Lebanon grow on the lawns around the abbey and the yew tree is one which has been recorded over many centuries. The claim by some that it dates from the building of the abbey seems far fetched. Robert Hutchinson describes the tree in the nineteenth century. The abbey overlooks other big free-standing trees, particularly limes, in the surrounding lands.

Thirteen kilometres (8 miles) south-west of Peebles at Stobo, Dawyck Botanic Gardens were created by Sir James Nasmyth in 1720 under the considerable influence of his mentor Linneaus, the great Swedish botanist. There is an extensive collection of

conifers, maples and many other rare trees. The original *Dawyck beech*, an upright-growing form of the common beech, was first grown here in 1860. It has become popular over the last few decades in formal planting schemes and resembles the shape of the Lombardy poplar. Some of the first larches in Scotland were planted here in the 1720s. There are magnificent woodland walks down the Scrape Burn Glen and a Dutch bridge stands above an attractive waterfall. The Botanic Garden at the heart of the estate is now maintained by the Royal Botanic Garden of Edinburgh.

At Posso, near Peebles grow two of Britain's greatest sycamores, the *Posso sycamores*. Only discovered recently by Jim Paterson, these great trees show that many giants are still growing in remote areas

Whittinghame yew – historical tree with evil connections (J Paterson)

awaiting discovery. We still do not know everything! The distinctive feature of the Posso trees is the great root buttresses that form the strong structure on which the giant crowns have grown. They were found by accident when surveying work on ruined castles was being carried out. They grow near a remote farmhouse.

EAST LOTHIAN

East of Edinburgh and Dalkeith in East Lothian at Ormiston Hall is the *Ormiston*

yew, first mentioned in 1474. Some years ago, amongst papers belonging to the Earl of Hopetown, which had been sent to him by the Cockburn family, there was the record of a lease of a piece of ground granted by the head of a religious establishment at Ormiston, which had been signed under the yew tree in 1474.

In 1846 Sir Thomas Dick Launder described the tree in flowing style: 'at the moment the yew is in the fullest vigour of growth, and presents, perhaps one of the

finest objects, as a vegetable production that can exhibit'.

Jim Paterson measured the tree in 1987 at 6 metres (19.7 feet) in the girth at 1.5 metres (5 feet) high compared to the 1834 measurement of 5.4 metres (17.7 feet). In 153 years there was little difference in size. A remarkable aspect of the tree is its vast limbs that grow out from the trunk horizontally in all directions creating a dense shade over 18 metres across.

It was at Ormiston in January 1546 that George Wishart, the Scottish reformer, was seized by Earl Patrick and sent to St Andrews where he was burnt at the stake under the direction of Cardinal Beaton, for which the cardinal was later murdered.

Another historical yew of great dimensions, at East Linton in East Lothian, is the *Whittinghame yew*. In the words of Robert Hutchinson:

it stands on the brow of a gentle eminence, sloping to the north, and which it entirely covers. In fact, it has less the appearance of a tree at a little distance than that of an enormous bank of the densest foliage. The circumference of its branches, which sweep the sward on all sides, is close on 100 yards.

Another great discovery by Hutchinson which links the tree with Celtic folklore was:

within this gloomy and dark leafy canopy there is, curiously enough, a spring of clear cold water, which is now imprisoned and conducted in a leaden pipe to a tap.

The great legend of the yew at Whittinghame is that in the adjacent castle of the Earl of Bothwell, Earls Morton, Ruthven, and others of the Scottish nobles opposed to Darnley (the husband of Mary Queen of Scots, her cousin whom she had

married in 1565), had met to discuss the means of getting rid of the detested consort of the Queen. They gathered in the great shade of the yew and entered into a bond to accomplish the death of Darnley at Kirk O'Field, Edinburgh in 1567. The Earl of Bothwell who was charming, powerful and ambitious, later abducted Mary and married her after a quick divorce from his wife. When Mary was deposed he escaped and ended up imprisoned in Denmark, where he died insane.

CITY OF EDINBURGH

On the western side of Edinburgh is a tree unique to Edinburgh, the *Corstophine sycamore*. This remarkable tree grows in a small garden on a busy street and also carries the name 'The White Lady'. The leaves are a pale gold in spring, as distinct from the customary light green of the common sycamore. As long ago as 1679 the tree was written about, and in 1906 Elwes wrote:

The tree has a romantic history, as being the only survivor of an avenue which formerly led to an old manor house belonging since 1376 to the Forrester family. James Baillie, second Lord Forrester, who took an active part against the Commonwealth and became involved in difficulties on account of a heavy fine laid on him by Cromwell, is said to have quarrelled with his sister-in-law on August 26th 1679, and to have been murdered by her at the foot of the tree.

There is an alternative story that recounts that:

the large and very beautiful tree at the corner of Dovecot Road and Sycamore Place was in grounds of what used to belong to the Forresters. Lord Forrester's daughter would meet her lover beneath the tree. Her father found out and, disapproving of her suitor, slew him one night at the meeting place. After that night the leaves of the sycamore turned a lighter colour, in fact almost white and the place was haunted by the ghost of the daughter.

LEFT:
Robbie Burns's sycamore grows beside Alloa churchyard (J Paterson)

The tree was measured in 1905 and had a girth of 3.3 metres (11 feet). It has increased little since then. It now stands at about 20 metres (66 feet) tall and has a girth exceeding 3.5 metres (11.5 feet). The dovecot attached to the tree has been there since at least the turn of the nineteenth century. Many grafts from the tree have proliferated the Corstophine or Golden sycamore.

At Moncrieffe House, another very large Corstophine sycamore grows. Taller than the Edinburgh tree but not as stout and without the same folklore.

RENFREWSHIRE

Off the M8 west of Glasgow at Bishopton, Dargavel House has several notable trees. The *Dargavel yew* is a fine tree measured by Hutchinson in 1890 at 3.7 metres (12.1 feet) in the girth at 1.5 metres (5 feet) and remeasured in 1992 at 4.9 metres (16 feet) at 0.3 metres (1 foot) (Paterson).

Another good yew stands in front of the house but the greatest attraction at Dargavel is the incredible layering hornbeam whose great spreading contorted branches twist and fall over a large area of the grounds. Several of the branches have props under them. This must be one of the most remarkable hornbeams that can be seen anywhere. It had a girth of 4 metres (13 feet) in 1992. The building of Dargavel House was started in the sixteenth century and has more recently been used as an Ordnance depot. A permit has to be obtained from the main gate for anyone wishing to see the trees.

South of Bishopton in the built-up area of Johnstone, near Paisley, the great Scottish yew tree recorder Robert Hutchinson found the *Craigends yew* on the banks of the River Gryffe. This yew was the largest yew on Hutchinson's list of 1890 and at that time had a girth of 6.4 metres (21 feet) at 0.3 metres (1 foot) above the ground. Where the old Craigends House once stood has now become a housing estate with the area around the tree now a rubbish dump. The yew is still very much alive but it has split,

with branches layering into the surrounding ground.

STIRLING

A great example of the weeping or West Felton yew grows at Arngomery House, Kippen, in the Stirling Region. This tree in fact is larger than the 'original' tree in Shropshire and, as with some other Scottish yews, layers from the main branches creating a crown circumference of over 100 metres (109 yards). The tree, *Taxus baccata* 'Dovastoniana', looks healthy and in full vigour. Its planting date is unknown but should be after the original tree in 1777, although strangely there is supposedly a measurement by a Professor Walker in 1762.

CLACKMANNANSHIRE

In the old Alloa churchyard, on the north side of the River Forth, Robbie Burns's father is buried. Growing against the wall of the churchyard is a leaning tree known as *Robbie Burns's sycamore*.

FIFE

Further north on the Firth of Tay estuary is the romantic ruin of Balmerino Abbey. It was founded for Cistercians in the thirteenth century by Alexander II whose mother is buried there. The last Lord Balmerino was a brave man, beheaded as a Jacobite in 1746. At the abbey is one of Scotland's oldest and biggest sweet chestnuts, which must be of considerable age. The *Balmerino chestnut* stands with the ruins off a side road from the village of Wormit, near Newport-on-Tay.

The largest girthed sweet chestnut though, indeed Scotland's largest girthed broadleafed tree, is found just west of Aberdour at Cochairney in Fife, a few miles from the famous Forth Road Bridge. The *Aberdour chestnut* has girth exceeding 8.5 metres (28 feet) measured at breast height.

RIGHT:
Balmarino chestnut – grows in the abbey grounds near the Firth of Tay (J Paterson)

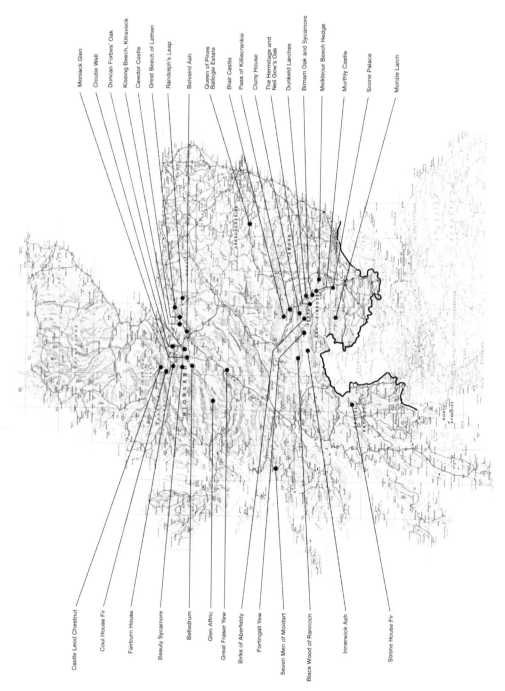

Moniack Glen
Cloutie Well
Duncan Forbes' Oak
Kissing Beech, Kilravock
Cawdor Castle
Great Beech of Lethen
Randolph's Leap
Balvaird Ash
Queen of Pines Ballogie Estate
Blair Castle
Pass of Killiecrankie
Cluny House
The Hermitage and Neil Gow's Oak
Dunkeld Larches
Birnam Oak and Sycamore
Meikleour Beech Hedge
Murthly Castle
Scone Palace
Monzie Larch

Castle Leod Chestnut
Coul House Fir
Fairburn House
Beauly Sycamore
Belladrum
Glen Affric
Great Fraser Yew
Birks of Aberfeldy
Fortingall Yew
Seven Men of Moidart
Black Wood of Rannoch
Innerwick Ash
Strone House Fir

Scottish Highlands

The full drama of the Highlands starts not far beyond the central belt. At the western end, the hills rise into the Trossacks. In the east, the waters from the lochs and highland peaks flow down from the Grampians and out into the rivers North and South Esk. One of the richest areas in Britain for trees is wonderful Tayside, once the home of that mysterious but vanished race, the Picts. The River Tay flows through a majestic landscape that includes Scone Palace, the ancestral home of the Scottish kings and once the home of the intrepid tree explorer David Douglas. The region has the biggest hedge in the world, the oldest yew tree, Dunkeld's larches, and Diana's Grove at Blair Athol. These are all jewels in this gateway to the highlands.

Further north, the great salmon rivers of the Spey, the Don and the Dee make their spectacular way along tree-lined banks through the Cairngorms. Around the capital of the Highlands, Inverness, on the Moray Firth are numerous tree treasures. A famous Shakespearean castle has a tree story second to none, conifers soar up into the sky and a holy well has trees festooned with prayer rags. Castle Leod has the largest tree on its latitude anywhere in the world and a tree with the earliest recorded planting date. Further inland are reminders of the great forest of Caledon. Scots pines with red, rugged bark, and delicate birches with their rich autumn colours of gold are unmatched anywhere.

From Inverness the Great Glen slices across the country and on the banks of Loch Ness is a remote and ancient yew belonging to a famous Scottish clan. Majestic landscape is all around and the glen finally reaches a coastline very different from that of the east. In the shelter of Ardnamurchan, the most stirring of ruins, Castle Tioram, stands on a rock promontory and the Seven Men of Moidart beeches commemorate the landing of the Young Pretender in 1745.

In the far north, and warmed by the Gulf Stream, Inverewe Gardens has trees more in keeping with Tresco than with the Scottish Highlands.

It is the magnificent trees of the great estates and vast landscapes that add to the splendour of this special region of Britain.

ARGYLL AND BUTE

On the west of Scotland at Cairndow, by Loch Fyne, the Strone House Pinetum in Argyll has one of Britain's most incredible conifers. The *Strone silver fir* (*Abies alba*) has four gigantic stems of up to 46 metres (151 feet). They leave the main trunk at about 4 metres (13 feet) up. The tree grows beside a burn which flows into the River Finglas, which in turn flows into the Loch. It was originally planted as part of an avenue in about 1790. Most of that avenue has now disappeared but the sheer enormity of the trunk, root buttresses and four stems, and the structure of this particular fir make it one of Britain's most outstanding conifers. The Pinetum was planted about 1875. It is always open to the public and also has an extremely tall hybrid larch and a record fitzroya.

PERTH AND KINROSS

A notable collection in this tree rich area is at Scone Palace, Perth which has a 16 hectare (40-acre) arboretum. Here may be seen one of the original Douglas firs, grown from the seeds sent home by the explorer David Douglas to his father who was head gardener at Scone. David Douglas's adventures have now become engrained in our tree history and folklore. He encountered hostile Red Indians, whom he later befriended and worked with to find his plants. He lost four years of valuable notes while negotiating rapids and was eventually gored to death in a wild bull pit in Hawaii.

His amazing exploits, and his fight against illness and failing eyesight, provide a strange parallel to the apparently gentle art of plant hunting.

David Douglas is forever remembered in the fir that bears his name. Another one of the original firs stands at Walcot Park, South Shropshire.

Also at Scone, plantings of silver firs, wellingtonias, and sitka spruce were laid to a simple grid pattern in 1860 to supplement the older arboretum. Amongst the record-breaking trees at Scone are spruces, Scots

Scone Palace – Sitka spruces in old pinetum

and Jeffrey's pines and western hemlocks.

In Strathearn, north of Crieff, stands Monzie Castle (pronounced Monie) Monzie means 'field of corn' and it is easy to understand when visiting why there has been habitation in this lovely sheltered valley since early times.

The oldest part of the castle dates from 1634 built by the Graham family on the site of a previous dwelling. The Grahams subsequently sold Monzie to their cousins the Campbells of Taymouth. The present owners, the Crichton family bought the castle and grounds in the 1850s.

Growing by the lake behind the castle is one of the original European larches brought to Scotland early in the 18th century by Colonel Menzies of Glen Lyon. The *Monzie larch* is a beautiful stately tree, a true giant of great historical importance. It stands at over 35 metres (115 feet) tall and has a girth exceeding 6 metres (20 feet) making it Britain's largest larch tree. Its great branches sweep gracefully down to the waters edge where moorhens nest in the branch tips. There were several other larches planted along with the survivor. They are now gone but the stump of one remains as a reminder of the original group.

Monzie Castle and grounds is usually open to visitors during selected days each May.

North of Perth on the A93 to Braemar, and before the small town of Rattray, is the *Meikleour beech hedge*, the tallest beech hedge in the world at between 26 and 28 metres (85 and 92 feet) in height.

The 'hedge' is over 550 metres (600 yards) in length and stands on the west side of the road heading north, not far from the River Tay.

It was planted in 1745 and is a most impressive sight, especially in spring when the young green leaves appear, and again in autumn when the colours are rich reds,

RIGHT:
Monzie larch – magnificent original tree from the early eighteenth century

browns and golds.

Not far from the village of Meikleour, on the other side of the Tay, is Murthly, which has many huge conifers of record size, including Sakhalin and Serbian spruces. There are in fact three Serbian spruces (*Picea omorika*) of great size. Two of these trees – the graceful weeping conifers, much admired by all who see them – are Britain's biggest.

The sinister Dead Man's Walk at Murthly Castle is an avenue of yews leading towards the Catholic chapel, the oldest in Scotland. Reputedly for over 400 years no Laird of Murthly has travelled down the avenue until after death. The Fotheringham family are the Lairds of Murthly and have always been keen tree enthusiasts. Permission to visit the delights of the estate must be obtained via

LEFT: *Beech hedge, Meikleour – the tallest beech hedge in the world*

Meikleour hedge – old photo

Murthly – towering conifers near the River Tay (J Paterson)

Murthly – record Serbian spruces by River Tay

the estate office.

Further upstream on the Tay and to the west, where the highlands eventually meet the richer agricultural lands, is Dunkeld, a place rich in tree history. Dunkeld, often called 'The Gateway to the Highlands', is worth exploring. It has many treasures, especially its tree history. Down Cathedral Street

from the Square, stands the old Cathedral, whose origins go back to 1318. An Arts Festival is held in June in the Cathedral grounds, which sweep down to the River Tay. Near here is the record-breaking and rare Japanese tree *Alcock's spruce*.

From near the Cathedral the 'Larch Walk' leads into woods at the rear of the grounds. Here can be found the *Parent larch*, the last survivor from a group of five planted by the second Duke of Athol in 1738. It is named the *Parent larch* because from these early trees, the natural hybrid between the European and Japanese larches occurred, thus producing the vigorous tree used extensively in forestry to this day.

The old larch stands at over 20 metres (66 feet) tall. Nearby are other huge conifers, including a record Douglas fir. In the woods can be seen red squirrels along with the introduced greys. The walk leads past great larches and on up to the King's Seat, where a beautiful view of the woods and river can be enjoyed.

At Dunkeld House, now a hotel, is a record girthed Japanese larch and also one of the famous 'Pedestal' larches, which grows on a bank above the driveway at the rear of the hotel. On the far southern bank, opposite Dunkeld House Hotel, stands the oak tree associated with the famous Scottish fiddler, Neil Gow.

He lived at Inver and was said to have sat by this tree both composing and playing his haunting, melancholy airs. *Neil Gow's oak* can be visited on the 'Inver Walk'.

The Hermitage, which runs alongside the tumbling River Braan, was originally intended as a tree garden and was planted in the eighteenth century. Most of the original trees have gone, but the Douglas firs, which were the most successful here, remain. One of the firs is now deemed to be the joint tallest tree in Britain at 64.5 metres (212 feet) and it grows from a steep bank by the Black Linn falls. They gave inspiration to the painter Millais, who rented a cottage nearby. Try visiting them in the late autumn, when there are fewer people round and the

Dead Man's walk, Murthly Castle

Parent larch, Dunkeld

Perthshire colours are magnificent.

Further downstream on the Tay, past Thomas Telford's elegant bridge, is Birnam, popular since Victorian times as a resort. The buildings reflect that period. Beatrix Potter loved this place, where she spent many happy hours on holiday. No doubt the surrounding landscape influenced her later, charming stories. The Telford bridge replaced a toll ferry in 1879, and down from that point close to the river side stand two famous trees.

The *Birnam oak*, complete with its props, is a huge, old hollow tree, over 6 metres (20 feet) in girth. Very close is the even bigger *Birnam sycamore*, one of the largest girthed sycamores in Britain at over 7 metres (23 feet). Its height exceeds 30 metres (98 feet). Birnam Woods and landscape are widely believed to be the setting for Shakespeare's *Macbeth*. Taking a walk in the evening, when the sun is going down, does not dissuade you from this belief. Further downstream, the walk passes an attractive beech avenue. It can then be continued up to Birnam Hill, where black grouse and roe deer are present. Fine

165

Pedestal larch, Dunkeld House Hotel

In the birks of Aberfeldy.
(Robbie Burns, The Birks of Aberfeldy*)*

trees can be seen right back up the river to Loch Tay.

The 'Birks of Aberfeldy' are stands of birch, with an excellent walk from the stream starting from the town.

Let fortune's gifts at random free,
They ne'er shall draw a wish frae me,
Supremely blest wi' love and thee,

On the north bank of the Tay Valley, to the east of Aberfeldy, is the beautiful woodland garden at Cluny House. In this magnificent setting grow two massive wellingtonias. The larger of the two is the British record holder and has a girth of almost 11 metres (36 feet) (1994). In 1985 it measured 36 metres (118 feet) tall.

Beyond Kenmore, on the northern side of the Loch close to the smaller River Lyon, is the settlement of Fortingall. This unassuming locality is the site of the *Fortingall yew*, reputedly the oldest living thing in Europe. The yew tree, close by the little church and the hotel, is now enclosed by a stone wall and a metal fence. The only way to look closely at the trunk is to gain access through the locked gate. The tree is now in two distinct pieces, with the old shell sending new, healthy growth above the surrounding wall.

Measured in 1796 by Pennant, the girth

The Hermitage – the record breaking Douglas fir clings precariously to the banks of the River Braan by the Black Linn falls

Birnam sycamore – by the side of the River Tay near to the Birnam oak

It leads one to agree with the theory that there must be some yews today in England and Wales which are vastly over their estimated age because so much of the original tree is missing.

The other fascination of the site at Fortingall is that at Glen Lyon, a few hundred metres down the lane, is a Bronze Age mound that may well have close association with the yew tree. An old notice on the wall beside the yew reads:

No-one can say how long the tree has grown here, but distinguished botanists say it is a specimen of the Primeval Forest, and therefore 3,000 years old (as old as the time of King Solomon), and is believed to be the most ancient piece of vegetation in Europe

Over 2 centuries ago its circumference was 17 metres (56 feet). The trunk became fragmented and over the years suffered at the hands of vandals – hence the protecting wall and pillars.

Cluny House – a beautiful woodland garden

was 17 metres (56 feet). Later, the French botanist De Candolle was most impressed by the tree and its possible age. The tree has often been subjected to rough treatment, with fires being lit around the basal area. The ritual of Celtic 'Beltane' fires probably damaged parts of the tree, although this practice must have occurred over many centuries.

The wall was built in the middle of the nineteenth century to create a sanctuary for the undisturbed growth of the yew and, viewing it now, one can probably say that this has worked. Without the earlier records it would be difficult now to determine the surviving pieces as one tree, but there are many observations to confirm that it is. Colonel Campbell who, in the late eighteenth century lived close by at Glen Lyon, confirmed that this was so.

Under the branches is the burial ground of the Stewarts of Garth, and behind it is that of Sir David Currie of Garth, Glenlyon and Chesthill, who in 1900 replaced the Pre-Reformation Church with the present building. There has been a place of worship on the site since the 7th century.

In 1994 building work was underway on the chapel.

The other mystery of the yew at Fortingall is that it is by far the largest ancient yew known in Scotland. All the other truly ancients are in England and Wales.

Also, the girth of more than 15 metres (49 feet) is well over 3 metres (10 feet) larger than any other yew in the world.

Some great ash trees grow in Scotland and none bigger than the *Innerwick ash*, standing in remote hills by the road through Glen Lyon. The ash is a considerable age and has many battered and torn branches. The younger healthy stems have sprouted from the lichen-covered bole that has an enormous girth, for an ash, of 6.7 metres (22 feet) (1993). One suspects that if pollarded, the tree would last for many a long year yet.

Further north, beyond the Glengoulandie Deer Park, is that great mountain The Schiehallion, and through the beech and birch woods by Loch Rannoch can be found some fascinating remnants of the Caledonian pine forests. Here, at Blackwood, beautiful old and young pines are growing in an almost natural state. It is interesting to look at the different forms and bark patterns, particularly beyond Rannoch School heading west. The boggy ground of the forest is very uneven, with bilberry, heather, birch and juniper accompanying the pines. The Black Wood of Rannoch is now a national nature reserve, but by using the parking areas and proper paths, a sense of what part of the old landscape of Scotland must once have looked like can be experienced.

The Dukes of Atholl have been pioneers in forestry and tree collecting for several

Black Wood of Rannoch – native pines near to the loch

centuries. At their ancestral home of Blair Castle, near the village of Blair Atholl, Perthshire, many huge conifers up to 45 metres (148 feet) tall grow in Diana's Grove, including a Japanese larch (*Larix kaempferi*), the rare red fir from Oregon (*Abies magnifica*), and white fir (*Abies concolor, v lowiana*) – all British record trees. The entrance to the castle is through an impressive avenue of old limes, since added to with younger plantings. The association of the Atholls with the European larch is well documented and Colonel Menzies of Glen Lyon was also involved in the early introduction of the larches from the Tyrol. In 1988, the tenth Duke planted commemorative larches on the estate.

Three miles south of Blair Atholl you enter the top of the densely wooded gorge called the Pass of Killiecrankie, a place famous for the battle that took place around the gorge in 1689. The valley has been cut by the River Garry that tumbles along far below the road. The hanging woodlands that clothe the valley side have spectacular walks through them, and in the autumn the colours of the woodlands make a beautiful picture that contrasts with the violent history of the pass. The battle of 1689 was between Graham of Claverhouse, 'Bonnie Dundee', leading his brave Jacobite Highlanders, and the British Army led by General Mackay. 'Bonnie Dundee' wished to depose William of Orange and restore James VII/II to the throne. The British were almost annihilated by the wild Highlanders, but Claverhouse was mortally wounded and his death left the army he led without his inspired direction. His body was taken to Blair Castle. Three weeks later the government troops gained a decisive revenge victory at Dunkeld.

Between Blair Atholl and Killiecrankie at Urrard House are *Bonnie Dundee's larches*, a line of old larch trees named after the brave and revered leader of the Highlanders.

ABERDEENSHIRE

West of Banchory on the Ballogie Estate, which is south of the great River Dee, grows the *Queen of pines*, one of the finest Scot's pines in Britain and with a known planting date of 1792. The tree grows by the main drive and has been measured five times this century. The measurements, which are of interest to the dendrologist and lay man alike, are as follows:

1913	Royal Scot. For. Ass.	33m. (108ft.) tall 3.5m. (11.5ft.) girth

Pass of Killiecrankie – autumn colours at the scene of the battle in 1689

1931	Conifer Con. Report	32m. (104ft.) tall 3.9m. (12.8ft.) girth
1987	A. Mitchell	37m. (121ft.) tall 4.4m. (14.4ft.) girth
1992	J. Paterson	39m. (128ft.) tall 4.5m. (14.8ft.) girth
1994	J. Paterson	39m. (128ft.) tall 4.6m. (15ft.) girth

The last 200 years has produced this great pine which, one suspects, will not put on too much top growth in future, but may well become stouter.

MORAY

About 13 kilometres (8 miles) south of Forres, through Darnaway Forest, is Logie on the B9007. Here is a celebrated spot on one of Scotland's most beautiful rivers, the Findhorn. Robert the Bruce gave land belonging to the Cummings to Thomas Randolph, Earl of Moray. The Cummings raided Darnaway Castle in retaliation but were forced to flee. Alistair Cummings leapt over the dramatic narrow gap above the river gorge to escape from his pursuers. Despite it being a Cummings who leapt, the spot is called Randolph's Leap.

Upstream and in clear view from the lookout by the leap, are two giant conifers growing side by side. The Sitka spruce is the slightly taller of the two at over 60 metres (197 feet). The Douglas fir, measured early in the 1990s was just below at 59.8 metres (196 feet).

There is probably nowhere else in Britain that two different species of such height grow so close together.

On the path from the pull-in on the roadside is a stone marked with the date 1829. This was the flood water level mark of the great flood of 1829 which caused great destruction down the whole valley. It is difficult to believe when standing here and looking down on the Findhorn in the gorge that the torrent could have been so great that it reached this mark.

HIGHLAND

At Lethen House near Nairn grows the *Great beech of Lethen*, one of north Scotland's most wonderful trees. This tree is truly a 'character'. Carved on its mighty bole are initials and dates going back over 200 years, a history of the Brodie family of Lethen who have lived there since 1634. 'To stand under the circuit of the branches and to look around is to seem encircled by a writhing mass of pythons and shows us in living form such stuff as dreams are made of' writes Jim Paterson of the great tree that is estimated at well over 350 years old.

Valentine's of Dundee, famed for post-

Bonnie Dundee's larches, Urrard – named after the revered leader, Graham of Claverhouse (J Paterson)

cards, photographed the tree in 1884 and it looked remarkably similar to today, apart from the absence of the intricate wooden seat that used to encircle the base of the trunk. The date '1779' carved on the main trunk is clearly visible on the old photograph. In *The History of Nairnshire* by George Bain (1893) the beech was written about and its position plotted on an old estate map. Constance Brodie writing in the *Lethen History* says of the tree: 'The oldest date on the very old beech at the foot of the garden

Great beech of Lethen – Jim Paterson stands below the old giant

is 1701 just above the large knot on the north of the trunk of the tree.'

The many carvings, including the depiction of the beech itself, have very gradually 'callused' over, but are still readable. This gives authenticity to the date of the carvings. The old age of the tree and lack of vigour have preserved the carvings. On a younger beech they probably would have disappeared as the bark grew. Although the tree is in decline, with some of the layered branches now

dying, the *Great beech of Lethen* is the very antithesis of an individual historical tree, full of character.

Eight kilometres (5 miles) east of Culloden, at the ancestral home of the Rose family of Kilravock Castle (pronounced Kilrawk), another great beech of similar but not quite so distinguished appearance is the

Kissing beech. It was so named for it was the site of an illicit embrace between a member of the family and a housemaid, witnessed by another servant some decades ago. The beech is of considerable age and its drooping branches layer into the ground on a bank near the entrance into the castle grounds. A giant sitka spruce grows on the edge of the lawn in front of the castle.

Rose of Kilravock entertained Bonnie Prince Charlie before the battle at Culloden. He was not a Jacobite, but the Prince had ridden over to call on him and no true Highlander refuses hospitality.

Prince Charles walked with his host around the grounds and watched young trees being planted. They would not have seen the sitka being planted, it was introduced later, but they could have seen the

Kissing beech – layered branches are an indication of the great age of the beech at Kilravock

The many carvings on the trunk of the Lethen beech stretch back over the centuries

young beech and some of the giants of today going into the ground as young trees. Kilravock Castle is now run as a hotel.

Prince Charles Edward Stuart (Bonnie Prince Charlie) and his 5,000 exhausted Highlanders were defeated by the Duke of Cumberland, son of George II and his 9,000 highly trained troops at the Culloden battlefield in April 1746. At least 1,200 Highlanders were killed in the massacre. It is still a painful memory to many Highlanders. The battlefield, a wild moorland site, has many interpretive displays and a visitor's centre. On the western edge of the moorland is the old *Balvaird ash*, where the Bonnie Prince retreated and watched the

Duncan Forbes' oak, Bunchcrew (J. Paterson)

terrible end of the battle. The windblown tree grows on a farm track near private farm buildings off a minor road.

There are well-known oaks in the area. The oak on the rail bridge at Smithiton, near Inverness, stands next to a huge stone and makes one wonder how vehicles crossed the bridge in times gone by. The *Duncan Forbes' oak* is a squat old tree with a table-top crown and bottle-shaped trunk. It grows in a field near Bunchcrew at Beauly Firth. Lord Forbes was Lord President at the time of Culloden and it was in his Jacobean castle near Culloden that Bonnie Prince Charlie made his headquarters for two months

before the battle. The building is now The Culloden House Hotel. The oak is where Forbes used to sit planning his ambitions when a younger man.

Cawdor was immortalised by William Shakespeare in *Macbeth* as the scene of Duncan's murder. The history of the castle, however, is colourful enough. It dates from 1372 when the central tower was built. The domestic buildings were added in the sixteenth century. Carbon dating by Cambridge and other research has confirmed that the remains of a dead tree, now railed off in the castle's basement, are in fact older than the building itself. Intriguingly, it fits in with the old legend that the original founder, Thane William, was granted a licence to build himself a castle. He was 'instructed' in a dream in 1370 to load a donkey with panniers of gold and build his castle where the donkey stopped. The donkey stopped twice before finally settling under the shade of a thorn tree. Thane William built his fortress around the thorn. The one new fact discovered about the story is that carbon dating has revealed the thorn is in fact a holly! In the 'Hawthorn Room' the 'semi-petrified' tree reaches from floor to ceiling. A fascinating story!

Outside, across the bridge are excellent big conifers and in front of the castle are some fine old lime trees. There has also been plenty of new planting at Cawdor, which is open daily in the summer season. The castle lies to the south-west of Nairn, near the B9090.

A walk through the Moniack Glen near the Beauly Firth will reveal to the observer a sight of incredibly tall trees. At least three of the Douglas firs at the top end of the walk near the bridge are over 60 metres (197 feet) tall and growing. Others are following and, in this sheltered valley ideal for the conifers to grow in, record trees of the future are reaching the top of the valley sides. These are amongst the tallest trees in Britain and Europe. The other trees in the glen are firs, spruce, larch and native broadleaved trees. A small car park, not far from the Moniack Castle Winery, is an ideal base for this not-to-be-missed place.

Great conifers abound in this area. At Belladrum, just to the south-west, Britain's largest western red cedar (*Thuja plicata*) grows near a stream on the estate.

At Beaufort Castle, ancestral home of the Lovat family, the old beautiful estate on the Beauly River contains many good trees. None more so than the tree pines growing close to the huge old walled garden – Corsican pine (*Pinus nigra var. maritima*), Austrian pine (*Pinus nigra var. nigra*) and

Moniack Glen — huge conifers grow in the sheltered valley, roots cling to the banks of the stream for firm anchorage

Crimean pine (*Pinus nigra var. caramatica*) – carefully selected when planted and seen together nowhere else in Britain. Within the great but decaying circular walled garden grows an old Lombardy poplar and one of Scotland's earliest cedars of Lebanon, now broken and declining, and probably planted about 1725. In the open parkland a giant beech, Britain's biggest, once stood until blown down in a particularly bad storm some years ago. Nothing now remains of the old tree.

LEFT: *The great old sycamore at Beauly Priory*

The Lovat family have a rich and fascinating history littered with heroics and tragedy. They are the traditional Chiefs of the Clan Fraser. In recent years the family have had terrible times with successive deaths of the sons of Lord Lovat in 1994 and his own death in 1995. The estate is private and permission to see the trees can only be obtained by prior arrangement.

The Lovat family came to Britain with the Normans and it was their French influence that inspired the name Beauly (Beau Lieu). The village of that name near Beaufort Castle is an attractive and much visited location. The ruin of Beauly Priory, at the north end of the market-place, is approached through iron gates and dominating the view is the huge old *Beauly sycamore*. This great old hulk is many centuries old, some say as old as the beginnings of the priory in 1231. This is doubtful, but it has obviously been there a long, long time protected as it is in the confines of the priory grounds. Also to be found are several old burred elm pollards, a sight now rare in England since the elms' disease outbreak in the 1970s.

North of Inverness crossing the Beauly Firth on the A9 you enter the Black Isle, which is in fact a peninsula sticking out into the Moray Firth. Turning eastward on the A832 Fortrose–Cromarty road the straight road reaches Munlochy by the bay of that name. On the roadside before the village a strange sight meets the traveller. The woodland fringe is festooned with thousands of rags of varying sizes above the holy St Boniface's Well. The now more commonly used name of Cloutie Well has been an attraction for those wishing to have prayers answered for many centuries. This form of 'votive' offering, whereby the prayers may be answered by leaving the offering, has a story connecting with our Celtic pre-Christian past. This amazing place can be mirrored in St Ciaran's bush and similar thorns in Eire. The difference at the Cloutie

Well is the sheer numbers of rags decorating many trees, stones and the fence above the little spring that emerges from the bank by the roadside.

North of Beauly, in the magnificent scenery that is all around in these parts, at Fairburn House, near Marybank, a conifer extravaganza awaits the visitor. A most impressive spreading sitka spruce grows on

Cloutie Well – rags festooned over the trees above the holy well

grows one of the Douglas firs grown from David Douglas' original batch of seed in 1827. There are also big broadleaved trees in the region, none bigger than the record girthed wych elm (*Ulmus glabra*) near Braham House.

At Strathpeffer, a few miles north of Contin, Highland Games are held in the grounds of Castle Leod in early August each year. For the tree enthusiast and investigator, Castle Leod, home of the Earl of Cromarty, has a sweet chestnut of considerable distinction. It was recorded as having been planted in 1550 by John Mackenzie, Chief of Kintail 1486–1558. The records of the planting are kept in the castle's monument room. The

Old Douglas fir at Coul House near Contin

the lower lawn, noble fir, mountain hemlock and morinda spruce plus many other record-breaking conifers make this a special place for the conifer enthusiast. There is no doubt, Scotland can grow conifers of great proportions, probably due to the long summer daylight hours and rainfall levels. Fairburn is now a hospital and permission is required for those wishing to look at the trees.

Across the valley by the rivers Conon and Blackwater, and just in sight of Fairburn, is the Coul House Hotel, near Contin. Here, on the edge of the lawn in front of the hotel,

Sweet chestnut, Castle Leod – four hundred-year-old 'King of Strathpeffer'

Detail of the Strathpeffer chestnut bole

*In wild country above Loch Ness grows the Great
Fraser yew*

plaque by the chestnut tells us he was Privy
Counsellor to King James V and Queen
Mary. Grandfather to Sir Roderick
Mackenzie of Castle Leod, Conage and
Tarbet, ancestor of the Earls of Cromarty
1574–1826.

The measurements of this historic and
beautiful tree that grows with its characteristic spiralling bark in the fields near the
castle was 7.9 metres (25.9 feet) in the girth
at 1.5 metres (5 feet) in 1935. The *Strathpeffer
chestnut* is one of the earliest recorded trees
in Britain. At 160 metres (100 yards) north-
west of this spot is another chestnut which
is believed to have been planted at the same
date as the other tree. The second tree

measured 5.8 metres (19 feet) in the girth at
1.5 metres (5 feet) in 1935. Closer to the
castle are two giant wellingtonias. The tree
to the west is a monster and is one of the
tallest wellingtonias in the British Isles
standing at over 52 metres (170 feet) tall.
This tree is the largest tree on its latitude (57
40 N) anywhere in the world.

From the last car park at the head of Loch
Beinn a' Mheadhoin, there is a chance to see
a section of an old pinewood, the old Glen
Affric Forest. The complete walk is approximately 16 kilometres (10 miles) and gives a
glimpse of the beauty and atmosphere
created by the original Caledonian Pine
Forest.

On the banks of Loch Ness in the Great
Glen, the Woodland Trust now manages the
attractive estate of Balmacaan. Here, not far

The many-stemmed interior of the Great Fraser yew – first documented in 1876

from the loch, are an excellent collection of large conifers including a record western red cedar and many big broadleaves.

One of the most remarkable yews in Scotland grows on the southern banks of Loch Ness on the Knockie Lodge estate. This is at the Fort Augustus end of Stratherrick. To visit the historic *Great Fraser yew* requires a strenuous 3-mile walk over rough moorland and sheep tracks. The diffi-

culty in reaching the tree has in many ways protected it and given it an elusive quality. It is also necessary to obtain permission from the estate to go across the moor.

Tradition states that the yew was the gathering point in times of trouble for the Clan Fraser. The Stratherrick lands belonged to the clan since early times. The tree grows about 500 metres (550 yds) from the shoreline of Loch Ness in birch scrubland. The

such as *Ormiston, Dargavel, Whittinghame* and *Colquhalzie,* which send up growth from layered branches. The *Great Fraser yew* has been estimated at about 700 years old by tree authorities in Scotland. It was first documented in 1876 when H. Evershed wrote in the *Gardener's Chronicle:*

If proof were wanting of the indigenous growth of the yew tree in Scotland, we may quote the fact that a very large and aged yew grew about the year 1834, high among the hills, far from any cultivation and from any human dwelling, in the midst of the wild country between Loch Ness and the sources of the River Findhorn.

There can be few trees with such a distinguished and romantic connection as the *Great Fraser yew.*

Just north of Acharacle, sheltered by Ardnamurchan, an unmarked road to the left turns to the south channel of Loch Moidart. Here can be found one of Scotland's most romantic ruins. Castle Tioram (pronounced tiram) stands on a promontory overlooking the island Eilean Shona. This castle was built between the thirteenth and fourteenth centuries and was the home of the Macdonalds of Clanranald. A Jacobite chief burned the castle down in 1715 to prevent it from falling under government control. In 1984, an open air mass was held at the castle to rededicate the Clanranald banner, which had survived since Culloden. Jacobite associations are present everywhere and parallel to the Loch, near to the place where Bonnie Prince Charlie landed during the second Jacobite rising, are seven beech trees in a line. Known as the *Seven Men of Moidart,* they celebrate the seven men who accompanied the prince on his journey. One of the big beeches blew down some time ago and has now been replaced by a younger tree.

root system of the old yew projects out like a giant clock face and, from the roots which vary in length from 6 to 15 metres (20 to 50 feet), over twenty new stems of varying heights rise up. The outer circumference of the giant crown is approximately 110 metres (360 feet).

The unique nature of the *Great Fraser yew* is that the young growth springs from the roots and not as other famous Scottish yews

Mount Stewart

Crom Estate

Bedell's Sycamore

Tullynally Castle

Dancing Tree

St Patrick's Well and Ash Tree

National Botanical Gardens

King Oak, Charleville

Powerscourt

Mount Usher

The Money Tree

Abbeyleix Gardens

The Cotton Tree

John F. Kennedy Arboretum

Fota Island

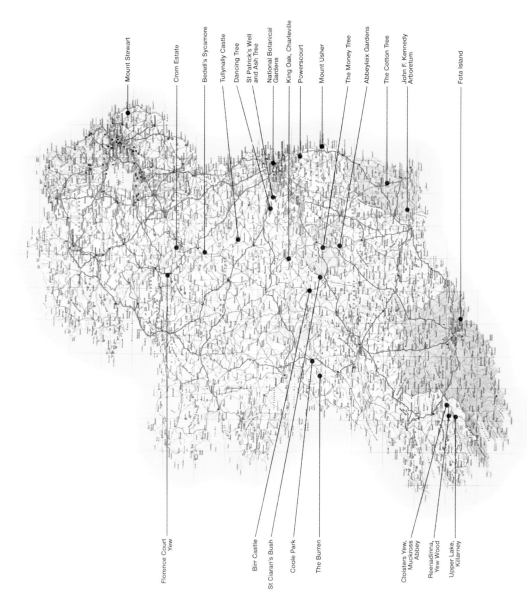

Florence Court Yew

Birr Castle

St Ciaran's Bush

Coole Park

The Burren

Cloisters Yew, Muckross Abbey

Reenadinna, Yew Wood

Upper Lake, Killarney

Ireland

The rivers Nore, Suir, Barrow and Slaney weave beautiful valleys through the lush rolling countryside of that mild corner of Ireland, the south-east. Here, in New Ross, a most ambitious modern tree park is dedicated to a past American president whose ancestral home was County Wexford. The Normans struggled to govern this land, but nevertheless left handsome legacies in Wexford, Waterford and Kilkenny, where nearby Inistioge on the river Nore has many tree treasures.

The south-west coast is warmed by the Gulf Stream, and the mild climate has allowed some exotic trees to flourish. On an island near Cork there is a great pinetum. Killarney and the west has a rugged moist landscape where one of Europe's best yew woods grows and a very straight yew stands in the centre of a ruined abbey. By the wonderful lakes, you can look for strawberry trees and find wild holly and oak woods.

Beyond the extraordinary and prehistoric Burren is a tree signed by the literary famous, and the midland counties around the Shannon basin still have their 'fairy' and 'holy' trees. Great tree collections of international importance dot the whole of Ireland, from Powerscourt and Mount Usher in the lovely Wicklow mountains to Mount Stewart and Florence Court, with its unique upright Irish yew, in the north.

In the centre of Ireland are the renowned grounds of Birr Castle and its great and rare trees, Tullynally Castle, Tullamore and its *King oak*, Abbeyleix Gardens and in the east the lively city of Dublin has a gem of a botanic garden.

In the north-west, the wild bare mountains of Donegal have a distinctive beauty of their own and at Slieve League, one of Europe's finest cliffs plunges 550 metres (1,800 feet) from mountain to sea.

Glenveagh National Park has a remnant ancient woodland consisting of oak, birch and holly.

The countryside of north-east Ireland is made up partly of lake-filled lowlands, the higher hills of the Antrim plateau and the mountains of Mourne. The region also has the great inland sea of Lough Neagh. Some unique yews grow in Northern Ireland, and at Scarva, Co. Down are still the remains of the immense sweet chestnut used as a gathering place before the Battle of the Boyne, 1680.

Throughout the whole of Ireland there is much to tempt the tree traveller in this beautiful and varied land.

WEXFORD

The *Cotton tree, Crann Critheac* or the *Quivering tree* grew in Enniscorthy, Co. Wexford. It was felled in 1991 and was a black poplar, not very common in Ireland outside of Dublin. The tree stood on the town side of the old Slaney Bridge at Slaney Place and was well-known for its association with the Battle of Vinegar Hill. The hill being a local landmark overlooking the cathedral town of Enniscorthy. The popular name for the tree is the *Cotton tree*, because the seeds on poplars are borne on white down resembling cotton. The *Quivering tree* refers to the leaves' habit of rustling in the slightest wind.

During the uprising by the Wexford people against the British, Father John Murphy, with his patriots, captured Enniscorthy and camped on Vinegar Hill. The British troops formed under the *Cotton tree* to receive their instructions and they tethered their horses to its branches. The patriots fought a long battle to retain the hill and town, but against huge odds eventually lost.

*The Cotton Tree Pub, Enniscorthy – a reminder of
the Battle of Vinegar Hill*

*John F Kennedy Arboretum, Co Wexford – a superb
young arboretum on the southern slopes of Slieve
Coillte*

In the Town Square is Oliver Shepard's
classic bronze memorial to the heroes of
Vinegar Hill. In 1991, the old Slaney
Bridge, originally built in 1775 by the
Oriel brothers, was subject to roadworks
on the western side. Great local debate
ensued over the *Cotton tree* and its reten-
tion. Tree surgeons were called in to
inspect it and rot was discovered in the
trunk. The decision was taken to fell the
tree and so it was taken down, its roots
grubbed out by excavator, and the wood
was given to a local craftsman, who then
used it to carve pieces for souvenirs. The
Cotton Tree pub, opposite to where the
tree once stood, remains as a reminder of
the tree.

The castle in Enniscorthy houses an
excellent museum illustrating local history
and interest. In the cellar is a ring of wood
from the *Cotton tree*.

Thirteen kilometres (8 miles) from New
Ross, Co. Wexford is the magnificent
memorial park to the former President of
the United States, the John F Kennedy
Arboretum. It is situated on the southern
slopes of Slieve Coillte, near the original

home of the Kennedys at Dunganstown.

The park covers over 245 hectares (600 acres) and was formally opened in May 1968. The whole ambitious project is developing well and the beautiful visitor's centre and administrative buildings invite you to explore the parkland further. It is a popular and an inspiring place to visit. There is a viewing point on Slieve Coillte for a spectacular vista of the park. The arboretum is now noted for its collection of Eucalypts, with over seven species which are British Isles record breakers.

CORK

On Fota Island in Cork Harbour is a world famous arboretum, lying within the grounds of Fota House and started in 1820. The mild climate and sheltered position allows normally tender trees and shrubs to flourish here. It is notable for its collections from China, Japan and Chile. Notable trees include a Persian ironwood (*Parotica persica*), the tallest Chinese tulip tree in Britain (*Liriodendron chinese*), *Northofagus moorei*, the biggest in Britain, the rare *Cuppressus lusitanica*, *Cuppressus sempervirens*, *Juniperus*

Killarney National Park – strawberry tree near the upper lakes

procera, and many more rare and record trees.

KERRY

In Ireland there is a plant called the strawberry tree, which is an evergreen with translucent flowers. During September and October the flowers hang alongside the ripening fruits that give the tree its name, 'Caithne' or strawberry tree. The plant is actually a member of the heather family (*Ericaceae*) and the species name is *Arbutus unedo*.

The name 'Caithne' is found in place names and the word Quin is also associated with the tree.

The growing range of the strawberry tree is from Turkey, through the Mediterranean countries, to Portugal, and it is found locally in parts of France including Britanny, and in Ireland. Here it is at its most numerous around the Lakes of Killarney, but can also be found at Sneem, Cloone Loughs, Glengatriff, Skibbereen and Fron Fota in Co. Cork. Further north in Co. Sligo, it grows on the shores of Lough Gill.

It would appear that at one time the tree was more widespread. Nevertheless, in Killarney National Park it is relatively common. A walk around the Upper Lake will reveal one, usually growing in a wild craggy place at the edge of the holly or oak woods. Here, in the more inaccessible parts of the Upper Lake, the searcher will be rewarded by finding truly wild woods, some purely of holly, where wonderful, old, gnarled trees grow, and also untouched oak woods that grow in this mild, damp climate. The trees take on a magical appearance and create a dream-like atmosphere.

On the Muckross Peninsula leading from Muckross House, you eventually enter a natural yew wood, the only surviving pure yew wood in Ireland. It is called Reenadinna Wood and can be approached from Muckross House and Gardens. This is a dark wood, with mosses growing everywhere. In places the deer have stripped the bark from some trees, but the general appearance is similar to Kingley Vale in Hampshire, only damper and softer underfoot. The place is very atmospheric and well worth a visit.

Natural yew growth can also be found on the Burren, and dwarf growth of yew found clinging to the crevices on the limestone pavement. Muckross Gardens contain some impressive trees grown over the past 100 to 150 years and the arboretum is being added to all the time.

Nearby, at Muckross Abbey, or the Friary of Irrelagh, stands a remarkable tree known as the *Cloisters yew*. It grows exactly in the centre of the Cloister garth of the ruined abbey buildings. It is indeed a strange sight!

Arthur Young, writing in his *Tour in Ireland* (1780) was very impressed with the tree, and stated that it was the most prodigious he had ever seen. This seems strange, as standing outside the ruins is a yew with greater proportions. He must, as are all who see it, have been impressed by the clear, straight bole and the place of its growth.

Reenadinna Wood – the pure yew wood on the Muckross peninsula

BELOW: *Cloisters yew, Muckross Abbey –
remarkable tree in the romantic ruins*

ABOVE: *Muckross House – fine grounds with
excellent specimen trees*

Dwarf yew on the Burren's limestone pavement

189

Young estimated the tree to be 0.6 metres (2 feet) in diameter, with an approximate height of 4.3 metres (14 feet).

Percival Hunter, writing in 1836, stated that the tree had been stripped of all lower branches, so as not to interfere with the cloisters.

The situation of the tree leads one to believe that it was deliberately planted in its position. Whether that was before or after the friary was burned by Cromwellian troops in 1652 is open to debate. What is known is that the friary was founded in 1448 by Donald McCarthy, and was added to in 1621. Its founder's tomb, and that of other Kerry chieftains, is in the choir area. So also are the graves of the Gaelic poets, O'Rahilly, O'Sullivan, Ferriher and O'Donoghue. The *Cloister yew* is one of several yews, but is by far the most remarkable, for its position of growth gives an added attraction to a fascinating place. The site, only a short walk from the jaunting car gate, is now managed by the Irish Office of Public Works.

GALWAY

In Co. Galway, south of Galway city near Gort, can be found Coole Park. This estate was purchased in 1768 by Robert Gregory on his return to Ireland after working with the East India Company. It remained with the Gregory family until 1927, when it was sold to the State.

Living there at that time was Lady Augusta Gregory, a famous dramatist, folklorist, and co-founder, with W.B. Yeats and Edward Martyn, of the Abbey Theatre. Within the grounds of the Park is a magnificent copper beech, standing on the lawned area. This is the celebrated *Autograph tree*. The signatures of Lady Gregory's friends and visitors can be seen on the trunk. These include people as well known as George Bernard Shaw, John Masefield, Augustus John, Sean O'Casey, W.B. Yeats, A.E. Russell and J.B. Morton. There are many others, and the tree has a plaque offering a description of them all.

Coole Park – entrance through avenue of Holm oaks

Nearby is a fallen, but still growing, Catalpa tree (*Catalpa bignonoides*), which was once Lady Gregory's favourite tree. Here, on her regular walks around the garden, she used to pause to sit and contemplate.

The whole of Coole Park is excellent.

There are huge old limes, beeches and two notable Oriental planes, one close by where the old house stood. The celebrated 'Seven Woods', as described by Yeats, are now part of a nature trail, taking in such habitats as turloughs, lakes, woodlands, limestone outcrops and prehistoric sites. In the woods live red squirrels, pine martens and badgers, and on Coole Lake, the wild swans, (one of Yeats' most celebrated poems) are still frequent autumn and winter visitors. The following poem was written by Lady Gregory about Coole:

> *These woods have been well*
> *loved, well*
> *tended by some who came before me, and*
> *my affection has been no less*
> *than theirs. The generations of*
> *trees have been my care, my*
> *comforters. Their companionship has often*
> *brought me peace.*
> *(Lady Gregory, 1852–1932)*

OFFALY

In Ireland (and the Isle of Man) solitary thorn trees are associated with fairies for whom it is a trysting or meeting tree. The thorn as a miniature tree is said to be very suitable for the 'Little People', its small gnarled rounded habit making it little more than a bush.

Fairies who gathered around a thorn tree are thought to be earth spirits and as a precaution no evil thing is ever said of them for fear of retribution. The old belief that any damage done to their trysting tree will bring misfortune to the doer has not died out and farmers still laboriously cultivate around them. In several instances it has been impossible to persuade workmen to remove a thorn tree from the route of a new road or footpath, and there is a widespread belief that

Fairy tree – at a road junction in rural Ireland

to cut a thorn would bring ill luck on the person 'injuring' the tree and possibly death.

Apart from 'Fairy thorns' there is another category of thorns which overhang holy wells. These are equally venerated and many are connected with fifth and sixth century saints. Often such thorns have a collection of rags attached to them as it is the custom to leave some article of clothing on a branch.

Some of these wells were places of pilgrimage at the time of the Christian Mission to Ireland and were most probably pre-Christian sites of pagan veneration. Pilgrims to the wells hang medals, crucifixes, rosary beads or strips of cloth on the thorn bushes in acknowledgement of cures obtained there. These Raths, Bushes and Wells were in existence before St Patrick came to Ireland.

Rowans have similar superstitions about them. This is hardly surprising as the rowan was among the most sacred plant in pre-Christian times. Viking invaders also revered the tree. Rowans were thought to protect the home and farm, and this idea of them as 'protector' was carried on until recently by planting them near homesteads. A Gaelic name for rowan is 'fid na ndruad', which means the Druids' tree.

Located at Clareen, in the countryside to the east of Birr in the Irish Midlands, stands the small whitethorn known as *St Ciaran's bush* (sometimes spelt as Kieran). It is dressed in clothing rags and those who hang the rags offer prayers for special intentions. They believe that when the rags rot to nothing, their prayers and intentions will be answered. The nearest tradition in England is the Arbor Tree dressing at Aston-on-Clun in Shropshire, and in the practice of Well dressing in the Peak district and parts of Scotland. The bush at Clareen is linked with

St Ciaran's bush – the decorated thorn near Clareen in the Irish Midlands

the holy well in a nearby field. That in turn has associations with the old monastic settlement of St Ciaran, now in ruin.

The thorn does not appear to be particularly old, but a villager confirmed that the same bush had been decorated for at least 40 years. It is likely that the present thorn replaced an older one.

The local people did help to preserve the bush when it was in danger of being felled due to the re-alignment of the road some years ago. It now stands on an 'island' of grass, surrounded by low white railings, the old lane on the west side, the new road on the east.

Growing near the entrance to the Charleville estate at Tullamore, Co. Offaly is the tree known as the *King oak*. It is a pedunculate oak, which grows naturally around Tullamore. Old trees in local woods have been ring counted at between 350 and 450 years old.

The *King Oak* is a magnificent specimen, with four of its branches touching the ground, the longest of which is over 23 metres (75 feet) from the bole. Tradition holds that when a member of the Hutton-Bury family dies, a major branch falls from the tree. The tree stands over 21 metres (69 feet) tall and has a girth of 7 metres (23 feet).

According to Rev. D. Hutton-Bury, measuring it in 1993, the crown covers 1,350 sq. metres (1,615 sq. yards). The age would be between 450 and 500 years old and it is one of Ireland's largest oaks.

The *King Oak* is used by the young of Tullamore as a gathering place, and the sweeping branches make it an ideal place to rest. It may well be that the branches were trained to the ground with weights, a practice I was shown at Warmwell House near Infield, Co. Meath. Here, the previous owner had trained an old sycamore's lower branches towards the ground with pegs. The effect of sweeping branches is quite dramatic and provides a wonderful play area. The disadvantages are that weakness and water pockets can result in these lower 'trained' limbs.

The Tullamore estate is dotted with big, old oaks and close to the castle is the *Queen*

King oak, Charleville, Tullamore – one of Ireland's biggest oaks

oak which pre-dates the building.

The present castle was designed in 1798 by Francis Johnston, one of Ireland's famous architects. After years of being empty, it has now been re-occupied, and plans are in place to restore it to its former glory.

The most famous sycamore in Ireland, the *Bedell sycamore*, grows at the derelict castle at Kilmore, Co. Cavan. It is thought to have been planted in 1632 and is therefore one of the oldest sycamores in Ireland. The main claim to fame of the Bedell tree is that it was written about in the eighteenth century by Rev. William Henry. He described the grove of sycamores, of which this is one, and assigns their planting to Bishop Bedell in the seventeenth century. Other big sycamores in Ireland are at Birr Castle, Co. Offaly and at Headfort House, Co. Meath.

Birr Castle Demesne, situated as it is beside two rivers in the centre of Ireland, is filled with rare plants and trees. There was probably a medieval garden around the ancient fortress at Birr, but the main development of the garden and park was carried out by Sir Laurence Parsons in the seventeenth century.

Birr Castle – giant beech by the lake. Birr has many great trees

The great box hedge at Birr Castle

Plantings continued over the centuries, particularly by Michael, sixth Earl of Rosse and his wife Anne. They left meticulous notes and drawings of their introductions. From their own travels, they collected plants and seeds from Tibet, Mexico, China, New Zealand and Tasmania, to name but a few. There are many record trees at Birr, including rare maples, chestnuts, cotoneasters, beeches, and cherries. There are notable conifers too, such as junipers, cedars, and larches. The tallest box hedge in the world grows at Birr, standing at over 10 metres tall. The gardens, parkland and river walks are worthy of a visit, for it ranks amongst the best in Ireland for its plant and tree collection, and attractive surroundings.

LAOIS

The *Money tree* or *Well in the tree* is an old sycamore which had died and finally blew down in 1994. In the summer of that year, it was still lying in the old road next to the main Dublin–Limerick road, several miles to the east of Mountrath, at Clanenagh, Co. Laois. The rotten limbs of the tree used to hold rainwater, hence the name *Well in the tree*. It was associated with the old original well of St Fintan across the field and also with the nearby graveyard. The tree was once hung with prayer rags, but that developed into hammering coins into the trunk for wishes and for luck. Many hundreds of coins still adorned the remaining, fallen sections.

People also used to take pieces of the tree as souvenirs – no wonder it eventually fell. What will happen now remains to be seen. Possibly a replacement tree will be planted, but it will have to be substantial to withstand the coins!

MEATH

At St Patrick's Well, between Kilcock and Infield, Co. Meath, the well next to the old cemetery emerges from an old ash tree. In common with so many other wells, the water is claimed to cure eye problems.

Just past Infield on the road to Mullingar, the 'hotwell', associated with St Govan, had until recently an elm growing next to it. This tree is now dead, but the well remains and in a small boulder near the well are indentations that are supposed to be where St Govan knelt as he prayed at the well. The water level fluctuates but it is always supposed to be warm. The local farmer on whose land the well stands is very keen on trees and has planted many to provide for the future.

Sometimes the branches of a lone ash or rowan have a weeping habit. On a summer evening, with a breeze and with the sun setting behind them, the trees 'come alive' and appear is if they are dancing. These are the *Dancing Trees* of Ireland. Near to the well-kept churchyard to the east of Infield, Co. Meath, on the N.4, stands a Norman motte and bailey. On the top of the mound is such a tree, an old ash that has, according to local folk, grown on the hill for at least 80 years. The tree is best observed from the churchyard, approached from the old main road to Kilcock and Dublin.

The ash (*Fuinseog*) is a common tree in Ireland but it plays a prominent part in Irish mythology and many lovely specimens can be found in the hedgerows, fields and in special places. An ash, *Bile Tortan*, (probably Co. Meath) was said to have been an enormous tree that sheltered the men of Tortu and, according to legend, was visited by St Patrick who established a church nearby for Justian. It was said to have sprung from berries planted by St Fintan. The tree eventually fell in 600 AD. *Craeb Daithi* in Farbill, Co. Westmeath and *Bile Uisneg*, which stood at Usnagh, Co. Westmeath were supposedly two more of Fintan's 'magical trees'.

There are other stories of ancient ash trees in Ireland. The sacred well of Kilcrohane, at the extreme west of Co. Cork, had an ash tree growing above it and the ruined chapel. In 1945 it was recorded that the tree had fallen, but pilgrims continued to stick coins into the bark (as with the sycamore at Mountrath). The *Great Ash of Leix* grew at Emo, Co. Laois, between Monasterevin and Portarlington. A print of the old tree shows the enormity of the trunk and that it was a

Money tree, Clanenagh – remains of the sycamore showing the many coins pressed into the bark

focal point for the local community. The tree died in the early nineteenth century. When it was measured in 1792 by Samuel Hayes, the girth at 1.8 metres (6 feet) was 7.6 metres (25 feet) and was 12 metres (40.5 feet) at 0.3 metres (1 foot) from the ground.

At Kinnity, near Emo, was another well-known ash that was used as a resting place for funeral corteges. Under the *Kinnity ash* a prayer would be said and a stone thrown below the crown. Over the years a huge cairn had built up. It was 6.6 metres (21.8 feet) in the girth with a 5.2 metres (17 foot) clear stem.

At Bweenounagh, Co. Galway is the record of another ash with stones below the crown.

Also in Galway, at Clarecastle, was *The Old Ash of Donirey*. It reputedly measured over 12.2 metres (40 feet) in the girth and its hollow trunk was used as the village school!

There are no truly huge ash trees left in Ireland now, but good big ones can be seen at Abbeyleix Gardens (over 30 metres [98 feet] high in 1985) and at Castle Forbes, Co. Longford.

FERMANAGH

A distinctive and well-known tree in churchyards and cemeteries throughout the world, originates from the gardens of Florence Court in Northern Ireland. An account of the 'finding' of the tree makes a fascinating story:

> *Two young plants were originally found in Co. Fermanagh in a place called Carricknamaddow or 'The Rock of the Dog'. One, which the finder planted in his own garden, died in 1865. The second he took to his landlord, the Earl of Enniskillen at Florence Court, and it is from this plant that all the true Irish yews are descended by vegetative propagation. Cuttings were given to Lee of Hammersmith at an unrecorded date but probably around the turn of the century, since the Irish yew was available at a low price by 1838.* (Trees and Shrubs Hardy in the British Isles, Volume 4, p. 566) *W.J. Bean.*

The area where the upright yews were

found lies in a spot on the north-eastern side of Cuilcagh Mountain, which straddles the boundary between Fermanagh and Leitrim. Dr Nelson, of the Botanic Gardens, Glasnevin, and John Phillips, regional forest officer for Fermanagh, trekked the hills in 1980 looking for any other such yews. They found no trees at all in the area now known as Willis's Rock.

It would seem that the original date of the find by Willis was between 1740 and 1760 and that the 'two' trees were probably a multi-stemmed seedling that was later divided, with one plantlet being planted by Willis's house and the other in the estate of his landlord at Florence Court. Only the Florence Court tree survived into the twentieth century and still grows in a small glade

surrounded by laurel and taller trees by the Finglas River. This mother of all Irish yews is now a ragged looking specimen, hardly surprising when you consider it has received two centuries of pruning for new cuttings!

In 1780, John Loudon described two fine Irish yews growing at Comber in Co. Down which were planted about 1780. The original tree at Florence Court is a female 'berried' tree, therefore all its descendants raised by vegetative propagation must be female. Very occasionally, as with the common yew, a branch with male 'strobili' has been found. It is probably from such a branch of the upright form that male Irish yews were first propagated. Loudon illustrated such a branch in his work *Arboretum and Fruticetum Britannicum* (1838).

Dancing tree – old ash on motte and bailey, Co Meath

Some record trees

The following lists have been taken from the records held by TROBI. They show the botanical and common name, height and diameter, date measured and location of tree. The trees listed are the more common species and represent only a sample of the records kept.

Listing is alphabetical by genus and species. The entries are generally the stoutest specimens known. Occasionally there are more than one entry when there are more than one exceptional tree.

Measurements are metric with the height in metres and the diameter in centimetres. The diameter is derived from the girth measurement. Traditionally measurements have been taken at 1.5 metres (5 feet) above the ground, and on the upper side of any slope. A girth measurement in centimetres is converted to a diameter measurement by dividing by 3.14159. To convert girth measurements in feet and inches to centimetres diameter, change to inches and multiply by 0.8085. As a rough but useful guide, 1 foot of girth is equal to 9.7 cm. (almost 10 cm.) of diameter.

Throughout this book there are references to imperial measurements. The reason being of course, that all the old measurements were taken in this fashion. The metric system is now the internationally accepted manner of tree measuring.

BROADLEAVES

Botanical Name	Common Name	Location	Height x Diameter m cms	Date recorded
Acer campestre	Field maple	Sundridge Pk Golf Course Kent	18 x 62	1996
Acer cappadocicum	Cappadocian maple	Maidstone, Kent	18 x 121	1995
Acer griseum	Paper Bark maple	Dyffryn, South Glamorgan	11 x 62	1988
Acer lobilii	Lobel's maple	Eastnor Castle, Herefordshire	30 x 120	1989
Acer negundo	Box elder	Gladstone Park, Gt. London	17 x 100	1981
Acer opalus	Italian maple	Tortworth Court, Gloucestershire	19 x 104	1992
Acer palmatum	Japanese maple	Megginch Castle, Tayside	14 x 63	1993
Acer platanoides	Norway maple	Hafodunas Hall, Powys	26 x 137	1990
Acer Plat. 'Goldsworth Purple'	Norway maple (Purple)	Sotterley Lodge, Suffolk	18 x 47	1985
Acer pseudoplatanus	Sycamore	Posso House, nr Peebles, Borders	— x 275	1992
Acer saccarinum	Silver maple	Osterley Park, Gt. London	31 x 131	1995
Acer saccharum	Sugar maple	Belton House, Lincs	22 x 86	1992
Aesculus x carnea	Pink horse chestnut	Wrest Park, Beds.	15 x 104	1995
Aesculus hippocastanum	Horse chestnut	Hurstbourne Priors, Hampshire	34 x 221	1993
Aesculus indica	Indian horse chestnut	Endsleigh, Devon	26 x 97	1995
Aesculus pavia	Red Buck Eye	Goodwood House, Sussex	12 x 39	1980
Ailanthus altissima	Tree of Heaven	Chichester, W. Sussex	17 x 146	1997
Alnus cordata	Italian alder	Tottenham House, Wiltshire	12 x 124	1984
Alnus glutinosa	Common alder	Tretower Court, Powys	14 x 145	1995

Alnus glutinosa 'Laciniata'	Cut leafed alder	University Parks, Oxford	7 x 92	1993
Alnus incana	Grey alder	Castle Milk, Dumfries	24 x 61	1984
Arbutus x andrachnoides	Hybrid strawberry tree	Bodnant Gardens, Gwynedd	22 x 51	1990
Arbutus unedo	Strawberry tree	Colchester, Essex	9 x 82	1993
Betula ermanii	Erman's birch	Westonbirt Arboretum, Glos	22 x 105	1992
Betula papyrifera	Paper bark birch	Benmore, Strathclyde	20 x 92	1991
Betula pendula	Silver birch	Leith Hill, Surrey	26 x 133	1987
Betula pendula 'tristis'	Weeping birch	Edinburgh RBG	14 x 78	1987
Betula utilis	Himalayan birch	High Close, Grasmere, Cumbria	20 x 62	1994
Buxus sempervirens	Common box	Gunnersbury Park, London	8 x 28	1987
Carpinus betulus	Common hornbeam	Bath BG	32 x 109	1986
Castanea sativa	Sweet chestnut	Cowdray Pk, W. Sussex	25 x 364	1997
Catalpa bignonoides	Indian bean tree	St James Park, London	14 x 98	1994
Cercidiphyllum japonicum	Katsura tree	Sezincote, Gloucestershire	(at 0.2m) 18 x 143	1993
Cordyline australis	Cabbage tree	Tresco Abbey, Isles of Scilly	15 x 68	1987
Cercis silaquastrum	Judas tree	Canterbury, Kent	11 x 64	1995
Cornus controversa	Table dogwood	Forde Abbey, Dorset	19 x 42 + 46	1993
Corylus avellana	Common hazel	Barlavington Hanger, Sussex	22 x 99	1993
Corylus colurna	Turkish hazel	Syon Park, London	22 x 99	1997
Cotoneaster frigidus	Tree cotoneaster	Gulval Churchyard, Cornwall	13 x 60	1990
Crataegus monogyna	Hawthorn	Hatfield Forest, Essex	16 x 116	1989
Davidia involucrata	Dove tree	Hergest Croft, Herefordshire	16 x 70	1995
Embothrium coccineum	Chilean fire bush	Mount Usher, Co. Wicklow	12 x 58	1989
Eucalyptus gunnii	Cider gum	Sidbury Manor, Devon	33 x 163	1994
Fagus sylvatica	Common beech	Eridge Park, Sussex (at 1.1m)	26 x 284	1994
		Tullynally Castle, Co. Westmeath	40 x 217	1990
Fagus sylvatica 'Dawyck'	Dawyck beech	Dawyck, Borders (at 0.3m)	29 x 86	1992
Fagus sylvatica 'Pendula'	Weeping beech	Endsleigh, Devon	29 x 164	1995
Fag. sylvatica 'Purpurea'	Copper beech	The Park, Mogerhanger, Beds. (at 1m)	21 x 193	1990
Ficus carica	Fig	St James Park, London	x 46	1987
Fraxinus augustifolia	Narrow leafed ash	Ray Pk, Woodford, London	28 x 116	1995
Fraxinus excelsior	Common ash	Clapton Court, Somerset	12 x 183	1995
		Talley Abbey, Dyfed (not T.R.O.B.I.)	20 x 180	1993
Fraxinus excel. 'Pendula'	Weeping ash	Bedgebury School, Kent	12 x 186	1989
Fraxinus ornus	Manna ash	Haynes, Beds. (at 1m)	17 x 115	1995
Gleditsia triacanthos	Honey locust	Wateringbury, Kent	25 x 86	1993
Ilex aquifolium	Common holly	Finlarig Castle, Strathclyde	26 x 101	1989
Juglans nigra	Black walnut	Old Rectory, Much Hadham, Herts	36 x 204	1984
Juglans regia	Common walnut	Gayhurst, Bucks	20 x 196	1992
Laburnum alpinum	Scotch laburnum	Megginch Castle, Tayside	8 x 120	1993
Laburnum anagyroides	Laburnum	Abercynrig House, Powys	5 x 140	1988
Ligustrum lucidum	Chinese privet	Battersea Park, London	15 x 93	1989
Liquidambar formosana	Chinese sweet gum	Killerton, Devon	20 x 47	1991
Liquidambar styraciflua	Sweet gum	Stratfield Saye, Berks	28 x 99	1986
Liriodendron tulipifera	Tulip tree	Golden Grove, Dyfed	26 x 270	1993
		Claremont, Surrey (at 1.0m)	20 x 290	1992
Magnolia acuminata	Cucumber tree	Fawley Court, Oxford	18 x 104	1994
Magnolia campbellii	Campell's magnolia	Trebah, Cornwall	24 x 106	1991

Magnolia campbellii 'Charles Raffill'	Rafill's magnolia	Trengwainton, Cornwall	16 x 68	1993
Magnolia grandiflora	Evergreen magnolia	Nonsuch Pk. Epsom, Surrey	10 x 72	1989
Magnolia macrophylla	Large leafed cucumber tree	Killerton, Devon	18 x 30	1983
Malus floribunda	Japanese crab	Horsham Park, Sussex	12 x 56	1982
Malus sylvestris	Crab-apple	Felshamhall Wood, Suffolk	10 x 103	1991
Metrosideros excelsa	Pohutawawa	Tresco Abbey, Isles of Scilly	20 x 225	1987
Morus alba	White mulberry	Oxford UBG, Oxford	9 x 70	1996
Morus nigra	Black mulberry	Weathersdean House, Kent	9 x 98	1988
Myrtus luma	Orange Bark myrtle	Suarnarez Pk, Guernsey	10 x 102	1995
Northofagus procera	Roble beech	Braddick Cst., Arran, Strathclyde	30 x 131	1988
Northofagus obliqua	Raol beech	Ashbourne Hse, Co Cork	30 x 100	1987
Ostrya carpinfolia	Hop hornbeam	Killerton, Devon	22 x 56 +	1983
Parrotia persica	Persian ironwood	Endsleigh, Devon (at 0.3m)	15 x 53	1992
Platanus x acerifolia	London plane	Bishops Palace, Ely, Cambs.	35 x 287	1990
Platanus orientalis	Oriental plane	Chilton Foliat, Hungerford	23 x 290	1993
		Corsham Crt. Wilts	24 x 150	1995
Populus alba	White poplar	Eden Hall, Cumbria	27 x 65	1995
Poplus nigra var. betulifolia	Black poplar	Chelsworth, Suffolk	38 x 242	1992
		Longnor Hall, Shropshire	38 x 194	1984
Poplus nigra 'Italica'	Lombardy poplar	Haresfield, Glos	30 x 169	1993
		Lincoln Arb., Lincs.	44 x 119	1993
Poplus tremula	Aspen	Ardgay, Sutherland	20 x 89	1993
Prunus avium	Gean/wild cherry	Studley Royal, Yorkshire	17 x 182	1994
Prunus padus	Bird cherry	Achnagarry, Highlands	11 x 55	1988
Pterocarya fraxinifolia	Caucasian wingnut	Lacock Abbey, Wilts	26 x 193	1987
Pyrus communis	Wild pear	Bredwardine, Hereford	16 x 113	1993
Quercus mirbeckii	Mirbeck's oak	Ham Manor, Sussex	28 x 141	1979
Quercus castaneifolia	Chestnut leafed oak	Kew RBG, Surrey	33 x 216	1991
Quercus cerris	Turkey oak	Knightshayes, Devon	40 x 250	1991
Quercus coccinea	Scarlet oak	Newnham Pk, Oxford	19 x 108	1993
Quercus frainetto	Hungarian oak	Buxted Park, Sussex	29 x 174	1994
Quercus x hispanica 'Lucombeana'	Lucombe oak	Phear Pk, Exmouth, Devon	25 x 242	1990
Quercus ilex	Holm oak	Westbury Court, Glos (at 1m)	14 x 257	1993
Quercus macranthera	Caucasian oak	Melbury Pk, Dorset	26 x 101	1989
Quercus palustris	Pin oak	Kew RBG, London	31 x 101	1991
		Godington Park, Kent	16 x 111	1994
Quercus petraea	Sessile oak	Powis Castle, Powys	21 x 346	1989
		Cowdray Pk., W. Sussex (at 1m)	8 x 405	1997
Quercus robur	English oak	Bowthorp, Lincs. (at 1m)	12 x 406	1997
		Fredville Park, Kent	20 x 384	1993
Q. robur fastigiata	Cypress oak	Bicton, Devon	22 x 108	1983
Quercus rubra	Red oak	Cobham, Surrey	23 x 202	1990
Quercus suber	Cork oak	Mt. Edgecombe, Cornwall	26 x 163	1983
		Anthony Hse, Cornwall	20 x 169	1991
Quercus turneri	Turner's oak	Kew RBG, London	22 x 165	1989
		Golden Grove, Dyfed	27 x 174	1994
Robinia pseudoacacia	Locust tree	Kew R.B.G.	30 x 108	1992
Salix alba	White willow	Moreton-on-Lugg, Herefordshire	23 x 235	1989

Salix caprea	Goat willow	Ardross Castle, Highlands	16 x 115	1989
Salix fragilis	Crack willow	Wadhurst, Sussex	11 x 138	1994
Salix x pendulina	Weeping willow	Wings Meadow, Reading,		
v. elegantissima	'Elegant'	Berks	11 x 121	1988
Sambucus nigra	Common elder	Campbeltown, Strathclyde	4 x 43	1992
		Brook St, Lewes, Sussex	7 x 46	1994
		(at 1.2m)		
Sorbus aria	Whitebeam	Megginch Castle, Tayside	15 x 95	1993
		Battersea Park, London	20 x 61	1987
Sorbus aucuparia	Rowan/Mountain ash	Bellington Wood, Bucks.	28 x 56	1995
		(at 1.3m)		
Sorbus domestica	True service tree	Borde Hill, West Sussex	17 x 86	1995
Sorbus torminalis	Wild service tree	Udimore, Sussex	16 x 139	1993
		Markshall, Essex	26 x 124	1990
Tilia cordata	Small leafed lime	Haveningham Hall, Norfolk	19 x 184	1991
		Dallam House, Cumbria	22 x 256	1994
		(at 0.5m)		
Tilia x europaea	Common lime			
(x vulgaris)	(coppiced)	Holker Hall, Cumbria	22 x 230	1992
Tilia x europaea	Common lime			
(x vulgaris)	(coppiced)	Markswell Wood, Hants.	24 x 428	1993
Tilia platyphyllos	Large leafed lime	Pitchford Hall, Shropshire	14 x 236	1984
Tilia tomentosa	Silver lime	Tortworth Church, Glos.	35 x 144	1988
		Buckland House, Brecon,	28 x 181	1988
		Powys		
Tilia tomentosa 'Petoilaris'	Silver pendant lime	Toddington Manor, Beds	21 x 147	1993
Ulmus glabra	Wych elm	Brahan Hse, Highlands	28 x 217	1989
Ulmus x hollandica	Dutch elm	Abbots Rippon, Cambs.	34 x 158	1989
Ulmus minor (carpinifolia)	Small leafed elm	Kippencross Hse, Tayside	21 x 151	1987
Ulmus minor				
(vulgaris procera)	Hybrid elm	Preston Park, Sussex	12 x 199	1988
Zelkova carpinifolia	Caucasian elm	Worlingham, Suffolk	22 x 222	1990
		Pitt Farm, Chudleigh, Devon	34 x 198	1984
Zelkova serrata	Keaki	Horsted Keynes, W. Sussex	19 x 101	1997
Zelkova sinica	Chinese zelkova	Woburn Park, Beds (at 0.8m)	17 x 71	1992

CONIFERS

Botanical Name	Common Name	Location	Height x Diameter m cms	Date recorded
Abies alba	Silver fir	Strone House, Ardinglas,		
		Argyll & Bute	46 x 298	1994
Abies concolor				
v. lowiana	Low's fir	Blair Castle, Tayside	53 x 125	1989
Abies celphalonica	Grecian fir	Dalemain, Cumbria	52 x 159	1989
Abies firma	Momi fir	Balfour Hse, Devon	31 x 113	1979
Abies grandis	Grand fir	Balmacaan Highlands	53 x 244	1993
Abies magnifica	Red fir	Blair Castle, Tayside	37 x 157	1989
Abies nordmanniana	Causican fir	Endsleigh, Devon	32 x 165	1991
Abies procera	Noble fir	Uig, Benmore, Strath.	50 x 165	1983
		Glenferness, Grampian	39 x 167	1987
Araucaria araucana	Monkey Puzzle	Bicton, Devon	30 x 128	1991
Calocedrus decurrens	Incense cedar	Doune House, Tayside	38 x 187	1988

Cedrus atlantica	Atlas cedar	Cirencester Park, Glos	29 x 176	1989
Cedrus atlantica 'glauca'	Blue Atlas cedar	Brockhampton Pk, Hereford	38 x 136	1978
Cedrus deodara	Deodar cedar	Higham Court, Glos.	30 x 245	1992
Cedrus libani	Cedar of Lebanon	Goodwood Park, Sussex	32 x 292	1997
		(at 0.5m)		
Chamaecyparis lawsoniana	Lawson's cypress	Gregynog Hall, Powys	29 x 194	1993
Cham. lawsoniana 'Erecta'	Lawson's cypress 'Erecta'	Bodnant Gdns, Gwynedd	33 x 140	1990
Cham. nootkatensis	Nootka cypress	Eastnor Castle, Hereford	27 x 103	1989
Cupresso cyparis leylandii	Leyland cypress	Leighton Park, Powys	33 x 127	1988
Cuppressus macrocarpa	Monterey cypress	Johnstown Castle Co. Wexford	40 x 255	1989
		Strete Raleigh, Devon	36 x 320	1990
Ginkgo biloba	Maidenhair tree	Whitfield Hse, Hereford	21 x 140	1995
Juniperus virginiana	Pencil cedar	Painshill Park, Surrey	26 x 153	1989
Larix decidua	European larch	Monzie Castle, Tayside	35 x 192	1991
Larix x eurolepis	Hybrid larch	Blair Castle, Tayside	24 x 100	1988
Larix kaempferi	Japanese larch	Dunkeld House, Tayside	29 x 105	1990
Larix x pendula	Weeping larch	Tunbridge Wells, Kent	24 x 88	1995
Metasequoia glyptostoboides	Dawn redwood	Central Gdns, Bournemouth, Dorset	24 x 108	1993
Picea abies	Norway spruce	Lingholm, Cumbria	40 x 146	1995
Picea omorika	Serbian spruce	Murthly Castle, Tayside	28 x 68	1990
Picea orientalis	Oriental spruce	Cortachy Castle, Tayside	28 x 125	1981
Picea sitchensis	Sitka spruce	Castlehill, Devon	46 x 258	1989
Picea smithiana	Morinda spruce	Taymouth Castle, Tayside	35 x 145	1990
Pinus ayacahuite	Mexican white pine	Bodnant Gdns. Gwynedd	25 x 110	1989
Pinus contorta	Shore pine	Errol House, Tayside	26 x 114	1982
Pinus coulteri	Big cone pine	Stanway, Glos.	21 x 92	1982
Pinus x holfordiana	Holford's pine	RHS Gdns, Wisley, Surrey	24 x 111	1993
Pinus jeffreyi	Jeffery's pine	Scone Palace, Tayside	36 x 135	1988
Pinus lambertiana	Sugar pine	Hawkstone Park, Shrop	23 x 99	1992
Pinus muricata	Bishops pine	Ebernoe Hse, Sussex	29 x 134	1983
Pinus nigra caramanica	Crimean pine	Beaufort Castle, Highlands	37 x 162	1983
Pinus nigra v maritima	Corsican pine	Dropmore, Bucks.	37 x 144	1982
		Llanfachreth, Dolgellau, Gwynedd	33 x 179	1991
Pinus nigra v nigra	Austrian pine	Keir Castle, Tayside	26 x 145	1985
Pinus pinaster	Maritime pine	Carey, Dorset	25 x 133	1986
Pinus peuce	Macedonian pine	Stourhead, Wilts	34 x 134	1992
Pinus ponderosa	Western yellow pine	Powis Castle, Powys	22 x 112	1991
Pinus pinea	Stone pine	Victoria Park, Bath	23 x 70	1988
Pinus radiata	Monterey pine	Mount Stewart, Co. Down	31 x 220	1993
Pinus strobus	Weymouth pine	Cannop, Forest of Dean, Glos	38 x 118	1992
Pinus sylvestris	Scots pine	Balogie, S. Deeside	39 x 114	1994
		Scone Palace, Tayside	34 x 185	1987
Pinus wallichiana	Bhutan pine	Fota, Co. Cork (at 0.7m)	31 x 140	1994
		Kilruddery Pk, Co. Wicklow	30 x 139	1989
Pseudotsuga menziesii	Douglas fir	Dunans, Strathclyde	64.5 x 175	1992
		The Hermitage, Dunkeld Tayside	64.5 x 132	1993
		(Tallest Trees in UK)		

Sequoia sempervens	Giant redwood	Woodstock, Co. Kilkenny	42 x 247	1992
Sequoia dendron giganteum	Wellingtonia	Clunie Hse Gdns, Tayside	36 x 345	1988
Taxodium distichum	Swamp cypress	Broadlands, Hants	36 x 159	1986
Taxus baccata	Common yew	Ulcombe Church, Kent (at ground)	13 x 317	1995
		Defynnog Church, Kent (at 0.3m)	9 x 342	1989
		Kenn Church, Devon (not T.R.O.B.I.) (at 1m)	12 x 310	1993
Taxus baccata 'Dovastoniana'	West Felton yew	West Felton, Shrops	17 x 117	1983
Thuja plicata	Western red cedar	Balmacaan, Highland	41 x 195	1993
Tsuga Canadensis	Eastern hemlock	Hawkstone Park, Shrops.	27 x 134	1984
Tsuga heterophylla	Western hemlock	Scone Palace, Tayside	41 x 201	1988

Champion Trees Nov. 1997 Copyright T.R.O.B.I., 1997

Bibliography

AA Book of British Villages
Britain's Green Mantle A.G. Tinsley
British Trees Rex Vicat Cole
Cadogan Guide to Scotland Richenda Miers
Celtic Britain L. Laing
Famous Trees; R. St. Barbe Baker
Gardens of England & Wales; N.G.S. Char. Trust
Historic Thorn Trees in the British Isles; Vaughan Cornish
Landscape into Art Kenneth Clark
Landscape with Trees Miles Hadfield
Man, Myth & Magic BBC Publications
Origins of Britain L. Laing & J. Laing
O.S. Woodland Walks Gerald Wilkinson
Pagan Celtic Britain Anne Ross.
The Country Churchyards of Wales Donald Gregory
The Lore of the Forest; Alexander Porteous
The Shell Guide to Scotland. Edited by Donald Lamond Machtie and Moray McLaren
The Golden Bough Sir James Frazer
The Great Yew Forest Richard Williamson
The King's England – Herefordshire – Arthur Mee
The History of the Countryside – Oliver Rackham
The English Counties Odhams Press Ltd
The English Landscape Wm. Beach Thomas.
The Churchyard Yew & Immortality Vaughan Cornish
The Making of the English Landscape W.G. Hoskins
The Tree Book J. Edward Milner
Trees of Cumbria Amy Bradshaw
The Trees of Bedfordshire, David Alderman
The New Forest Galley Press
The Living Isles Peter Crawford
The Yew Trees of G.B. & Ireland John Lowe
The Sacred Yew Anand Chetan & Diane Brueton
The Trees of G.B. & Ireland Elwes and Henry
Transactions of the Worcestershire Naturalists Club 1897–1899
Trees & Woodlands in the British Landscape Oliver Rackham
Trees of Ireland E.C. Nelson, W.F. Walsh
Trees in Britain J.F. Brimble
Trees in Britain Alexander L. Howard
Trees of Britain & N. Europe Alan Mitchell
Trees of Britain in History & Legend G.H. Wilks
The Shell Guide to Gardens Arthur Hellyer
The Shell Guide to England Edited by John Hadfield
The Natural History of an English Forest Norman Hickin
Yew Trees of Old England E.W. Swanton

Index